Profit from Your Money-Making Ideas

PROFIT
FROM YOUR
MONEY-MAKING IDEAS

How to Build a New Business or Expand an Existing One

HERMAN HOLTZ

A DIVISION OF AMERICAN MANAGEMENT ASSOCIATIONS

Library of Congress Cataloging in Publication Data

Holtz, Herman.
  Profit from your money-making ideas.

  Includes index.
  1. Success. 2. Self-employed. 3. Small
business. I. Title.
HF5386.H676   658'.041   80-65880
ISBN 0-8144-5590-5

First Printing

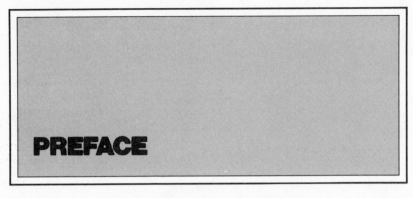

PREFACE

Why is it we get so soon oldt und so late schmardt?
—Pennsylvania Dutch saying

Who hasn't often mumbled, "If I knew then what I know now . . ."? After more than twoscore years of working for a living, sometimes as someone else's employee, sometimes as my own employee, I am still mumbling it bitterly.

It seems so simple now. There are so many ways to be self-employed, to earn a good living—even *money,* if one wants to work *that* hard.

The first time, I sold my house to get starting capital—and lost most of it in the first six months. And it wasn't the only time I lost some money. But the money I lost was well spent: the practical education I got was worth many times the cost.

Of course, there was no way I could have "known then what I know now." I was just beginning to get the necessary education. It really is not at all difficult to start a small business, even without capital . . . working at home, if you like (I recommend it) . . . full-time or in your spare time. What *is* difficult, or at least time-consuming and expensive, is getting that education—if you insist on getting it the way I got it, through trial and error (mostly error).

That's why I conceived the idea of this book. Perhaps I can help you to "know then" rather than "now." Perhaps I can save you that lengthy and costly learning process, or some part of it at least. Perhaps you can get some of your business education from my own experiences and the experiences of

v

many others who have been kind enough to pass on word of their own travails and things learned.

Over the years, after that disastrous first business, I tried my hand at many small businesses, all of which earned me a good living, at worst, without excessive effort. As I expanded and enriched my business education, my businesses grew increasingly easier to start and easier to operate. I was learning both what to do and what not to do. But perhaps even more important, I was learning that there is an almost infinite number of ways to be self-employed—to start a business, particularly in these changing times, where there are few businesses which remotely resemble businesses of as little as ten years ago. The change itself is opportunity: it *creates* opportunities, almost daily. My own memory goes back to a time before computers, television, dishwashers, automatic clothes washers and dryers, electric kitchen appliances, pocket calculators, high-speed airplanes, offset printing, office copiers, and myriads of other devices, many of which form the basis for both large and small businesses today. Over the years, I got involved in the TV and appliance repair business and even was a designer-installer-contractor for another relatively recent invention, the tub and shower sliding-glass-door enclosure, earning a good living from each business.

I have also done well as an independent government contractor, consultant, newsletter publisher, lecturer, seminar entrepreneur, and free-lance writer, while operating a small mail order enterprise. In fact, I conceived and tried out a great many business ideas, simply out of curiosity, to see how well they would work. Most of them worked so well that I was reluctant to drop them, despite the fact that I had too many irons in the fire already and couldn't really attend to all of them properly!

I found that every idea had within it the seeds of another idea which would either produce extra income or perhaps be the basis for still another enterprise. For example, when I was in TV service, I ran into a good many curious service problems. Each time I did, I made it the subject of an article, which

I sold readily to the popular magazines dealing with the subject. So now I began to prepare a series of reports on the various business ideas I had developed, and sold the reports by mail—and they sold rather well. Then I moved on to other things, which occupied so much of my time that I really had no time to advertise and sell the reports. But I tried out another idea, because I hated to see those reports sitting idly on the shelf: I offered to license others to reprint and sell those reports. And that worked too!

And so this book is a rather natural culmination of effort to pass on as much as possible of what I have learned in all these enterprises and efforts. It finally occurred to me that this book was necessary.

I started this with a rather naive idea of preparing a book on "how to get money-making ideas." But as I began to research and outline, I soon came to realize that getting ideas was less than one-half the battle. Almost everyone gets good ideas, now and then; but most people never *do* anything with their ideas. And even the best idea is not worth a copper penny if it's not put to work. But putting ideas to work—that is, *making money* with your ideas—is "where it's at."

Take King Gillette, for example. He had a great idea: the safety razor. He planned to put an end to the drudgery of the dangerous straight razor. He fully expected that men would welcome his new, simple, and safe method of shaving. He was shocked to discover that men resisted change, even to something infinitely better than what they had become used to. His great idea was foundering rapidly.

But then he had his second great idea, the one which would make the first great idea work: he reasoned that there was no big money in selling the *razors;* the money was in selling the *blades,* that consumable item which men would buy over and over. In fact, to sell the blades, he could afford to give the razor away. And he did, thereby breaking down sales resistance and starting his success story.

Perhaps the Gillette safety razor would have caught on eventually by itself; perhaps not. But for the time, at least, the product idea was not worth much without the business idea—the *marketing* idea. On the other hand, sometimes the marketing idea *is* the main idea—better ways to market goods.

You will find in these pages a potpourri of ideas—ideas for products, ideas for services, ideas for marketing. There are business ideas scattered throughout the chapters, along with discussions of vital information on conducting business, sales promotion, advertising, and other important matters having to do with what to *do* with your idea, after you have developed it, borrowed it, or "stolen" it. (Ideas per se are neither copyrightable nor patentable, so they can usually be appropriated wholly, in part, or with modifications.) In fact, this book devotes at least as much time to what to do with ideas as it does to how to get ideas. Moreover, the population of viable business ideas is so vast that no single book could possibly cover them all. Therefore, I have also included a chapter on where else to find ideas that will stimulate your own creative imagination.

There is, I hope, something here for everyone—for the wage earner who wants to start a spare-time, second-income enterprise, for the individual ready to plunge full-time into a new business, for the established business person who wants to get some new ideas for expansion, for the executive planning a new division, for the housewife who wants to earn some pin money, and even for the retired person who just wants to have some fun. For it is great fun to experiment with starting small businesses, and I hope that you have as much fun at it as I have had and am still having.

Herman Holtz

CONTENTS

1 HOW DO YOU KNOW WHEN YOU'VE GOT A MONEY-MAKING IDEA?

Gary Dahl was in a casual bar-room conversation. The talk was about the high cost of keeping a pet today. Someone—it's not clear whether it was Dahl or someone else—sniggered that the only pet which wouldn't cost a great deal of money to keep would be a pet rock.

Dahl was intrigued. For his own amusement—he was an unemployed advertising copywriter—he sat down at home and wrote an entertaining booklet on the care and feeding of a pet rock.

He had an idea. He gathered up some smooth beach pebbles—he lived on the California coast—put them into little cage-like boxes, had his little brochure printed up, and invested $25 in a booth at a trade show. A *Time* reporter saw his exhibit, was amused, and wrote a story for *Time* magazine. A million dollars' worth of free publicity—and a million dollars for Dahl within 90 days, as a result of the ensuing Pet Rock fad.

Thetford Corporation makes $30 million a year building what are probably the best and most advanced portable toilets made, many different models for different applications. They're the result of a problem one of the founders of the corporation had and solved. His wife was handicapped and couldn't get around easily. This was a problem when they traveled in their Winnebago vehicle. A former General Motors engineer, he applied his engineering mind to the problem and devised a practical toilet, which he built and installed in his vehicle. It worked so well that he was about to suggest the

1

idea to the trailer manufacturer, when he discovered it was hard at work trying to invent what he had already created! It launched him into a business which is still growing and leading its field.

Hubert K. Simon had quit his job and was trying desperately to earn a living as a free-lance something or other (he wasn't yet sure just what). He knew that some radio stations would accept "P.I." deals—run commercials on a commission basis—while others would not. Almost by accident, he hit on the idea of buying the names of companies that wanted P.I. (per inquiry) deals from radio stations that wouldn't take P.I. deals and hence had no use for the names of customers who asked for them. The stations were happy to sell the names to Simon for a small sum. And when he made the deal, Hubert says, he wasn't yet sure how he would cash in on all those names.

His next step was to write to advertising agencies and offer to swap names of radio stations that accepted P.I. deals with them, one for one—for each one they sent him, he would send them one they didn't have on their list. (Radio stations are notoriously secretive about accepting such deals because they are afraid that if the word gets out, it will hurt their sale of advertising time.) He soon collected the names of a great many radio stations that would accept P.I. deals, to go along with the growing number of names of companies that wanted P.I. advertising. For $37, Simon compiled a list of 400 stations that would accept P.I. ads. And he still wasn't sure how to cash in on it.

It was his wife who triggered him by suggesting that there must be people who would like to buy his list. After he scathingly advised her to let him do the thinking, he reasoned out a plan. He compiled a folio, including the list of 400 stations and instructions—many advertising agencies, even major ones, didn't know about P.I. deals because station owners were secretive about it—and sent out 300 letters to advertising agencies other than those he had gotten names from. He offered his folio for $50 a copy.

Before it was over, Hubert pyramided that original $37 into $26,000 and launched the successful business he operates today.

These three success stories share one factor: each was based on an original idea. Yet, there are differences, too. Pet Rocks was a temporary thing, a 90-day fad, but it earned its creator more in 90 days than most of us earn in a lifetime. The portable toilet was an invention. The P.I. package was an idea developed slowly and laboriously, with its originator never being sure what the next step would be.

But there is one other common factor, a most important one: in each case, the individual *did something* with his idea. Millions of good ideas are lost because the originators never do anything about their great ideas after they develop them. Unless an idea is put to work, it may as well have never occurred.

NOTIONS VERSUS IDEAS

As the manager of a large group of people, I found employees coming to me frequently with their ideas. Only most of these ideas weren't really thought out; they were merely vague notions. I didn't want to discourage imagination or offend well-intentioned people; yet, I found myself constantly frustrated by such things as this:

We were a technical-services firm, doing most of our business with government agencies. One day, one of the people on my staff came into my office and showed me a newspaper item advising the world that the Department of the Interior was assigned responsibility for cleaning up water pollution. (This was before EPA was formed.) She gave me an "idea": "Let's go and get a contract to help Interior do this job." That was it. That was her great "idea." How could I turn her off this impractical notion without making her feel put down, humiliated?

I finally hit on a foolproof way to handle such situations, which arose quite often: I agreed that the idea was a great one, and asked the offeror of the great idea to now prepare a reasonably detailed *plan* to begin doing something concrete about implementing the idea! Without exception, I never heard from one of these idea-offerors again.

This leads me to the firm belief that unless you can back up your thought with a plan for action, you do not yet have an idea. You have only a notion. And there is no money in a notion.

When an employee came to me with a justified complaint about the way his group was organized and said it should be reorganized, I agreed. I authorized him to draw up a reorganization plan. Complete and everlasting silence followed.

When an eager staff person came to me to report that the new Department of Transportation had a large beginning budget, I authorized him to draw up a marketing plan, identifying specific targets within the new Transportation Department, and plans for pursuing the targets. I never heard about it again.

To this day, I test all notions which come my way—whether I originate them or they are suggested to me—by immediately considering possible practical applications. If I can't come up with any, I shelve the notion, at least until I can find an application.

Getting an idea is not even one-half the battle. It's probably not more than 10 percent, in most cases. It's only the beginning of the battle. The rest is devising an application, developing a practical, detailed plan of action, and putting the idea and plan to work.

You'll find that's true in every case you read about in this book. And you'll ultimately realize that the ability to conceive applications and develop plans to implement the idea and its application is even more important than the idea itself.

THE ELEMENTS

The title of this book was designed, frankly, to entice your interest. After all, doesn't everyone get good ideas, now and then? And shouldn't the conceiver of a good idea be entitled to make money from his or her idea?

Certainly. You should be able to make money from your good ideas. That's the purpose of this entire book—to help you get ideas and make money from those ideas. But if you believe that the world will beat a path to your door when you invent the better mousetrap, and press their damp dollars into your eager little hands—forget it! It's a fable. You just might get lucky, as Gary Dahl did. But don't count on it. Anyway, Gary Dahl didn't "just get lucky" at all. *He put himself into a position to get lucky* by making up a package and renting a booth at a trade show where he could be seen. He had developed a plan and was beginning to work it when Fate stepped in with a smile, in the person of that *Time* reporter.

Here are the several elements you will need to turn that great idea into folding money in your pocket and a row of zeros inscribed in your bank book:

1. Get—or copy, borrow, steal—your basic idea. (It doesn't have to be "different" or original.)
2. Decide how you will use it to make money by selling it or something deriving from it.
3. Work out your plan for "packaging" the product/service for which you are to be paid.
4. Develop your marketing plan—advertising and/or other sales promotion.
5. Do it.

Those are the things we want to talk about in all the pages that follow.

2

INNOVATE OR IMITATE?

Study what some other successful person is doing and do the same.
—John D. Rockefeller, Sr.

John D. Rockefeller, Sr. is reputed to have offered the above advice to many people. His thought was that emulating a successful business took much of the risk out of a new enterprise, and almost ensured success.

Successful businesses have been built imitating other people's ideas, introducing new ideas, and adapting old ideas. As they taught me in the Infantry School at Fort Benning, Georgia, during the Great Unpleasantness currently abbreviated as "WW II," anything that works is right.

The three examples used in the first chapter to introduce you to the subject were all original ideas—perhaps not "new" in the strictest sense of the word (but what is totally and completely new?) but original at least.

On the other hand, Joe Cossman returned from that Second World War keenly aware of the post-war shortage of consumer goods in Europe, stumbled across a ready supply of soap for which he could readily find a European buyer, and quit his $35-a-week job to put his first deal across and launch his career, which was to make him a millionaire. It wasn't a new idea at all—he simply matched a need with a means to satisfy the need. That's a basic business principle.

Remington-Rand hired one of the inventors of the electronic digital computer and offered the world its first commercial computer, but IBM seized the idea and became the number one (by far) computer manufacturer in the world.

An engineer intrigued with the characteristics of a special new spring his company had produced for a special application took one home to fool around with it. His children loved it, especially when they discovered that it could "walk" down stairs. He marketed it successfully as a children's toy under the name "Slinky."

"Silly Putty" was a new plastic with unusual characteristics and no apparent practical use—until someone decided to offer it as a children's toy.

WHAT IS IT YOU SELL?

Let's take a look at some of the successful ideas and businesses we've talked about so far. Just what was it that was sold—that the customers bought?

In some cases, it was a completely new product—the digital computer, for example. There had been mechanical "computers" around for some time, although they were not exactly lightning-fast or very sophisticated. In fact, they were pretty much Rube Goldberg kinds of machines, full of complex levers, wheels, gears, and cams. And there had even been some "analog" computers around, but they were more or less limited to specific jobs for which they had been designed; they didn't have the flexibility of the new digital computers, which are able to take on almost any kind of computing job. Nor did they have the speed of this new machine, which had virtually no moving parts except for input and output devices.

Remington-Rand was first on the market with it, after hiring one of the two men who had worked at the University of Pennsylvania to develop this remarkable new machine for the government, as part of the war effort (WW II). How then did IBM catch up with Remington-Rand and then get so far ahead that the Remington-Rand official statement one year was a wish to "be a better Number Two" in the computer field?

IBM had—and has—two things going for it: superb marketing organization and superb service organization. And part of IBM's secret of success in marketing is the quality of its service: customers who know IBM buy with complete confidence that IBM will be Johnny-on-the-spot with service, when needed. And that's no small matter in these days of steadily declining service and customer-be-damned attitudes. The customer doesn't really care about an argument for the technical superiority of one highly sophisticated product versus another. The computer is a "black box," as far as the customer is concerned, and the chief difference between the two black boxes is the service needed to keep them operating without undue interruption.

Superb service is almost a new idea these days. When customers buy IBM, that's what they buy—superb service.

The "Slinky" was not a new product, but offering it as a children's toy was a new idea—a successful new idea.

Customers bought Pet Rocks because they were a novelty—amusing and "in." The thing made a nice present, and it was a conversation piece.

"Mood rings" were also a short-lived fad that made a great deal of money for a number of people. And the gadget wasn't even new. It had been around for years, until someone came up with the idea of setting the mineral stone into cheap rings and thinking up a catchy name.

Thetford brought a kind of respectability to portable toilets, as well as a great increase in convenience. Today's portable toilets are attractive, clean, and odorless, unlike the early models. The comforts of home.

To make money, the item being sold does not need to be new or different. The packaging, promotion, name, or something else about it can be new or different—or even if not new and different, merely better, more effective, than what is presently offered.

WHAT'S WRONG WITH THIS PICTURE?

Joe Neophyte has come up with a brand-new idea: He has discovered a new and unknown foreign import, an electronic room-air purifier. He's got an exclusive on this sensational new device, and he's going to go to town on it. People will be breaking his front door down to be the first to own one.

What's wrong with this picture is that it's not likely to happen—although Joe may be able to *make* it happen, if he's a genius promoter, has lots of money to spend, and/or gets lucky. But the probabilities are that he will have an uphill fight to win acceptance of his product, if he manages to at all.

New products, like new ideas, take customers aback. Everyone tends to resist change, almost instinctively. What is familiar we feel secure with; what is new and strange represents potential hazard, insecurity. It puts us on the defensive.

That's one distinct disadvantage of offering something really new. In many ways, it's easier when you have plenty of competition for this simple reason: all your competitors have participated in educating the public to the product or idea, so that it is no longer a strange one. This removes that one obstacle (sales resistance to a new idea) at least.

There are two basic selling problems you will face. If the product/service/idea you offer is really new and different, you will have to educate your prospects and break down that resistance to new ideas before you can persuade them to buy. If what you offer is something familiar—another brand, perhaps, but something which is recognizable as similar to something people presently buy—your selling problem is to persuade them to buy *your* brand, or buy even the same brand, but from *you* rather than from someone else.

In short, a market must be created for every product/service—a demand for it—and competitors help you create that market through their advertising and sales promotion. Too, when you go up against established competition, you have the comfort of knowing that there *is* a demand, a market.

Do not be too quick to assume, therefore, that having a new and different idea is necessarily a shortcut to success. It may be a shortcut to heartbreak.

Yet, there are ways to have your cake and eat it too—to get the advantages of something new and different without fighting against the disadvantages. It would be premature to get into that yet. For the moment, recognize that you will probably meet with some resistance to change when you offer something new, but that there are ways to overcome this problem.

What has this to do with *getting* money-making ideas? Just this: When you develop those money-making ideas, you must keep the selling problem in mind—it's an integral part of the idea-generating process. You must remember that the more radically different the idea, the more problems you face in selling it—unless you can apply some of the remedies you'll learn about later in these pages.

Just remember that your objective is not to be new and different for the sake of being new and different—for the sake of being clever—but for the sake of making money. The chief question is, will it make money? Will people buy it?

Here is one of my favorite quotations, attributed to Calvin Coolidge, President of the United States from 1923 to 1928. He was known as "Silent Cal" because he said little. But he said a mouthful here:

> Nothing in the world can take the place of persistence. Talent will not; nothing is more common than unsuccessful men with talent. Genius will not; unrewarded genius is almost a proverb. Education will not; the world is full of educated derelicts. Persistence and determination alone are omnipotent.

I hope that as we proceed through these pages, you will come to appreciate the wisdom in that brief paragraph. All you will learn here, all the ideas you will read about and generate, all the knowledge you will acquire will not be quite as important to your ultimate success as the words of that taciturn but wise man.

3

CREATIVITY: WHAT IS IT?

Genius is one percent inspiration and ninety-nine percent perspiration.

—Thomas Edison

GREAT ACCOMPLISHMENTS ARE ALWAYS IMPOSSIBLE

Charles "Boss" Kettering was hired to create the self-starter for the Oldsmobile automobile by Ransom Olds, who knew that he would never sell automobiles to women as long as cars had to be started with a hand crank. And Kettering knew that the self-starter was a practical impossibility. All engineers knew that. They knew—and could easily prove—that the starter motor had to be as large as the engine it was to start, or it would overheat. Moveover, there were no storage batteries available capable of supplying enough current to such a starting motor.

Nevertheless, Kettering did design and build a satisfactory starting motor that was only a fraction the size of the engine and could fit easily under the hood of an automobile. And he went on to improve the storage batteries of that day, too.

There was no escaping the basic fact. A starting motor smaller than the engine *would* overheat. Period. And since there was no escape from that fundamental fact, and Kettering had as a second fact that he must and would design a workable starting motor, Kettering simply decided to *accept* overheating as a condition to be expected and designed for! (Some call that "finessing the problem.")

What Kettering saw and others did not was this: Under practical operating conditions, overheating could be accepted. A starter would operate for only a minute or two at a time, and would not be called upon for some time after, allowing it ample time to cool down again. Ergo, it need only be designed to withstand some overheating without doing it permanent damage. And to this day, starters overheat, but it does them no serious damage if they are not run continuously or for extended periods.

That lesson was not lost on the aerospace engineers of our times when NASA set about designing "re-entry vehicles" in the space program. Everyone knew that there was no way of slowing down a re-entry vehicle to a point where it would not encounter serious friction with the atmosphere and overheat badly. Extended overheating at high temperatures had to be accepted. It was a difficult problem, but not an insoluble one: the answer was an "ablative" nose cone—in practice, a ceramic shield which would, by design, be burned up during re-entry, protecting the metal container it covered. Some of our modern ceramic ovenware is the result of the search for and development of a suitable ceramic for the purpose.

Moral: When you tackle a problem which is logically impossible because of some inescapable facts, *accept* those facts. Accept those conditions. And design your solution to work, *despite* those conditions.

All great inventions have been impossible dreams. Edison was ridiculed by those experts who knew that the electric light was an impractical idea. Governor Earle of Pennsylvania was denounced as a fool when he approved the high-speed Pennsylvania Turnpike, because all the experts knew that automobile tires could not stand up under sustained speeds over 35 miles per hour. Pasteur was called a madman for challenging the accepted idea of "spontaneous generation." And Semmelweiss was persecuted for insisting that doctors who didn't wash their hands between examinations were transmitting diseases from one patient to another. (Did you know that the Polaroid Land color camera works on the "impossible" idea of using only two primary colors?)

Some men are almost-bottomless pools of creative ideas. Edison went on to invent many more things after he succeeded with the electric light. And Kettering was also the developer/inventor of many new devices, including the first electric cash register. Yet, creativity is not the exclusive province of a few men and women. Everyone is capable of creative thought—intellectually. But there are obstacles, for many of us. Thinking creatively requires a certain amount of courage and self-confidence. To be creative is to be different, to challenge the status quo and decide that there is a better way, to reject accepted methods and practices, to brave ridicule by the self-appointed "experts" who are always waiting in the wings to jeer at anything new and different.

Education gets in the way, too. Breakthroughs are often made by those who are too ignorant, too uninformed to know that it can't be done! Studies of creativity have indicated rather clearly that the greater or more advanced an education the individual has, the less likely he is to come up with new and different ideas.

Kettering himself said that education was "all right" if one didn't allow it to interfere with thinking. What he meant, of course, was that one must not allow acquired knowledge to substitute for independent thought. Despite the fact that many advances are made by scholarly individuals, the highly educated are less likely to challenge accepted notions than are the lesser educated. Even today, in this era of sophisticated technology, many patent holders of sophisticated devices are not even college graduates.

So do not let the lack of an advanced education discourage you from thinking great thoughts about better ways; that lack may even be an advantage.

THE NATURE OF THE CREATIVE PROCESS

Research into the nature of creativity suggests strongly that there are three phases or elements in the process of developing new ideas: concentration, incubation, and illumination.

In interviews, inventors and other creative people revealed that first they thought, hard and long, about a problem or a new way to do something. Then they dismissed the thought from their minds entirely, going on to other things. And ultimately, at some future time—and frequently when they were relaxing—an answer or new idea flashed into their minds spontaneously, as if by magic.

A commonly accepted explanation for this phenomenon is this: The concentration—that long and deep *conscious* thought—is a means of transferring the problem to the human *subconscious* mind. In effect, it says to the subconscious: "Here is a problem for you, with all I know about it. Work on it and tell me what you think, when you are ready." During incubation, the subconscious is working on the problem—perhaps for a few hours, or a few weeks or months. The illumination, or "inspiration," as it is often referred to, is the act of the subconscious saying to the conscious mind: "Here is the best answer I have been able to come up with. Try this."

Evidently, there is no direct link between the conscious and the subconscious. It takes intense concentration for an individual to transfer ideas from his conscious to his subconscious mind. But communication between the two is greatly facilitated when the conscious mind is relaxed and not engaged in active or deep concentration. That's when the communication between the two minds is most easily accomplished. (Which explains hypnosis neatly.)

Obviously, you cannot assign a task to your subconscious without identifying and explaining what the subconscious is to do—therefore, the need for the concentration phase. But then you must dismiss the problem from your conscious thoughts.

This theory of the creative process explains why you can sit up in bed suddenly with the answer to something which has troubled you, or why you suddenly recall a name you have been unable to recall—after you have quit trying.

Hypnosis demonstrates that the subconscious retains information that has been lost to the conscious mind—forgotten, that is. The subconscious is therefore in a better position to work on a problem: it has more information at its disposal. It is also not so bound by emotional biases and prejudicial ideals as is the conscious mind, but appears to be far more objective.

Man still does not know too well how the human mind works, but it is rather well established that there is a conscious and a subconscious (or unconscious) mind, and that under hypnosis, individuals can remember things they cannot remember consciously, and perform feats they cannot perform consciously. This latter is significant. It demonstrates that to a large extent, what we can do depends largely on what we *think* we can do. Under hypnosis, we can extend an arm, make it as rigid as a bar of steel, and hold it in that position for a long period—something we could not do in a fully conscious state. We can will our bodies and our conscious minds to do things suggested by a hypnotist, such as remembering or forgetting events, developing a revulsion for cigarettes, or responding to cues.

WHAT "POSITIVE THINKING" REALLY MEANS

There are countless proponents of "positive thinking." Unfortunately, too many make it appear to be some sort of mysticism, which it is certainly not. It is, in fact, another thing which characterizes creative people: they have confidence in their own abilities and in their quests. Thomas Edison never doubted that he would ultimately succeed in finding a material which would serve as a satisfactory filament for his electric light. It is reported that he tested some 10,000 materials, never doubting once that he would ultimately find at least one that would work. And he never considered it a failure when a tested material did not work—it was a success, the successful elimination of one more candidate material, and a step forward to finding the material which would work.

That's persistence, perseverance. But it arises out of confidence, faith. Without that faith in your eventual success, it is impossible to persevere in the face of disappointments and setbacks. And with that faith, it is impossible not to persevere: the two are inseparable.

There have been dozens of books written on the subject of "positive thinking." But in the end, they all come down to that same point: if you *believe,* you will be able to survive all the disappointments and find your way through, over, or around all obstacles. Successful people rarely become successful overnight. The overnight success you hear about often is the climax of years of effort, of many struggles, disappointments, and setbacks. When the breakthrough finally comes, those who do not know the story tend to regard it as pure good fortune. But let's have a look at some of those overnight successes.

Elisha G. Otis seemed destined to failure. With no taste for farming, but born to a farmer, he left home to seek a different career. He built and ran a grist mill, which failed. He then built carriages, surviving for seven years, until this too failed. Inventive and "mechanical" by nature, he next built a plant to manufacture machines, which survived for only two years. He then became a master mechanic in a bedstead factory in Yonkers, New York, but the bedstead factory eventually failed. However, during his tenure with the bedstead manufacturer, Elisha had devised several new machines, including a hoist with a safety feature which would automatically stop its fall should the hoisting rope break.

With the failure of the bedstead factory, Otis founded the elevator company that bears his name today and grosses some $300 million a year. And even then, the company's greatest success came after Otis passed on, leaving the factory to his sons. But for some 20 years previously, Elisha Otis experienced one failure after another, and only his great faith in himself enabled him to go on to new ventures.

Imagine yourself at the age of 51, having finally, after long effort, developed a method for preserving milk. You're deep in debt, carrying on your experiments in the basement of a friend. Your family lives with relatives hundreds of miles away, because, being already deeply in debt, you can't support them. Now, you have developed your method, and the product is far better than anything competitive. You apply for a patent, but it is denied. It is to be three long years of struggle before you win your battle for a patent. Even then, you have many problems. The public is not quick to accept your new product, which, though better, is far different from what they have become accustomed to. (That resistance to change again!) Your two backers, without whose financial support you could not survive at all, become discouraged and withdraw, one selling his share to his father-in-law, the other buying out one-half your patent right, which was so difficult to win in the first place. Your factory closes.

But months later you try again, persuading your former partners to another effort. And now, as you seem to be succeeding, comes the Panic of 1857, and all appears lost again.

But now you have the good fortune to meet a successful businessman who agrees to buy out your partners and back you, for a one-half interest. And this infusion of money enables you to ride out the Panic.

And yet your troubles are not over. Accustomed to buying doctored milk (commonly referred to as "swill milk") that is adulterated with chalk, watered down, and thickened with molasses, a newspaperman attacks your product, placing it in a class with the adulterated milk sold elsewhere. And it is a bold move by you that begins your first real breakthrough: you write a powerful rebuttal and place it as an advertisement in the very paper in which you were attacked.

Your name is Gail Borden, and you founded what is today known as The Borden Company. You suffered through some eight or nine years of bitter setbacks before even sighting eventual success. Only determination—stubbornness, even— has kept you going. That and the knowledge that you have developed a worthwhile product.

Hershey, Pennsylvania, is named after Milton S. Hershey. It's a company town, of course, and you can smell the characteristic bouquet of chocolate even before you reach the environs of the Hershey buildings. Milton S. Hershey rarely knew anything but adversity in his life, from the time he trudged two miles to the country school near Lancaster, Pennsylvania, to the time when he started and failed in one candy-manufacturing business after another.

First there was the penny-candy business in Philadelphia, which was a brisk enough enterprise but could not expand into a truly worthwhile business without the capital Hershey did not have. And the long, hard hours broke his health to a point where it was almost a miracle that he finally pulled through and survived. Next, there was the caramel manufacturing in Chicago, retailing the product through street vendors, again working long hours to earn enough for survival. Then there was the shop in Denver, which survived for only a short while. Next, a shop in New York and a return to caramel making—apparent success, such as it was, but again, failure and bankruptcy.

And now, another caramel-making venture, this time returning to Lancaster, apparently a good move, for success now smiles. Backed with some outside capital by relatives, the Lancaster Caramel Co. begins to grow. A later sale of this company for $1 million provided Hershey with the capital for his subsequent venture into chocolate, with results that everyone today knows.

Charles N. Aronson, almost on the spur of the moment, founded the Aronson Machine Company in Arcade, New York, in a decrepit building whose sign still said it was "Zimmer's Garage," although it had long since ceased to be. Aronson could tote up perhaps $4,000 in assets, if he included his 1940 Ford (the year was 1946), a 12-inch bench lathe, and his hand tools.

It was a race with disaster from the beginning. The lone bank in town would not take a mortgage on the place, except for about one-half its minimum value, and then backed out of even that due to the pressure of competitors, who didn't want a rival business established in Arcade. He had no place to live, since he had been living in a place owned by his former employer, and had to vacate that. And when Aronson managed to swing a mortgage with the proprietor of the building, and used a corner of the old garage for his own living quarters, he discovered that the orders he had to start with had been canceled through the machinations of a competitor.

So, instead of manufacturing the fixtures Aronson had planned to manufacture, he found himself compelled to pursue "job shop" work, which is so cutthroat that it has been the death of more than one small machine shop such as Aronson had just opened without capital, equipment, or customers.

Three things saved the infant Aronson Machine Company: Aronson's own iron will and unshakable belief in himself, his fantastic capacity for work, and his true genius as a designer/inventor. With only a high-school education, Aronson could and did design one machine after another, many of them involving new inventions for which he was able to get patents, and all of them built directly from his drawings, without prototypes.

It took years of his iron will and capacity to work 18 yours a day, seven days a week before Aronson Machine Company could be said to have a firm footing. But in the end, Aronson sold his company for approximately $2.5 million and retired gracefully, after 23 years of struggle. Never did he doubt that he would be successful. He *knew* that he could do it, and he did it. (Ultimately, Aronson Machine Company settled on becoming the manufacturer of the world's best welding positioners, and remained in that business from that time on.)

Each of these successful entrepreneurs was creative, in his own way, although not all were inventors. Each, however, addressed a need.

4
THE COMMON
DENOMINATOR: NEEDS

The admonition to find a need and fill it is one of the oldest clichés offered to those seeking business success. It's almost as helpful a piece of advice as Bernard Baruch's famous easy formula for stock market success: "Buy low and sell high."

As individuals, we all have a number of basic needs. Our direct, physical needs are for food, shelter, clothing, medical care, transportation, and many other material goods and services. But we have emotional needs, too. They were recognized informally for many years, made the subjects of intense studies by Sigmund Freud, and formalized by Maslow in his hierarchy of needs. As Maslow and others pointed out, everyone needs love, happiness, security, and self-esteem.

The advertising industry has long since recognized and put these emotional needs to use. Products advertised by the Madison Avenue experts offer to bring the user affection, admiration, money, security, peace of mind, respect, prestige, happiness, fun, and all the other psyche-satisfying benefits of modern products.

But we all have needs at different levels of consciousness. While we may go to an automobile showroom to look at new cars because we have a need for a new car, we have some psychological/emotional needs that can be satisfied only by the *right* car for us. The driver of a Volkswagen has the same transportation capability as the driver of a new Continental, and at lesser cost, too. And while the Volkswagen owner may have bought the vehicle because he wished to economize on both acquisition and operating costs, he may also have selected the VW because it is a symbol to him. For some people, a VW

20

is a status symbol, just as a Continental is a status symbol to others, and as a low-slung, expensive sports model is to still others.

We can't discount the possibility that some people make a buying decision on purely logical, rational grounds. But a great many buyers are influenced by subtle factors, such as pride and the need to present an image. And that need is no less a true need than the practical need to have an automobile.

Some marketing experts speak of *creating* a need. At first glance, this seems to be impossible. How can you make someone decide to want something? Customers either have a given need or they do not, right—a need they already *feel?* If the customer did not feel this need, he would not be in your place of business talking to you. Or would he?

Experience proves that a large percentage of automobile buyers—perhaps even a majority—did not enter automobile showrooms with the conscious intention of buying. They were just "looking." And looking turned into buying in a great many cases. (I bought my first new automobile while just "looking" at the new models.)

FELT NEEDS VERSUS CREATED NEEDS

The fact is that there are two kinds of needs which we ought to recognize and be acutely aware of: felt needs and created or unconscious needs. The car buyer may have had a felt need for a car, but he probably had an unconscious need for some *kind* of a car. Or he may not have actually felt a need for a car, but he had an unconscious need for a new status symbol, perhaps to reflect his promotion to a higher-level job.

Look about your house to see how many products you have which did not even exist a few years ago. A young couple setting up housekeeping today has a TV on the immediate-needs list. How could a household exist without a TV? Yet, TV did not exist in the youth of a large portion of our present population. It could hardly have been a need, felt or otherwise, when it did not exist.

The introduction of something new often creates the corresponding need by the mere fact of its existence.

For some years now, the threat of energy shortage has plagued us, with the use of oil overtaking the rate of production and the known reserves in the ground. One of the uses of oil is to heat homes equipped with oil burners. Prior to the advent of the oil burner, most homes were heated with coal. Coal was a need. Few homes use coal today; oil is a need—except for homes built in recent years, most of which are heated with gas. Gas is a need today.

It's not exactly an accident or a coincidence that movement to the suburbs, the disappearance of the "Mom and Pop store," the appearance of the supermarket, and the swift rise of shopping centers and malls have all taken place in the same era. Two inventions are chiefly responsible for all: the electric refrigerator and the automobile. The refrigerator and the freezer have made it possible to shop for a week or more at a time, instead of every day, by providing the means in the home for storing food without spoilage, spurring the rise of the supermarkets, which first appeared in the cities, where most of us lived. But the fast rise in automobile ownership sped the move to the suburbs, with shopping centers and malls, and as parking in the cities became more and more impossible, the easy parking at shopping centers brought more and more people to the suburbs.

We have been assured that two things are inevitable: death and taxes. But we may add to that, *change*. Change is inevitable. Change is constant, all about us, particularly in the dynamics of American society and industry.

And yet, the more it changes, the more it is the same, as the French put it so eloquently: our *basic needs* do not change, much as they may appear to! Whether we heat our homes by coal, oil, or gas—or even by modern solar panels—the basic need is still heat. When an 18th-century townsman splurged on a silver snuff box instead of a brass one, he did so to command respect and satisfy his ego by showing off his affluence. Some men today drive a Mercedes for the same reason.

So, to fill needs, you must understand what those needs

are—both the conscious, felt needs and the unconscious needs. The understanding of this is the basis for success in business, whatever the business. All business succeeds to the extent that it satisfies the needs of its customers. And it can satisfy the needs of its customers only to the extent that the operators of the business understand and cater to the needs of its customer—*all* those needs.

This works down to all levels, from the basic orientation of the business itself to the approaches used by its salesmen. Here is a good example of the difference between two salesmen, one of whom made an effort to discover his prospect's need, and the other of whom did not.

My automobile had developed an ominous knock, which worried me. I thought I was ready for a new car, and I especially needed a dependable one, since I traveled regularly at the time. I therefore sped off Saturday morning to the showrooms of a large suburban dealer who had several franchises and did a quite enormous business.

I drove up to the Chevrolet showroom, parked, and walked inside to inspect the cars on display. A salesman approached me.

"Looking for a Chevvy?"

I shrugged. "I'm not sure what I'm looking for."

He handed me his card and said, "I'll be around when you decide what you're interested in."

My mouth dropped open. I couldn't believe that he would give up on a fresh prospect that easily. I turned, in utter disgust, about to leave the showroom and try another dealer, when a second salesman approached me.

"What kind of car are you interested in?"

"I'm not sure," I said. "Anything reliable. I don't want to spend a lot of money, but I want something dependable, and the brand name isn't especially important to me."

He asked for the keys to my car, offering to get me a swift appraisal. I surrendered them, and he disappeared, promising to be back in a few minutes. When he came back, he grinned at me. "Bearing knock."

I nodded. "That's why I want to get rid of it."

"You want a Chevvy especially?"

I shook my head. "Not especially."

"You're driving a Dodge. I can give you a hell of a deal on a Dart. Lot more than I can give you on a Chevvy."

To shorten the story, he took me into the Dodge showroom and sold me a white Dart, which I drove with complete satisfaction for the next five years. And the first salesman could have made that sale easily, if he had made even a modest effort. I didn't have to be "sold." I had come in to buy. All I wanted was some help. All the salesman had to do was find out what my need was.

It was unlike the first time I had bought a new car, when I had really come in just "to look," but had met a shrewd salesman who guessed my need when he said to me, "We could sew this up in less than an hour. You can drive out with your new car tonight." I glanced out the window at the decrepit thing I had been driving—it had gotten a flat tire while I was in the showroom—and thought to myself, "Gee, I'll never have to push that old wreck around again," as I reached for my checkbook to make the down payment. That salesman had also looked out at my old clunker, seen the flat on it, and guessed that I'd like nothing better than to never sit in it again. My need was for the peace of mind, the comfort, and the sheer joy of owning a new one, for the first time in my life. Had he not offered to have me drive out immediately with a new one, he could never have sold me. (In those days, it usually required several days to clear credit and make delivery of a new car.)

Gail Borden knew that there was a need for a better preserved milk when he went on his quest, and although he also had to fight adversity and prejudice against change, he never faltered because he knew the need was real.

Before Elisha Otis invented the safety feature for his elevator, elevators were used only to raise materials; they weren't safe enough for people. Otis could not have foreseen today's tall office buildings and high-rise apartment complexes and hotels. But without the safety elevator, they would not be possible at all. Otis anticipated a need which was just beginning in his time.

Charles Aronson knew there was a need for better machine design than was available, and he later learned that nowhere was that need greater than in the field of welding positioners, many of which were shoddy, unsafe contraptions, assembled by companies more interested in a cheap product and a fast profit than in meeting the *true* needs of their customers for better quality and safer designs. And in spite of his somewhat higher prices, Aronson's machines eventually established his reputation for meeting needs better than his competitors did. (He also lived up to his delivery promises, which most of his competitors failed to do, again meeting the customers' needs.)

WHAT IS THE TRUE NEED?

People never need a product or a service per se. Their true need is always for what the product or service *does* for them. You will see this idea come up again and again. When you go to a restaurant, you go to fill your stomach. But you go for more than that, or you would buy a can of beans or a bag of popcorn. Or, at least, you would go to the cheapest restaurant you could find. You also go for the atmosphere, the pleasure of good food well-prepared, the comfort of an attractive dining room full of attractive people, the sense of security that comes from eating in a highly reputed establishment, or for whatever else you seek—that is, you have a need in addition to sustenance.

To determine what the true need is, you must always ask: What does the customer want this thing (service) to *do* for him?

Identifying true need is a common denominator in many ways, and the search for it shows up in many occupations and professions. In value engineering it is called the "basic function," and a major portion of a value engineering analysis is devoted to identifying it—in fact, it is the major focus of the entire analytical effort. In the advertising business, it is the objective of "motivational research," for which millions of dollars are spent and great effort is invested. It is the essence of management by objectives, which is considered to be a major breakthrough in the art of management. It lies at the heart of systems analysis. It is what *every* business is all about.

Peter Drucker, well-known management consultant and author of numerous books on the art of management, addresses this by pointing out that far too many proprietors and executives do not know what business they are in. But other writers on the subject, particularly those writing on the subject of marketing, point out that *every* business is a service business. And, in the final analysis, they are right, of course. People buy things for what they *do* rather than for what they *are*.

Take, for example, even the objects which do not have a directly practical function, such as a ring or necklace. Why does a customer buy jewelry? What does jewelry do for the buyer? The benefits of jewelry are chiefly psychological benefits, of course—feelings of satisfaction and ego-gratification, a sense of security in the possession of an expensive gem, the pleasure of drawing attention and even envy, the sustenance of one's "image" or "position," and so forth (although some buy diamonds for investment).

Some years ago I talked with a young man who owned a $250 suit—an outrageously high price for a suit at that time— which he wore on the rarest of special occasions, such as when he was scheduled to be interviewed for a position. He considered that $250 a sound investment, and it undoubtedly was, for him. He explained that when he wore that suit, he was a transformed personality. He *felt* successful, and he was in a far better position psychologically to handle himself in an interview or other important meeting. The knowledge that he was wearing a suit which only very successful men could ordinarily afford to wear gave him enormous self-confidence.

Such a consideration transcends price and practical functions for the customer. When a customer wants or needs something enough, price is rarely a consideration—*as long as the customer agrees that the item does indeed satisfy the need.*

At the heart of most emotional needs lies the need for security. Money represents security. Love represents security. Respect, prestige, admiration represent security. Insurance represents security. Education represents security. Job promotion represents security. Honors bestowed represent security. Just about every human desire or need translates ultimately into security—or, perhaps more precisely, into a *sense* of security. And that appears to be true even when you subdivide security into such categories as financial security, physical security, and emotional security. In fact, such classification makes the truth of it even more apparent.

The success of any business is related directly to how effectively the business offer matches the conscious and/or unconscious needs of its customers, *in the customers' perceptions.* It is not the proprietor's perception that is important here, but the customer's perception. If the customer does not agree that you are satisfying his need, it doesn't really matter whether, in actuality, you are or are not; you will not be favored with his business.

The case of IBM computers was mentioned earlier: we could argue endlessly about the engineering merits of IBM computers versus anyone else's computers, and we might even be able to make a good case for technical superiority of one of the rival computers. Yet, the argument would not be particularly effective, because specific engineering superiority is of little significance to the customer. The typical customer is concerned only with function—what the computer does or does not do for him. The IBM better-idea is a simple one: *service.* Swift, dependable response when the customer needs service. Most customers are not so sure that anyone else is that dependable, for service generally has deteriorated seriously in modern times. And Mr. Typical Customer rationalizes thusly:

Maybe Rival X's computer is a splendid technological machine which rarely breaks down, but it's bound to break down occasionally. What happens then? Can I get fast service and get it back into operation quickly, before my whole system begins to deteriorate? Even if IBM's computer were to fail more often that Rival X's machine, wouldn't IBM's service mean that I would have a greater overall reliability?

Whether true or not, this is the *perception* of many IBM customers. (It's *my* perception of IBM and the reason *I* use IBM typewriters.)

When I started a newsletter several years ago, I carefully refrained from using "Vol. 1, No. 1" on it because I did not want to draw attention to the fact that it was a new publication. It's hard enough to get subscriptions, without the added burden of inviting people to subscribe to something new and untried. With the history of several years of continued publication behind me, I began to inscribe a volume and issue number, because now that would work *for* me by revealing that the publication had been in existence successfully for several years. (Ergo, it was not risky to subscribe to it for a year ahead.) I was much concerned with my customers' perceptions of my stability as a newsletter publisher. The newsletter not only had to serve their needs in its content but had to give them some reasonable assurance that it would remain in existence long enough to complete the year's subscription they were being asked to pay for in advance—that is, it had to serve their need for confidence in what they were buying.

5

WHAT COMES FIRST—
THE CHICKEN OR THE EGG?

*Pioneers are the fellows who get arrows in their backs, and
missionaries are the ones who wind up in the pot.*

—Don Dible

CUSTOMER PERCEPTIONS
REVISITED

Gary Dahl (Pet Rocks) found an idea and, with the help of
Time magazine, created a need for it. Thetford Corporation
was founded by a man who found a need and created a product to satisfy the need. Both were successful businesses, although Pet Rocks peaked very rapidly.

Hubert Simon also discovered a need. In his case, his customers recognized the value of what he offered and eagerly
seized the opportunity to buy and take advantage of his offer.
On the other hand, Gail Borden had great difficulty in persuading prospects of the value of his product in satisfying their
need, as did Elisha Otis.

The difference here is, again, a matter of customer perceptions: owners of advertising agencies readily recognized a need
for the names of radio stations that would accept P.I. advertising; their problem had always been the difficulty of getting
such a list. But condensed/evaporated milk was a new product,
and Borden faced that traditional resistance to change when he
offered his new product to the world, as did Elisha Otis. (Elevators had always been for goods, not for people.)

So we have here, first, the basic difference between dis-
covering a need and finding a product or service that satisfies a

29

need not yet "felt" by customers. Borden knew there was a need for preserving milk, in some manner, but not many customers knew it yet. They couldn't feel the need because they didn't have the faintest notion that such a product was possible in the middle of the nineteenth century. Borden's problem therefore was complicated by two negative factors: he had to "create"—make people aware of—a need for milk which could be stored on the shelf for long periods of time, and he had to make them agree that his product satisfied that need. (Customers resisted because his canned milk tasted a bit different from the adulterated fresh milk people were buying in those days.) The way of the pioneer is usually hard, which may be a good argument for Rockefeller's advice to emulate someone already successful.

It isn't always so, however. Thetford's new portable toilet did not experience that traditional customer resistance, because the new idea was a *new application* of a *familiar product*. The idea of a portable toilet was not new; its adaptation to a trailer home was. Customers could readily recognize the desirability of the application. It satisfied a need without requiring the customer to accept the risk of being the first to try out a brand-new concept.

Once upon a time people had to heat their homes, room by room, with stoves or fireplaces. And most ordinary people heated only one or two rooms, usually the kitchen, with the kitchen stove, and the sitting room, with a fireplace. Only the wealthy could afford to have fireplaces in all the rooms. It was not too difficult to persuade people to switch over to central heating, when that became a practical possibility, with a coal stove in the basement and radiators in the various rooms. And when oil came along, it wasn't too difficult to persuade people to switch over to oil, and it was even easier to switch them over to gas, later.

A POWERFUL MOTIVATOR

Through each of the change cycles in heating homes, the basic need was the same: the need for heat, for the comfort of heated rooms. Whether delivered by fireplace or central plant, whether fired by coal, oil, or gas, the need being satisfied was the same: heat. But another need was being served, which helps explain the ease with which these changes were accepted. In each case, a basic need was being satisfied with greater *convenience* than ever before. This also explains why the new Thetford product was so readily acceptable. Don't underestimate the power of convenience as a buying motivation. Convenience is a well-recognized need.

Perhaps belatedly, we should accept the term "need" as synonomous with "desire" when we speak of customer motivation. In everyday terms, you might say to yourself, when faced with a new and attractive, but expensive, gadget, "Oh, I really don't *need* it." But what you are saying to yourself, really, is that while you may *desire* the new gadget, it isn't attractive enough for you to part with the money it will cost. (Although you may change your mind in a little while.) That is to say, the term "need" is not used in any kind of absolute sense, but refers strictly to a customer's perception. The customer might be the first to agree that he doesn't "need" a new refrigerator, but if he decides to buy one anyway, then that desire is a need in the sense used here.

Convenience, then, is a need with most people and especially with the American public. The rapid success of 7-11 stores was due to the fact that they offered the convenience of late-hour shopping when most supermarkets closed at 9 PM or even earlier. And even today, with supermarkets open all night in many places, 7-11 stores still do well, because one can park close to the front door and the stores are small, not requiring long hikes up and down multiple aisles to find what one is looking for.

The downtown area of Silver Spring, Maryland, found itself losing business rapidly to the new Wheaton Plaza shopping center a few miles away. It did not require very intensive study to discover why: parking was difficult in downtown Silver Spring, whereas it was abundantly available at the Wheaton Plaza. The Silver Spring municipal authorities hastened to build large parking facilities throughout the downtown area and quickly recovered most of the business they had lost. Again, convenience was the decisive issue.

Once shopping centers were firmly established, entrepreneurs began to build shopping malls—shopping centers enclosed by walls and heated or air-conditioned, with the seasons. This led to at least a partial exodus of shoppers from the open-air shopping centers, particularly in inclement weather. In at least one case, a plaza countered appropriately: the Prince Georges shopping center in suburban Maryland enclosed and roofed over its shops, converting the center into a mall.

The convenience motivator works at all levels. A mail order dealer compiled a list of free government publications and mailed out a circular announcing quite frankly that all the titles listed were available free of charge from various U.S. government agencies. However, if the customer wished some assistance in getting these, the dealer would be happy to arrange to have the publications sent directly to the customer for a small service fee of 50¢ for each title checked off. The customers responded, sending orders as large as $25 for the convenience of having someone else order free publications for them.

Combine convenience with a recognized or felt need, then, and you immediately have an excellent chance for success. You have only to look around your own household to see the truth of that—an electric can opener for $20 or more to replace the 75¢ can opener of old, automatic coffee makers, microwave ovens, electric frying pans, electric brooms, clock radios, light dimmers, dishwashers, automatic dryers, and dozens of other items which cost money but make life easier and more pleasant.

But it's not only in the home that customers pay for convenience. Most stores today have electronic cash registers that automatically advise the cashier how much change he or she owes the customer, and some have even more advanced features. And some supermarket checkouts today have electronic checkers, which also automatically verify a customer's check-cashing authorization and make inventory postings. Everyone is interested in greater convenience and will pay for it.

Sometimes convenience means speed. We pay the Postal Service extra money for certain express services it offers, and one of the most successful new businesses is a company called Federal Express, which guarantees overnight service on an airfreight package.

One woman makes a profitable business of catering private dinner parties in the home. For a fee, she prepares and serves lobster dinners, and her customers have the convenience of having guests for dinner and being "guests" at their own dinner parties.

In many cities, college students earn money by running valet parking services at private parties. For a fee, they will take over the guests' cars and find parking places for them in adjoining streets, and retrieve the cars when the guests are ready to leave.

BASIC NEEDS AND SECONDARY NEEDS

Basic needs do not change. We shall always have the same basic needs for food, clothing, shelter, love, security, and the like. *Ways* of satisfying those needs and *degrees* to which they may be satisfied do change. In some of the examples we have just reviewed, a basic need was being satisfied at greater convenience to the customer, while in others, convenience itself was the primary need—that is, it was the *convenience* which was being sold.

For example, you can get an express shipment via the Postal Service at about $5 cost, for a small parcel, by taking it to the post office. But for a $14 charge, Federal Express will pick it up. Many people will satisfy that need for express delivery by paying an extra $9 to enjoy the greater convenience of having the shipment picked up.

On the other hand, anyone can drive around the streets and find a parking place, eventually. But many will pay for the convenience of having someone else do it. (One man hires teenagers to drive his car to gas stations and wait in lines during gas shortages.)

So we ought to recognize that needs are at two levels: basic and secondary. We have our personal basic needs, as defined, but we have many secondary needs: convenience, greater speed, greater confidence in the product/service, and so on. And these are often the determinant when a customer is facing several alternative ways of satisfying a need. Which is the most efficient, lowest-cost, most rapid, most dependable, most convenient solution?

The ability to satisfy a secondary need is often the sole determinant of success or failure of an idea.

MUST AN IDEA BE NEW?

By now we should have established that an idea need not necessarily be new. It can be an old idea in new clothes, with a new twist of some sort to improve the idea and/or improve the way it is sold. That is, the "new idea" need not necessarily be a new product or service, but may well be a better way of advertising, promoting, distributing, packaging, or presenting the product or service. Or it may even be a different application of the product/service.

When John Pemberton invented a new drink, he had only the most modest success with it, selling it to a few Atlanta soda-fountain operators to dispense to their customers. He sold out to another man, who did somewhat better with the business than Pemberton had done. But it was only when two other fellows came along with the idea of bottling the drink that Coca-Cola's real success story began.

Before Walter A. Sheaffer invented and marketed the fountain pen which was to make his name famous, he sold organs, which he carried to the prospects' homes by horse and wagon. And one of his most resistant customers was a prosperous farmer named Hockersmith. Sheaffer spent many weary hours demonstrating the organ and still failed to close the sale.

One day, out of sheer frustration, Sheaffer loaded up the most expensive model in his line and drove the team past Hockersmith's place. Hockersmith's wife called out to him, asking him if he was delivering the instrument to Hocker-smith's neighbor, Hartwick.

Sheaffer shrugged deliberately. "This is the best organ in the line. Who else could afford to own it?"

Hockersmith insisted that Sheaffer owed him, Hocker-smith, the privilege of buying the best organ in the line. And Sheaffer learned about people's needs to keep up with the Joneses, something he would use again and again in his later businesses.

A viable adaptation, then, is to give an item prestige value. Many people have that need—to prove to themselves and to anyone watching that they are as successful and have as dis-criminating a taste as anyone else, or that they can afford the very best.

Of course, there are other people who look to low rather than high price. They are not necessarily people who can't af-ford to buy higher-priced items or are miserly. Many individ-uals have a need to find bargains: they're the people to whom sales always appeal. Some businesses take advantage of this syndrome by running sales constantly. The week does not pass that they do not offer sale items. And their customers love to brag to friends about the "great buys" they've gotten.

The Robert Hall clothing chain built an enterprise that was successful initially (although the chain failed a number of years later because it didn't keep pace with changing markets) through appealing to that latter class of customer. The new approach introduced by the chain was to display clothing on "plain pipe racks" to enhance the bargain aspect of its offers.

EXACTLY WHAT DOES THE CUSTOMER BUY?

Earlier, I pointed out that all businesses are service busi-nesses, and that all customers buy what things *do* for them. But there is always the matter of customer perceptions, as I also pointed out: the customers must agree that they are get-ting what they want. Or, to put it another way, they must have some rational basis for *believing* that they're getting what they want.

Let's take the customer who was attracted to Robert Hall because he sought a bargain. For some of Robert Hall's customers, the low prices appealed simply because they couldn't afford more; others wanted the satisfaction many people get out of believing they've gotten a substantial bargain—some feeling of success, some sense of being shrewd buyers. The "plain pipe rack" idea helped them believe that they were buying clothes at substantial discounts from the regular prices. Of course, the pipe-rack fixtures did not reduce Robert Hall's costs by a significant amount. But they did help create the image Robert Hall sought. They did help the customer believe that this austerity made real bargains possible. The "plain pipe rack" was a successful *marketing* idea. It was what some marketing people refer to as "sales psychology" or "customer psychology."

In a broad sense, then, the customer "bought" the plain pipe racks. Robert Hall stressed plain pipe racks so much that it was obvious that *that* was what the chain was really selling.

In the case of Pet Rocks, the customers were buying not the rocks per se, but the amusing little booklet Gary Dahl had written. *That* was what they found to be worth $4.

Like Robert Hall, Korvette's was a successful chain, selling a variety of goods at prices alleged to be below the market. But while Robert Hall laid the stress on low overhead (plain pipe racks) to convince the customer that the prices were indeed low, Korvette took another tack: it was the first major chain to offer "discount" prices. And the chain's success was so great that it had many, many imitators, which exist to this day. The "discount" rationale was highly convincing, and an entire generation of customers will buy only from stores that promise discount prices. They have been sold the discount psychology.

Customers are not completely naive, however. The claim of a discounted price may not convince them. Most are not expert enough, after all, to examine a piece of merchandise and judge its fair market value. How are they to judge whether it is truly a bargain? Convincers are needed, even though the item may truly be well under the normal market or truly discounted below the normal selling price.

One convincer in common use is the claim that the item is a "factory second"—that it has some minor defect, undetectable by anybody except an expert, and is discounted because of it. Another is that it is a closeout or odd-lot item, perhaps even an overstock. Or it may be the subject of a special sale—a fire sale, closeout sale, going-out-of-business sale, bankruptcy sale (bankrupt manufacturer, that is), and so on. In all these cases, the object is to give customers some reason to believe that they are indeed getting a bargain. It is that rationale that is being sold.

SOFTENING RESISTANCE TO NEW IDEAS

A new idea may be a product or service offered, the manner in which it is offered, what it will do for the buyer, how it is packaged, some method of promotion, or a combination of these. To reduce the normal resistance to something new and strange, several approaches are possible.

A large, well-recognized firm, such as General Electric, may simply trade on its size and prestige, knowing the customer will have some faith in that long-established image and reputation. A newer or less-known firm can't use that approach effectively, but there are others possible. One of these is to present the offering in such manner as to make it appear reasonably familiar and "respectable." The Amana Company did just that when it introduced its microwave ovens by calling them "Radar Ranges." By this time, everyone had heard of radar, whether he knew what it was or not, and "Radar Range" was certainly a more familiar term than was "microwave oven."

A name or a slogan can be a new idea and an effective force in leading a business to success. Later, when we discuss advertising and sales promotion methods, you'll learn of other ways to accomplish this in making presentations. Even for the most prosaic items, it's possible to find new ideas that will increase success. Let's take the selling of insurance, an extremely competitive field which would appear to offer the individual salesman or broker relatively little opportunity to be innovative.

Frank Bettger, a ball player who suffered a knee injury that ended his baseball career, undertook to sell insurance. For a long time, he found himself singularly unsuccessful at it. But he persisted doggedly, keeping careful records of every call he made. On Saturdays he went to his office to review his week's work and plan the work for the following week.

One day, as he studied his large stock of index cards, on which he had recorded all his calls, he was struck with a pattern: he found that he had made virtually all his sales on the second or third calls on the prospect! Rarely had he completed a sale on the first call, and rarely after the third call. He resolved immediately that he would put this discovery to work: he would drop a prospect after three calls and spend the extra time calling on new prospects. Immediately, his sales began to increase.

Bettger was, eventually, the first insurance salesman to sell $1 million worth of insurance in a single year, although many have since joined the "million dollar round table." In his autobiography, he reveals yet another idea which was to prove a valuable asset. When he judged that an important prospect was about ready to sign up, given a bit of an extra push, he would call on his prospect and make this startling announcement:

"Mr. _____, I can do something for you this morning that no one else in the entire world can do." (Pause, while Mr. _____ responds with a startled look.)

"Why, what's that, Mr. Bettger?"

"I can have you covered in one-half hour. I've taken the liberty to arrange your medical exam this morning. If you'll get your hat and come with me, we can have your family protected immediately."

It was a successful tactic, we are told.

Successful ideas do not have to be complicated. In fact, some of the most successful ideas are quite simple. The story is told of P. T. Barnum that when he organized his first show in New York City, he experienced difficulty in getting the spectators to leave the building so that he could sell tickets and bring another group in. He hit on a simple solution: Over the exit door he hung a sign which said, "THIS WAY TO THE EGRESS."

HOW TO STAY OUT OF THE STEWPOT

It is pretty obvious that it takes more effort to sell a $25 item than it does to sell a $2 item, and still more to sell a $1,000 item. And it should be equally clear that when you ask a prospect to gamble with you on something new, the price tag is a major factor in the amount of gamble the customer will take. He might gamble $2 out of sheer curiosity, but he is not likely to gamble $25 just to satisfy curiosity.

The same reasoning applies to the degree of difference in what you offer: The more "different" the item or service is, the more selling it will take to persuade the prospect. Hence, the more different the item, the greater the need for making the customer feel comfortable with the idea. To put it another way, if you want to avoid getting those arrows in the back or winding up in the stewpot, don't announce blatantly that you are a pioneer or missionary—act as if you *belong there.*

There are several ways to get a prospect interested in something new and different. One way is to appeal directly to a compelling and well-recognized need. If you are offering some new kind of coffee maker, for example, don't promise "better" coffee, for who knows what "better" is? Your prospects are probably well content with the coffee they have right now. And it would probably arouse only yawns to offer a faster way to make coffee, for modern coffee makers are pretty fast and convenient to use. What really disturbs many people today about coffee is its price. If you can offer a coffee maker that uses less coffee—that is, a less expensive cup of coffee—you probably have a better place to stand with your sales argument. In short, appeal to a *familiar* idea.

Another way is to make the strange seem familiar by comparison with something well known. Manufacturers of oleomargarine for a long time referred to it as a "spread," and to its competitor, butter, as "the more expensive spread." But many people didn't get the allusion at all, and were simply puzzled by the code words. If you mean "butter," say "butter." Mystifying your prospect as to what you are offering is a sure way of losing his interest swiftly.

Makers of coffee-cream substitutes have a habit of referring to their product as a "whitener." Sounds pretty chemical to me. Might as well use white paint. What's wrong with "coffee-cream substitute"? Better yet: "Less fattening than coffee cream." Put a bit of sales argument into the message. Or "contains fewer calories than natural cream in your coffee."

Suppose you are offering a home wine-making kit. Wine has become a familiar item to most Americans today, and most Americans are now aware that California is the great American wine-making state and that California produces many wines equal to or better than imported wines. Why not advertise your new wine-maker's kit with something such as, "Make California-style wines in your own home"?

One woman in Washington has been quite successful selling imitation diamonds. But she doesn't call them "imitation"; she calls them "counterfeit" diamonds! Her ads are slightly humorous, feature "Lady Wellington," and are different enough to command attention, yet not cryptic at all—what she is offering is made quite plain. The product is nothing new, but the marketing approach is. She made imitation diamonds highly respectable rather than slightly shameful.

Robert Townsend wrote a sensational book, which attracted a great deal of attention, *Up the Organization!* Donald M. Dible wrote a highly successful book, *Up Your OWN Organization!* Anyone who read and liked the first book was all but compelled to buy and read the second one.

We'll return to this subject later, when we discuss advertising and sales promotion.

6

WHERE AND HOW
TO SEARCH FOR IDEAS

A wise man makes more opportunities than he finds.
—Francis Bacon

OUTSIDE SOURCES AND STIMULATORS

Brainstorms is the name of a newsletter published by Hubert K. Simon. (He's that fellow we told you about earlier, with his radio P.I. deals, remember?) It's one of several enterprises he operates. In *Brainstorms,* he brings readers a number of ideas every month—clever advertisements which have worked recently, for example, answers to questions subscribers send in, and ideas of many kinds.

George Haylings publishes his *Money-Making Communiqué* and Thad Stevenson publishes *Opportunity Knocks* every month, two other newsletters chock-full of business ideas. Jim Straw publishes the *Business Opportunities Digest* and the *Business Intelligence Network,* two more publications which bring readers news, tips, leads, and ideas.

These and many others of similar nature are listed in the final chapter of this book as references. Such publications help you develop ideas. By keeping you up with what others are doing, they also help you decide whether an idea you have is really new. However, these are *other people's ideas* you will be reading about, and one of our prime purposes in this book is to steer you into thinking up some ideas of your own.

IDEAS FOR SOLVING PROBLEMS

Everyone has problems, and everyone looks for help in solving those problems. In fact, that's one of the secrets of successful salesmanship: approach prospects as an expert consultant to help them solve their problems, and you'll find a welcome sign out.

The big job is to identify the problem. One of the newsletters I started several years ago was the *Government Marketing News,* and I scoured my sources every month to bring my readers news, tips, and leads which would help them in some way in winning government contracts. Still, despite a reasonable degree of success with this newsletter, I found the larger companies highly resistant to my sales appeals, much to my mystification.

After a great deal of experimentation, and almost by accident, I discovered why the big companies were not too interested: a monthly newsletter really couldn't bring them *news.* Moreover, the larger companies had full-time marketing departments that were collecting much of the same information independently. But what many of them didn't have, I found, was a well-developed capability for writing proposals. And writing effective proposals is a must-must for the larger contracts.

I therefore redirected the orientation of my newsletter to information and general assistance in the art of proposal writing, and almost immediately began to win readership in the larger corporations.

Here again, the customer must agree that what you are addressing with your offer is important to him. That is, *it's a problem only if the customer agrees that it's a problem*—even if he's wrong about it!

Searching out common problems identifies the need, of course: some means for solving the problem. And many successful enterprises are launched on that basis.

The 7-11 stores solved a problem for those individuals

who needed to get some shopping done when the big stores were closed for the day. (Remember, these stores started in the suburbs, where there were no "corner groceries.")

Washington Researchers started a successful business helping individuals and organizations find information in Washington, D.C., which is the largest information store in the world but a hopeless maze to those who don't know where and how to begin.

Dozens of individuals and even small companies write resumes for people who need them but don't know how to write them.

Applying for a federal government job is a laborious undertaking, because there is no good central source for news of job openings—the seeker has to go to many sources. One enterprising gentleman in Reston, Virginia, James Hawkins, publishes a popular bi-weekly newsletter that gives a complete list of federal openings, tips on applying, and other information far more helpful than anything available from official sources. He's been so successful that he's spawned imitative competitors.

FIRST IDENTIFY THE PROBLEM

Look around you at common problems. Think about your own problems, problems of your friends and relatives. Don't allow yourself to confuse problems with symptoms. It's easy to do, but it leads you down the garden path, away from the solution rather than to it.

I once accepted a position as editorial director of a group dedicated to the custom development of training programs. I inherited the group with all its troubles. As one of my first acts, I sat down with my assistant editorial director, who had been in that position for some time, to investigate the set of troubles which awaited me.

"What's your most serious problem?" I asked.

"Our biggest problem," my inherited assistant told me,

"is that we never seem to be able to get a job done on schedule or within the budget for it."

"That's a good set of symptoms," I responded. "But what's the problem?"

Of course, we had an immediate argument, my unsophisticated and unthinking assistant firmly maintained that he had described the problem to me. I finally said, "Look, we have unqualified staff, poor planning, poor estimating, poor management, or perhaps some combination of several of those. When we find out which of those are the cause of our poor performance, we'll know what the problem is and what to do about it."

As it turned out, after extensive troubleshooting, our principal problem was inadequate management, with some weakness in staff qualifications, both of which we were able to correct once we had identified them.

The fact is that the solutions are all but self-evident once you have correctly identified the problem. And unless one or more solutions all but suggest themselves to you, it is probable that you have not yet identified or defined the problem.

DOES YOUR SOLUTION HAVE COMMERCIAL POTENTIAL?

Once you are satisfied that you have identified the problem, you need to ask yourself two questions about it: Is it a common enough problem to represent an adequate market—number of potential customers who will buy relief from the problem? Will those people agree with me that this is a problem they would like to solve and for whose solution they will spend money? You need "yes" answers to both of those before you go further. Let me show you why.

U.S. Industries, a large corporation, had an automation division, which specialized in designing automatic equipment for commercial customers. One of the contracts it enjoyed called for the design and manufacture of an automatic candy packer for a large Canadian candy company. After months of effort, the division produced its automatic candy packer, a half-million-dollar machine, and delivered it. In the meanwhile, one of the salesmen went out and got another order for a similar machine from another large candy company, and while that one was being built, another salesman brought in such an order.

Delighted with its success, the division went on to build two more machines so as to be in a position to fill the additional orders it now could expect. But the two spares stood idle, as the sales staff tried in vain to find additional buyers. It was only at this point that the sales manager began to do the market analysis. To his horror, he discovered that there were only six candy companies in the world large enough to afford such a machine!

There are many cases where you know of a common problem and can offer a viable solution, but the customer prospects do not recognize the problem and hence are not likely to want to buy your solution. My own offer to help large companies write better proposals for government contracts suffered from that syndrome, to some degree: a great many companies have the notion that proposals are not the major decisive factor in contract competitions. To combat this, my sales literature had to *educate* the customer, to persuade him that he was wrong about this. And I could do that only if I could present strong evidence; otherwise, I would have to abandon the entire effort. Fortunately, in this case I happened to have the evidence which demonstrated the truth of what I was saying and thus enabled me to convince the prospect that he did have a problem and that I offered a solution worth the price I asked for it. (We'll discuss this further when we get to advertising and promotion.)

Suppose you decide to start a resume-writing service. The basic problem many people have is that almost all employers want applicants to submit resumes today, even for relatively low-level jobs, and few individuals can write good resumes, or even know exactly what should and should not be in a resume. You can write a good resume; your prospects are those who recognize that they need a resume written by a professional resume writer; ergo, you should have no difficulty making sales, right?

However, you are not the only resume writer in town: you have competition. Your problem is not so much finding prospects—there are plenty of those—but persuading prospects to call you rather than someone else.

Customer education is one way some of the resume writers do that. They remind prospects that job hunting is highly competitive—that the individual's resume is almost always only one of a large stack offered the employer and is often the needle lost in the haystack. The resume writer offers some sort of solution to this secondary problem—some way to prepare the individual's resume in such a way that it will stand out and get attention. There are several ways this can be done, including printing it on colored paper and using art work and/or a novel format (folded down, set up as a brochure, or typeset so as to simulate a telegram). A little imagination here helps your customers and helps you make sales. Again, what is needed is an analysis of both the general problem (need for a resume) and the specific problem (a resume that commands special attention).

By the way, resume writing appears to be a "growth industry," with more and more people entering the field as more and more employers demand resumes in an increasingly complex working environment. Many small companies command $150 and more for preparing resumes for senior people (executives and technical/professional specialists), and there is at least one company that commands $750 to $1,000 for preparing a resume for a high-level position. (The company works intensively on prospects to sell this.)

WHAT'S IN THE NEWS?

To get ideas, you have to stimulate your mind constantly with *input,* and there is no better source for input than reading newspapers and magazines. Many successful enterprises have been launched on the basis of something commanding public interest at the time. In many cases, this ties in directly with the problem-solution idea.

Although we have had a great many second thoughts about it and it now seems doubtful that we shall adopt the metric system in the United States, for a long time it appeared to be an imminent certainty, and a number of successful enterprises were launched on that basis. One man is still publishing his own successful booklet explaining metric measures and conversion of our present measures to metric equivalents, for example.

Gasoline shortages have stimulated sales of devices alleged to conserve gasoline by increasing automobile mileage.

Inflation has inspired many services and products designed to help shield the individual from its worst effects. One enterprising lady shops all the supermarkets for best buys every week and mails out a bulletin on the subject to a list of subscribers to help them conserve their shopping budgets. And inflation has spurred the growth of do-it-yourself products and instruction books.

The energy crisis in general has spurred development of alternative energy sources, such as solar energy cells and wind energy machines. A number of businesses have sprung up offering windmill ("wind machine") kits and instructions, and many people living in rural areas have bought these wind machines to drive pumps and generators.

Several people have invented log-splitting machines that can be operated from the jacked-up rear wheel of an automobile to help individuals cut wood for their fireplaces.

For those discontent with the overwhelming complexity of city life today, the highly successful *Mother Earth News* offers many pages of information and advice on "alternate lifestyles" every two months.

Such enterprises as these are using an indirect form of "free advertising"—newspaper and magazine articles that raise people's consciousness of these matters and make them more susceptible to offerings which promise to solve some of the modern problems of existence.

BE ON THE ALERT FOR IDEAS

If you consciously pursue ideas with a profit potential long enough, you will ultimately begin to be automatically on the alert for such ideas. One very successful entrepreneur, Joe Karbo, reveals that he stumbled across such an idea some years ago while struggling to solve his own problems. He found himself deeply in debt at the time, hard-pressed by creditors, searching for a way out. Eventually he did, and he has since become a millionaire. But at the time, in his searching for a way out, he discovered those special federal laws of personal bankruptcy which hard-pressed individuals could use to get the pressure off and win for themselves a "fresh start." And although he declined to escape his own debts in this manner, he stored the idea away in his memory and later sold it to others to use.

Occasionally, an idea will occur to you spontaneously, but if you train yourself to be watchful, you will have a store of ideas from which to sift and sort those which appear most promising.

I myself had conceived the idea of a newsletter announcing federal job openings several years before Jim Hawkins published such a newsletter, but I did nothing about it, while Hawkins did. Conceiving the idea was not especially difficult; it was the result of my own survey of federal job openings, during which I discovered that I had to visit a large number of government offices, since none of them—not even the main office of the Civil Service Commission (now the Office of Personnel Management)—had anything remotely resembling a comprehensive listing.

Every time you read about some new problem we citizens are experiencing, every time you yourself are frustrated by recurring troubles, every time you hear of a new fad, stop and ponder about it: where/what is the possible profit potential in

it? How can it be fitted into one of the types of business enterprise or profit-making moves listed in the pages of this
book?

Let's go and have a look at some of these kinds of enterprises one can launch without a great deal of capital or
special qualifications.

7

STARTING SMALL

HOW SMALL IS "SMALL"?

Best estimates are that there are approximately 13 million businesses in the United States, of which over 97 percent are classified as small business. And even that is deceiving: thousands of really small businesses are not even counted in the census.

There are many free-lance, one-person enterprises, both full-time and spare-time, which are not even referred to as "businesses," the proprietors being referred to as being "self-employed." However you designate these, they are enterprises, always with the possibility of great success.

William Shaw, an electronics engineer, began a spare-parts listing enterprise at his kitchen table approximately 30 years ago. Today he is the president of his own firm, which grew out of that kitchen-table beginning, operating branch offices around the United States and employing thousands of people.

Jack Folley is an engineer with a Ph.D. in psychology who also began a contracting business in his home, and who today employs over 50 people in an enterprise grossing well into seven figures each year.

Jim Straw got out of the U.S. Army and invested his first unemployment check in a small mail order idea, using his own home as an office. Today, he operates a thriving newsletter publishing business, complete with his own printing plant and staff of employees.

Laura Horowitz began spare-time typing and editing services from an office in her recreation room. Today she operates Editorial Experts, Inc., providing the services of a staff of both full- and part-time writers and editors.

A government-employed microbiologist who prefers anonymity started his spare-time publication, the *Want Ad,* as a mimeographed newsletter some years ago. In it, he offered free space for classified advertisements to anyone who had some personal possession to sell—a typewriter, old car, rug, lawn mower, or the like. He asked the advertiser to pay him 10 percent of the proceeds when the item was sold. Today, the *Want Ad* is a bound booklet, printed in the publisher's own modern printing plant and distributed in several major cities by the thousands, where it can be found on every newsstand.

Not everyone who made a modest start along these lines became big business. Not everyone wanted to become big business; many are quite content to earn a good living or even to simply earn extra money from their small at-home enterprises. And some have even started these enterprises in preparation for future retirement, because they wanted something to do which would keep them occupied and yet pay its own way.

One man operates a small printing press at home, enjoys doing it, and doesn't try seriously to make more than a most modest profit from it. He's quite contented with his job—he's a construction foreman—but he's not far from retirement and doesn't want a retirement of idleness.

Chuck Aronson—the Charles N. Aronson of the Aronson Machine Company, about whom I told you earlier—keeps happily occupied in his retirement publishing a newsletter he loves to refer to as "POP," which is the acronym for its title: *Peephole on People.* It's for fun, not for profit, but Chuck tries to make it pay its way. *POP* is 8 to 12 pages of Aronson's accumulated knowledge and wisdom every month. It's completely free-form, offering his thoughts on anything that occurs to him, from capital punishment to stocks and bonds, reporting his experiences and thoughts on weight control, favorite recipes, art, income taxes, and whatever else strikes his fancy during the month, including open letters to readers who have written him. Many people find it a delightful tour de force every month, and it will probably become a profitable enterprise, despite Aronson's low priority on profit in this small enterprise.

COMPLETE EVOLUTION OF AN IDEA—AND A BUSINESS

You met Hubert K. Simon a while ago, with his radio P.I. success and, later, with his *Brainstorms* newsletter, which is one of the several things he publishes successfully today. But between that initial $26,000 P.I. list success and his present successful business, Simon had a great many learning experiences.

Once he had saturated his market with that P.I. list, Simon cast about for a new venture. He found it in the form of a painting gadget whose inventor did not know how to market it. Simon discovered that there were 77 magazines with "New Products" columns, many of which would give him a listing—free advertising! He could buy the gadget for 25¢ and sell it for $1.25. But, more important, he now had a list of 77 national magazines that would provide free advertising for new products. His next successful venture was selling that list to the advertising agencies and public relations firms on his mailing list.

At that point, a friend asked Simon for some advice on how to start an at-home mail order business, and Mrs. Simon once again came up with the $64 question: why not write up the instructions as a general plan and sell that plan to many people? It was a winning idea, and Simon reports that he managed to sell $92,000 worth of his "Home Mail Order System."

Along the way, Simon had also had some experience in selling gift items and other merchandise by mail, and had developed some mail order know-how, in a day when little had been published on the subject. He had had to learn almost everything the hard way—by personal experience, through trial and error. Now he was mulling it over to find a path for the future. What had he done that was right? How could he extract an essence from that experience to guide him in building a permanent, successful business that did not depend on an occasional, fortuitous circumstance? (What business was he in?)

Concentration–incubation–illumination came to the rescue. After weeks of intense mulling, trying to find what he terms "the common denominator" of his most successful ventures, he woke one morning with the answer: the business he was in was selling specialized information by mail!

Mail order is a specialized undertaking in many ways, but especially in this way: the cost of getting orders is quite high—as much as 90 percent of the sale price may go into advertising, and it is not at all unusual to find that each order has cost you one-half its selling price in advertising/promotion. Therefore, large markup is usually essential to mail order. And "information"—words on paper—offers that markup, taking much of the risk out of the venture. Yet information, especially new ideas, has a value which cannot be measured by the intrinsic cost of the ink and paper.

Today, the H. K. Simon Company publishes a great many newsletters, bulletins, pamphlets, and other such products, all based on that single, simple idea of selling ideas—information—by mail. It's no longer a unique idea—there are many businesses based on this idea—but it was not a well-known concept when Simon developed it for himself.

THE CONSULTANT'S CONSULTANT

Frank Tennant is a retired Army officer who served for a time as a professor and director of the Instructional Television Center at West Point. It was still a new idea and unfamiliar to the faculty, so Frank had the task of making use of the TV center part of the teaching system. One way he did this was by conducting all-day workshops or seminars for the faculty, which turned out to be a highly successful approach.

Word spread beyond the academy, and before long Frank found himself being invited to aid others, as a consultant, in setting up and using instructional TV. And from that, after Frank retired, he had the idea of launching a second career as a full-time consultant, aiding others in public speaking, publications, and other functions in which he had become expert over the years.

It wasn't too long before Frank discovered that there were many people who were intrigued when Frank told them he was a consultant. People often asked, "Just what does a 'consultant' do?" Frank soon realized that what they were really asking was, "Could *I* be a consultant? And, if so, how do I go about it?"

Frank didn't have to incubate this idea very long, because he had already learned first hand how effective seminars and workshops can be in teaching. He soon began to develop a seminar/workshop to teach consulting to anyone interested. And he has made a successful enterprise of it, running one every month in Washington, D.C., an exceptionally good marketplace for seminars, but also in many other cities. Over the past several years, he has learned which cities are best at which times of year, how to advertise, and so on.

Joe Karbo, author of *The Lazy Man's Way to Riches* and a brilliant mail order entrepreneur (he prefers to call it a "Direct Response" way of doing business), has become a millionaire through his several entrepreneurial enterprises. You read, in the previous chapter, that he was deeply in debt and in desperate circumstances at one time. In his book he explains that he pulled himself out of it through what he calls "Dyna Psych," his own term for positive thinking. That and a great deal of hard work, of course.

One of the things he did to avoid bankruptcy was to hold a creditors' meeting and arrange a long-term payoff plan with them. Another was to put himself and his family on a firm budget and disciplined control of spending. And still another was to do extensive research into legal measures he could take, short of bankruptcy, to relieve himself of the pressures and get time to work his financial problems out. Out of that research, he found his solution, which included the creditors' meeting and a good many other things he had never heard of, and which most of us had never heard of.

Reflecting on all this, Karbo realized that he was not alone: a great many people find themselves in the same straits, but few of them could do what he, Karbo, did to find some answers. It was apparent to him that there should be a market for the kind of information he had so laboriously researched and assembled. He wrote a book, offering the fruits of his research to anyone else who was so troubled. He reports that he sold 100,000 copies of this book at $3.95 each.

TWO KINDS OF ENTREPRENEURS

There are, of course, more than two kinds of entrepreneur. But for purposes of making an important point here, let's consider these two: the fellow who develops a business idea and pursues it on a permanent basis, perhaps for the rest of his life, steadily building a business based on the idea, and the other fellow who develops an idea, exploits it for all it's worth for a period of time (several months to several years), and drops it or sells it off when he feels he has pretty well milked the major dollars out of it.

Joe Cossman and Joe Karbo are two good examples of the latter type of entrepreneur. Neither has visions, obviously, of building the multimillion-dollar corporation. Each seeks a viable idea, each is a skilled promoter who can find the marketing angle, and each seeks the next promotable idea when he feels he has pretty well exhausted the one he is working on at the time.

More significantly, the point is that some ideas lend themselves to long-term, permanent enterprises, while others simply do not. Karbo could well have built an entire library of helpful books and run a direct-response sales organization selling these, on a permanent basis, by adding new titles as older ones became obsolete. But he chose to select a single title and concentrate all his energies and efforts on it, suspending operations when it was exhausted—that is, when he had saturated the market.

Of course, you've got to decide for yourself, before you select your idea and business plan, which if these kinds of entrepreneur you prefer to be. You must remember that in our society today, change is inevitable and is almost continuous; it is a truism that no one can sell what he sold ten years ago. Even after only five years, most products and services show signs of obsolescence. I remember one dealer who got into TV retail sales early in the game, when the initial 7-inch TV sets were $200—quite a tidy sum of money in 1948—but was quite stubborn about closing them out at a sale price when the 10- and 12-inch sets began to appear. He was ultimately stuck with two of those 7-inch sets that had become obsolete, and it was almost impossible to even give them away.

ONE PRODUCT OR MANY?

Every field is full of "conventional wisdom"—the advice of the old-timers in the business, generally accepted as fact by those in the business. In the mail order or direct-response business, there are two schools of thought. One holds that the most effective sales-promotion focuses on a single item, and that the effort is vitiated by diluting it with other offers. The other maintains that the probability of getting orders is greater when there are several items being offered, and that this also offers a greater chance for repeat business.

Both approaches have their merits, and entrepreneurs have been highly successful at both approaches. But the decision as to which approach to use is not entirely arbitrary. Some products lend themselves to being the sole subject of a sales campaign, while others—for example, gift items—fit in well with many items and probably are not "strong" enough to carry a business on their own.

The odds against your business growing into a large one on the strength of a single product or service are relatively large, partially because of this: to combat obsolescence and keep up with the times, you usually must keep introducing new products/services and gradually phase out old ones. When something new in your industry comes along, you may find it necessary to "get aboard" immediately.

However, starting small often means starting with a single idea, item, or service and getting established before branching out into related lines. Many of America's largest companies started and grew in that pattern.

Deere and Company is a $500-million-a-year enterprise today, offering farmers some 300 products and bearing one of the leading names in such products as tractors. But the entire company grew out of John Deere's original handmade plow, developed to solve a farmer's need which Deere observed in Grand Detour, Illinois. After the first breaking and planting of the hitherto untilled land, the rich soil clung to the plows and refused to be shed. Scraping plow blades every few minutes made plowing an almost impossible job. Deere, a blacksmith, struggled to design a plow that would cleanse itself—shed the soil it turned. When he finally succeeded in finding a design that would work, he was forced to spend his full time thereafter making plows for the farmers in the area.

P. R. Mallory & Co., Inc. is today one of the best-known companies in the electronics industry, a major supplier of electronics components of many kinds. But it was organized originally to manufacture tungsten filament wire for the burgeoning electric light industry, which Thomas Edison's invention had fathered. A few years later, forced to discontinue tungsten wire manufacturing in a patent dispute, Philip Mallory turned to manufacturing vibrators, a device which made early automobile radios possible. From this product line, Mallory began to diversify into other electronic parts and components.

On the other hand, U.S. Industries was originally the U.S. Pressed Steel Car Company, organized by Diamond Jim Brady to manufacture railroad cars in the heyday of railroads. By the mid-1950s the company was rapidly becoming moribund, as the railroads began their slump, yielding to more modern modes of transportation. It was at this point that I. John Snyder stepped in and reorganized the company as U.S. Industries, abandoning the manufacture of railroad cars and diversifying into a variety of industrial enterprises in keeping with the times.

WHAT IS YOUR OBJECTIVE?

Each entrepreneur has his or her own objective. Some are trying to earn a personal fortune, some to build and operate an important business, others to reach the status of "tycoon," and still others merely to earn "a good living." It's fairly well established that to succeed at anything, you must have defined some specific objective. For if you don't know where you are going, how you can tell whether you're getting there?

This does not mean that your objective never changes. Many entrepreneurs start out with one goal and change that goal many times, as their progress and experience dictate. Bill Shaw (mentioned earlier), for example, started with the goal of being as big as the then-largest firm in his industry. Before many years had passed, he had become much larger than that firm—in fact, that firm ceased to even exist!

In fact, it is all but certain that you will change your goals and objectives as time goes on, for the very reason that change is inevitable and continuous, and circumstances beyond your control will dictate changes. But you must begin with goals, so that you can plan a route, an itinerary toward those goals, while still remaining flexible enough to change them when necessary. When Thomas Watson set out to become the master of the cash register business, he could of course not have foreseen that IBM would become dominant in the computer field. Nor could he have possibly foreseen, at a time when Remington and Underwood dominated the typewriter field, that IBM would become almost synonomous with "typewriter" one day. But while he was at the helm, he always knew where he intended to take his company.

The nature of business is to grow. But "growing" is not the same as swelling. "Growth" means something more than becoming larger. It means growing in your sophistication, in the quality of your products and service, in keeping up with what is happening in your industry. Failure to do so is usually fatal, eventually.

CAN ANY BUSINESS START SMALL?

"Small" is a relative term, of course. The fellow grossing $100,000 a year regards a competitor grossing $1 million a year as pretty big, but that latter fellow looks to other companies doing 10 to 20 times more than he.

The House Small Business Committee, in attempting to develop legislation to help small business compete successfully in the business world, has recognized this problem and has proposed to adopt the term and concept "mini-small" business to represent those firms which fall well below the size standards the Small Business Administration has established for identifying a "small business."

To some, "small" means being able to start a business at home, perhaps as a spare-time enterprise, with virtually no capital; to others, it means launching an enterprise with perhaps only $50,000 or $100,000 in capital. Therefore, it *is* possible for any business to start small, if we qualify that term. But it is not always possible for a business to start with no capital, using only spare time, and at home. Some can be started that way, but others simply require some substantial front-end capital—for example, it would be difficult to enter into the manufacture of computers without an industrial location, some equipment, and some capital. The small entrepreneur, therefore, must consider carefully what kind of enterprise he can launch, given his capital and other resources available.

There are a few exceptions. But they are invariably attributable to either unusual circumstances or most unusual people. James Ling is one example. After World War II, he began to sell shares in his one-man electrical-contracting business, peddling the shares laboriously to relatives, friends, and strangers, one by one. Ultimately, as he raised some operating capital in this manner, he began to trade, trading stock for companies, building steadily, issuing new stock for acquired and reorganized companies, and pyramiding his holdings to a point where he became a dominant industrial figure. This kind of industrial "empire building" is based on an ability to trade at high levels, rather than to build, and is possible only for certain unique individuals who have a peculiar genius for such transactions.

Chuck Aronson, of the Aronson Machine Company, started small too, founding his company with virtually nothing in assets except his own unique mechanical genius and remarkable personal strength. But where Ling was essentially a trader, Aronson was a builder. However, both were unusual individuals, and few of us are capable of doing what they did.

Before launching your great plan, then, take stock of yourself and your assets in light of the requirements of your plan. Here are some questions you must answer:

- *What is your main objective?* Are you trying to build a business, "turn a dollar," make a great deal of money, establish a second income, or what?
- *How much capital are you likely to need?*
- *How long should it take to start seeing some success?*
- *Can you put full time into this immediately,* or do you plan to start part time?
- *Will you have to draw a salary immediately,* or can you let everything remain in the business to help it grow?
- *Do you need any special training or knowledge/skills for this,* or can you learn on the job?
- *Are you willing to stick it out for the long haul,* or do you expect immediate success?

These are hard-nosed questions about yourself and your plans. But it is far better to ask them now, before you are committed, then to wait until you can no longer withdraw without heavy losses.

The hard facts are that few businesses earn any substantial money in their first year, many not until the third year or later. If you must put full time into the enterprise and have no other source of income or savings to carry you through the first year, the portents are not good. You are not likely to be able to draw much of a salary from a business that is new and probably undercapitalized to begin with.

All rules have exceptions, of course. There are successful entrepreneurs who have managed to build success without capital, managing their personal survival without drawing significant income from their new enterprises. One such man was Chuck Aronson, of whom you have read. Another was Gail Bordon, who sent his family to live with relatives because he couldn't support them during his long struggle to build a preserved-milk business. And still another was Nick Murray, publisher of the *Saltville Progress,* in Saltville, Virginia.

While Murray was struggling desperately to establish his weekly newspaper business, his wife, Allis, was often hard put to feed their family. She says, "During this period, we lived a rather frugal life. The vacant lot next door contained some pecan trees, and I must say that the pecans contributed substantially to our diet."

At one point, Nick couldn't have his shoes repaired, because he didn't have another pair. And when a patrol car stopped him for speeding, he was desperate to talk the officer out of giving him a ticket, because he wouldn't have been able to pay the fine. (Instead, he talked the officer into buying some advertising space for the officer's own spare-time business enterprise!)

Today, Nick is comfortably established, with a building and equipment free and clear, and a net worth of about $250,000.

These are all unusual people, people who struggled on in the face of adversity. Perhaps you are of the same mold, and can survive such odds. But it is more likely that if you have severely limited capital, you would do well to select an enterprise that you can work at in your spare time at home, keeping expenses to a minimum and hanging on to your job in the meanwhile. Many successful businesses start this way, and there are many businesses which can be operated this way.

A COMMON MISTAKE BEGINNERS MAKE

Once, while I was the manager of a firm providing engineering and related services to large companies, the head of one of my departments resigned to go into business for himself. Like many who do this, he expected to begin by taking a few of our best customers, with whom he had become acquainted while providing the services we sold those firms.

One firm he approached was a division of a large aircraft manufacturing firm. His approach went something like this:

"Mr. _____, as you know, I've always given you good service and good work, while I was with _____ Company. I'm in business for myself now, and I'd like to go on giving you that good service and good work, if I can have your account."

Mr. _____ responded somewhat as follows:

"Mr. _____, it wasn't *you* who gave us that good service and good work, but your company. Even though *you* did the actual work, your company provided the management and all the resources, and stood behind the commitment to us. I don't know at all that you're capable, as an independent contractor, of doing that for us."

He didn't get the account, nor any of the others he pursued. Nor did he succeed in his enterprise at all. Of course, morally he didn't deserve to, because he based his whole idea on stealing his former employer's customers—while still in his employ, in fact. But he made the mistake of believing that they had become *his* customers.

It's true that many new enterprises begin in just this manner. But it's also true that this approach fails quite often because the new entrepreneur deceives himself with wishful thinking; he believes "his" old customers will flock to him.

It's undeniably true that many new businesses are spin-offs

from existing companies—for example, TRW and Bunker-Ramo were spun off from Hughes Aircraft by dissatisfied employees. But they went out and started a business which succeeded on its own merits, and not by bribing or otherwise inducing Hughes's customers to enter into a conspiracy with them to switch from Hughes to their new company. Aside from the moral question, depending on the patronage of your employer's customers is a long gamble. It's much too thin a basis for establishing a new business. It isn't exactly what is meant in these pages by a money-making idea!

COMPETITION AND FREE ENTERPRISE

In all the many examples shown so far of successful enterprises, the enterprises succeeded because they answered a need and were *marketed* successfully. Otis's safety device for elevators was an idea whose time had come, or came shortly thereafter. Gail Borden answered a need for preserved milk. Aronson produced a *better product* (and delivered on his promise). Sheaffer answered a need of many for prestigious, high-quality merchandise. Joe Karbo offered help with a common problem of overextended consumers. Thetford Corporation anticipated a need just being felt at the time. Hubert Simon provided a very much appreciated service to those who had no idea such a service was possible.

Let's take a look now at how ideas are converted to businesses.

8

FIRST STEPS IN EVALUATING AN IDEA

SURE THINGS ARE AS RARE IN BUSINESS AS AT THE RACE TRACK

The platitude that some men are born great, some achieve greatness, and some have greatness thrust upon them has its counterpart in business: some ideas are naturals and take off to rapid success, almost out of control of the originator; some succeed only after lengthy and arduous work and tinkering; and some succeed because of lucky accidents or other unpredictable, outside forces.

Gary Dahl's Pet Rocks is an example of luck. Not that Dahl did not display initiative; he did, and he did something positive about his idea. But the *Time* magazine publicity was entirely fortuitous and was the primary reason for almost instant success. On the other hand, when Joe Cossman was plugging the "spud gun," he went to great pains to arrange for publicity, as he always does, having truckloads of potatoes dumped on the streets of New York and submitting to a fine for so doing. Publicity was no fortuitous circumstance but was carefully and skillfully engineered.

Probably everyone who comes up with a bright, new idea for a business believes that the idea is a natural—a "can't miss" idea. In some cases, the originators of these new ideas have been right; in others, wishful thinking has overwhelmed and buried logic and reason. In most cases, it is all but impossible to predict the success or failure of a new idea. Good evidence lies in such overnight sensations as hula hoops, mood rings, and pet rocks. All were great successes—for a short time. Each was a popular fad, which ran its course in a few weeks.

The only sound course is to evaluate carefully, to assume that your idea will have to be promoted skillfully and marketed through adequate effort. Most new businesses succeed only after a fairly long period of ground-breaking, especially if they are based on really new or different ideas—although there are exceptions, too, of course.

The computer was destined to be successful from the beginning, probably, as an idea whose time had come—the technology which made it possible was now at hand. Still, success did not come overnight, and some of the largest corporations in the United States found themselves compelled to withdraw from the computer field. General Electric and RCA are two examples of such withdrawals; Philco and other large corporations also tried their hands in the computer field and found themselves unable to get a secure lodging there.

Transistors furnish a somewhat analogous history, with many companies entering the field and later withdrawing from it. Still, that kind of history is also to be found in the case of almost every revolutonary new technological breakthrough. It happened in automobiles, in radio and TV receivers, and in many other new product lines.

Therefore, the fact that someone has made a great success with some business idea or new product is no assurance that you will succeed equally well. Here is still another case, relatively recent.

Dry copying on plain paper was a natural, once the technical problems were solved, and Xerox Corporation was inevitably bound for success when it introduced the early 914 model: there was already established demand, and there were no competitive products which could approach the 914 for ease and convenience. This is not to derogate Xerox Corporation's astute marketing, but the idea could hardly miss, once it became a practical possibility. From that time on, all competition was from machines which attempted to be as fast and convenient as the Xerox Corporation's machines. And today, despite the existence of many other machines which now can do the same job with the same convenience and speed, competitors all run a poor second to the leader (as do all competitors of IBM in the computer field). Being first on the market and capturing the market rapidly puts a company in a position which is hard to beat later.

You can count on it that if you are successful, you will have competitors. The more successful, the more competitors, too, of course, because the prize is greater. Most competitors will be imitators, too, trying to overtake you by being cheaper or faster, or simply catching the orts falling off your overcrowded table.

IF YOU ARE ALREADY
IN BUSINESS . . .

There are a large number of factors which you must take into account when you are considering a new idea. One of them concerns your own current situation, and it should have a definite effect on your judgment: is this an idea upon which a *new* business is to be based, or is it an expansion of your already existing business? That's an important consideration, if you are already in a business of some sort, because such "expansions" are not always expansions at all but may be *diversions,* doing you harm overall rather than good.

Here are some basic questions you ought to ask yourself when considering a new idea, to determine whether it is truly an expansion of your present business—a part of the business you're already in—or a brand-new business:

- Can I sell this new item to my present customers—do they have a need for it—or would I have to go in quest of an entirely new customer population?
- Can I sell this new item with my present marketing/sales force, or would I have to establish an entirely new (and additional) marketing/sales organization?
- Can I produce this item (or provide this service) with my

present production (service) organization, or must I create a new capability?

You can make these questions even more pointed by asking yourself not "if" but "how much"—that is, how much of your present marketing/sales force can you use, how many of your present customers would be prospects, and so on? (The answers to the first set of questions are not necessarily black-white or yes-no, but may be somewhere between the extremes.)

Unless that first set of questions produces an immediate go or no-go decision, you next must ask yourself what is going to be required to get this idea going successfully. Of course, at this point, the question of whether it is really a new business for you is somewhat academic, but the next steps in evaluation do vary somewhat according to those first answers.

If, for example, you have mostly yes answers, you probably do not have to concern yourself too much with the extent of new capital investment, since apparently you can market the new item with existing resources. But if the answers are no, and you want to study the matter further, you need to begin making at least some ballpark estimates on the new capitalization needed and the amount of your own time and energy you will have to divert to the new line.

THE HAZARDS OF NOT MAKING THIS EVALUATION

All too often, companies make themselves "pregnant," as a vice president of U.S. Industries often expressed it to me, by making a relatively small initial investment, without real study, and then find themselves forced to lose the initial investment or invest large additional sums to protect that initial investment. And even then, they run the risk of suddenly finding themselves in a business they never intended to be in! Here is a good example of how that may happen.

The company which employed me as its editorial chief found itself spending a substantial amount of money each year on printing, due to our expansion into new areas for the custom services the company offered. Unknown to me, the president of the company was a bit concerned over those growing bills for printing, although they were entirely in keeping with the nature and volume of work we were doing.

One day he came to me with a suggestion that we buy a reconditioned small printing press. It was offered to him by a salesman for only $800, he told me.

I was against the idea. I pointed out to him that we would either have to have some kind of plate-making equipment or use duplimat masters, which would create a lot of additional typing labor. Moreover, I told him, we would need a trained operator, whom we would have to keep busy every day, and some kind of binding equipment as well. Those $800, I told him, were only the beginning.

He didn't listen but went ahead and bought the reconditioned press. And, unfortunately, my predictions (which didn't require any great wisdom to make, of course) came true. Within a few weeks, my leader discovered that he couldn't keep the operator and the equipment busy 40 hours a week and that additional investments would be necessary to make the initial investment worthwhile. We weren't saving that much money, either, because (1) our printing requirements were not steady but had many peaks and valleys, and (2) we were getting good prices on our printing, and we couldn't do it ourselves for that much less.

Ultimately, he sold the press, at a loss, having decided to heed my original counsel and not make additional investments. Obviously, had he decided otherwise, we would have wound up trying to sell printing services to our customers, thereby getting into the printing business—an objective none of us had!

MAKE OR BUY?

In almost every business, you eventually come up against the traditional make-or-buy decision. Far too often, business people opt to make when they should opt to buy, for the very reason just outlined. It's essential that you remember what business you are in, and not go off on a tangent, tying up capital and other resources which you should invest in your own main business.

Take the example of supermarket chains. It's a common practice for many such chains to rent their buildings rather than buy them. Even when they build their new stores themselves to conform to their own designs, they commonly sell them to a bank or other investor and take back a long-term lease. This frees up their capital for inventory to sell, which is their business, rather than tying operating capital up in real estate, which is not their business. (There are also certain tax advantages, which is another consideration.)

Think carefully before you go off into a new venture, and determine whether you are truly expanding your business or getting yourself into an entirely different business that will make you pregnant.

BUT IF THIS IS YOUR INITIAL VENTURE . . .

On the other hand, if you are venturing into a new business, your initial evaluation is somewhat different. Here are some early questions you will have to ask yourself and answer for yourself, or find answers somewhere:

- Is there a need, already recognized by many people, for what this item will *do* (not necessarily for the item itself!)? That is, can a creditable case be made for this item contributing to a buyer's well-being—security, prestige, happiness, and so on?
- What other item is this similar or analogous to? Does it do whatever it does better than the other item does?
- How is it better? Quality? Price? Appearance? Other traits?
- Where, what is the market? (Who are the buyers? How can I reach them?)

- If it's a product, can I manufacture it without excessive investment? If not, have I a dependable source of supply lined up? An alternative source, should that prove necessary?
- If it's a service, can I handle a volume of business? Do it all myself? Will I need help? Can I find the right help? Train beginners adequately?
- Who, what is my competition? Can I compete effectively?
- Do I need a large initial investment, or can I start on a small scale, with little investment, and grow?
- Will I need any special permits or licenses? (You may have to check with local authorities if the product or service has alcohol or health aspects, or is a licensed professional service.)

These are screening questions. And you can't merely guess at the answers. You must check and be sure you have accurate answers before you make a decision to go further.

Suppose the business is to market a brand-new item—perhaps a new and inexpensive alarm system. How dependable is your source of supply for this item? Can you find a second source, if necessary? Or will you run the risk of investing your time and money and then be unable to follow through because your source of supply fails you? (Such things have happened to many people.)

You also want to know how stable and dependable the prices are that you have been quoted. A sudden price rise after you have advertised and got orders can be a fatal blow, making it impossible for you to deliver.

Only if and when your new idea passes the tests posed by these questions are you ready to examine other aspects of your proposed business, such as financing and marketing requirements to achieve success.

THE ROLE OF GREAT EXPECTATIONS

A great many writers, from Norman Vincent Peale to Napoleon Hill, have written about "positive thinking," al-

though each has had his own phrase to describe that characteristic (see Chapter 3). Call it what you will—positive thinking,
dynapsych, or plain stubbornness—it all comes down to having great expectations, to believing in what you are doing and
in your own ultimate success. It is only that kind of belief
which can sustain you through the disappointments and the
setbacks. It is the difference, for example, between the good
general and the great general. (One of the military lessons is
that in many battles the point arrives where it appears to each
command that he has lost the battle, but the final victory goes
to the more stubborn commander, the one who refuses to be
beaten.) As Chuck Aronson says in his autobiographical colos-
sus, *Free Enterprise,* "you can't beat a man who refuses to lose.
You can kill him, but you can't beat him." Like Nick Murray,
Chuck Aronson not only expected to win big, he simply
refused to accept anything less.

For men such as these, ordinary logic will not do. Logic,
as applied by most people, would dictate that they were quite
mad to expect success. They undertook to succeed at businesses requiring capital and experience, in highly competitive
industries; yet, neither had capital, and neither had the kind of
experience most of us would think necessary. Each succeeded
because of characteristics which defy ordinary logic and any
rules which you or I can conjure up to evaluate ideas and possibilities for success.

Someone observed that if we were to make an absolutely
equal division of all the money in the world, giving each
human on this globe a pro rata share (which would not be a
great sum of money when divided among some four billion
men, women, and children), in about ten years, most of the
money would be back in approximately the same hands. That
is to say, most successful people would do it all over again!
The drive and the personal characteristics which made them
successful originally would be applied to new initiatives, with
pretty much the same results. Perhaps that is true, but it
suggests that having the right idea (in the right place and at the
right time) is not necessarily the *sine qua non* for success, but

that personal drive and other characteristics of the individual are all that is necessary. Let's look at the evidence for that.

WILL YOU RECOGNIZE THE IDEA WHEN YOU SEE IT?

Ray Kroc was a musician, with some reasonable success, and also got into real estate and some other ventures later on. He always made out reasonably well. Yet, the big success he sought always seemed to evade him. Somehow, he knew that he would recognize the opportunity when it came along. But he was past 50—beyond the age where most men would consider starting a new career—and he still hadn't found that elusive great idea or opportunity.

By this time, he was sales manager for a company that sold milkshake mixers, including one model that handled up to six milkshakes at a time. An order came in from the California sales rep for eight of these machines for a single account. When he saw the order, Kroc was stunned. He had to see for himself the establishment that needed this kind of simultaneous milkshake-mixing capacity. So he decided to make the delivery personally to San Bernardino, where the customer's place of business was located.

He found it to be a roadside hamburger stand. Literally hordes of people were swarming around the counter, where milkshakes, hamburgers, and french fries were being dispensed in steady quantities.

It didn't take Kroc long to decide that here was an idea he'd been looking for, after he'd talked to the two proprietors and learned a bit more of the revolutionary success these fellows were making of the hamburger business. In a short time, Kroc bent his efforts to making a deal with the two brothers who owned the place, although he found them most reluctant.

If you haven't guessed it already, these were the McDonald brothers, and Ray Kroc is the man who launched a new industry—fast foods—which was to revolutionize eating habits and restaurant business in the United States, and in fact in the world.

It is doubtful that any man ever showed greater courage, more determination, or larger vision than did Ray Kroc in making McDonald's hamburgers and the whole fast-foods idea a new institution. Nor did any man ever face and overcome greater obstacles in carrying out his self-made mission. If ever faith was needed . . . .

Yet, Ray Kroc was the same man he had been when he was a musician, a real estate operator, a salesman, or a sales manager. He had succeeded, at least to some extent, at all these highly competitive and difficult occupations. But it wasn't until he met the McDonald brothers and combined their unusual pattern of food operation with his own ideas of cleanliness and service that he finally began to achieve that great success he had been seeking for so many years. It wasn't until he had the opportunity to combine his own success characteristics with the Big Idea that he forged that great success. But, again, he succeeded against all ordinary logic, doing what, probably, no ordinary man could have done.

You may be interested to know, also, that Ray Kroc is a firm believer in that "Press On" philosophy of Calvin Coolidge's (see the quote at the end of Chapter 2). He is, in fact, reported to have the statement framed and displayed prominently in his own office. Certainly, his entire life story and especially the story of how he built the McDonald's hamburger empire into what it is reflect his belief in the press-on philosophy.

IS "POSITIVE THINKING" ENOUGH?

Writers of success stories tend strongly to concentrate on never say die, positive thinking, don't give up the ship, and so forth, to the exclusion of those other traits commonly found in successful people. There is no doubt that faith and the perseverance which can be founded only on faith are important. But they are not all. There is at least one other important trait shared by successful people. And that is dedication—not to money, but to the Big Idea. Again and again it is made clear that successful people have focused their sights not on the financial rewards per se but on putting an idea to work and making it succeed.

Maurice L. Strauss expresses it in his own way: "Business is first. Worry about yourself second." He is today a retired— well, semiretired—millionaire.

Strauss was the son of a penniless immigrant who made a meager living with a pushcart in South Philadelphia. Maurice worked with his father at first, later became a cigar salesman and worked for several auto-supply companies, served in the World War I Navy, and decided in 1922 to go into his own business. Together with Emanuel Rosenfeld and W. Graham Jackson, he scraped up a few hundred dollars and started a retail auto-supply business.

Their first shabby little retail store was opened on the ground floor of the tiny house in South Philadelphia where Strauss, the elder, had opened a tiny chinaware store. Today, that first little store is represented by 104 modern stores selling auto supplies and related accessories throughout the United States, backed by an unpretentious warehouse in Philadelphia, which serves as corporate headquarters. Strauss never tried to make a personal fortune; that wasn't the idea at all. The idea was to build a business, catering to the huge market of automobile owners which Strauss had the foresight to envision.

The company soon became known as Pep Boys, Manny, Moe & Jack. Maurice Strauss was Moe, and he was the guiding genius of Pep Boys through all those years, following his creed of "business is first."

It's quite clear that the truly successful person pursues the idea, the business concept, not the dollar per se. In fact, such successful people never think of the dollar in personal terms but regard it as a tool of business, to be used in whatever fashion will most benefit the goal of making the big idea succeed.

The point of this is, do whatever it is you are doing, *better than anyone else has ever done it.* If you have a pizza parlor, make the biggest and best pizza anyone ever saw. If you clean carpets, give the best carpet cleaning service available anywhere. If you manufacture planters, manufacture the best planters in the world.

Ray Kroc decided that people wanted places where they knew the food would be not only inexpensive but fresh and wholesome, and of exactly the same flavor and quality no matter which McDonald's they stopped at. He decided, also, that it was difficult at best to find clean, convenient rest rooms—therefore his firm, almost fanatical, insistence on absolute cleanliness and strict adherence to the detailed procedures established for all McDonald franchises. He worried about the customer, not Ray Kroc, and the rewards to Ray Kroc, ultimately, were far beyond the wildest dreams of avarice.

That's exactly what Maurice Strauss worried about, too, when he said, "Business is first." He meant that the *customer* is first. Chuck Aronson felt the same way. He insisted on producing the highest-quality and safest machines possible, despite the fact that his competitors made cheaper machines. He had to fight hard for sales, since he had to charge a bit more, but he *always* kept his promises to his customers, delivered when he said he would—unlike most in his business—and was scrupulously honest in his dealings with everyone.

Nick Murray, introduced earlier as publisher of the *Saltville Progress,* sort of grew up in the newspaper business, because his parents operated several little weeklies in rural areas of the South, none of them very successful. Nick was one of five sons who provided virtually free labor for the struggling little newspaper chain, but still the enterprise was hanging on by its fingernails and not growing or showing much prospect of ever becoming more solvent. Nick, an obedient and faithful son, saw much that he thought was wrong with the business, but failed to prevail in the disagreements he had with his parents about it. For example, Nick believed (as did Henry Ford long before him) that low wages were a false economy and good wages a smart investment. And having only the best of staff is one of Nick's "secrets" of success today.

Nick Murray is a different kind of newspaper publisher. Customers subscribing to small-town weeklies don't expect Pulitzer-Prize quality in their newspaper, and rarely do they get it—except from Nick Murray. His staff members have won over 75 awards for excellence in less than five years, with the highest awards offered by the Virginia Press Association for 1976 and 1977.

We live in a time when service and quality are a matter of indifference to many business people, when cynical sophisticates sneer at old-fashioned values, such as patriotism, honor, loyalty, and honesty. But the record shows clearly that even those who sneer or pretend to sneer at such values treasure honesty, loyalty, and service when *they* are the customers!

In these days, good service, loyalty to your customers, honesty in your dealings, and sincere effort to be the best are themselves almost a new idea. They alone are enough to build a successful business. Just think of your favorite restaurant or favorite store of whatever kind. Why is it your favorite? What can you get there you can't get elsewhere? Better service? Better quality? Better treatment?

In Chapter 4 we talked about needs, and we made the point that a "need" is not a need unless the *customer* recognizes it as one. And that is the key to evaluating any business idea you have: you must evaluate it from the prospective customer's viewpoint, not yours.

When Gary Dahl had played out his string with the Pet Rocks—it was a fad, after all, as hula hoops and other things had been, and it ran its course rather quickly—he tried his hand at similar ideas. One of them was a device using beach sand instead of rocks. It didn't fly. Customers simply weren't interested. Probably Dahl was deceiving himself as to why customers had bought Pet Rocks and made him wealthy in a few short weeks. They simply had been amused and panicked into a fad created not by Gary Dahl, really, but by *Time* magazine, with its enormous influence. The public's "need" to be amused and to get aboard the newest fad had been sated by the Pet Rocks. And the lightning represented by the *Time* magazine piece didn't strike again.

Joe Karbo, with his successful "Lazy Man's Way to Riches" promotion, has tried to rebirth his earlier success by running his original advertisement again, but the results this time do not approach the original public response.

These and many other ideas are one-time ideas: they are rarely repeatable, and the entrepreneur must realize that in evaluating his idea. Some businesses are based on repeat sales, while others are by their nature good for only one sale to a customer.

LOCATION AS A FACTOR

For retail businesses, physical location is a major factor: what works well in one location may not work well at all a few blocks or a few miles away. Here are a few examples.

Outside Washington, in suburban Olney, Maryland, there stands a restaurant called "The Silo Inn." It serves meals buffet style, has live music in the evening, and has been growing steadily over the years, until today you need reservations on weekend evenings to be sure of a table.

The owner transplanted the idea to Hyattsville, Maryland, opening a similar establishment in a location where at least two prior restaurants had failed. He was sure that his successful Olney formula would work in nearby Hyattsville. It didn't, and he finally closed the second place, while the first place continued to become more and more successful.

At the corner of Connecticut Avenue and K Street in Northwest Washington stands a fast-foods place called "The Best of the Wurst." It's almost fantastically successful. But its branch on M Street, Northwest, a few blocks away in a busy downtown neighborhood, doesn't approach the volume of the original location.

Thompson Cafeterias are most successful in Chicago, but transplanted to Philadelphia, they were almost completely lackluster in their performance there. Conversely, the Horn & Hardart chain that originated in Philadelphia and did well there did not succeed in Chicago.

There is no accounting for some consumer preferences. You can hardly give away brown eggs in Washington and a number of other cities, whereas in Boston, the reverse is true: the public rejects white eggs!

It is impossible to say why an enterprise will succeed well at one location, yet fail at another. Location studies are not an exact science, but to at least some degree, locations can be tested. In fact, even before testing, there is often palpable evidence.

On the edge of one of Washington's busiest suburban intersections, there stood a branch of a well-known fast-foods establishment. For some reason, the establishment never did a large volume. Someone took over the lease, but not the franchise, establishing his own independent fast-food emporium. In doing this, he ignored the fact that earlier food enterprises had failed there and that the location was, therefore, at least suspect. The new enterprise lasted only a few months.

To study locations, you must decide what factors you need for success: Heavy foot traffic? Parking convenience? Window displays? Related neighboring businesses? Delivery service? Evening traffic? Morning traffic?

For example, often a small business survives solely because it is located near a large store which is customarily overcrowded. The smaller store offers a convenience and perhaps fast service to the overflow from the big store.

Obviously, if your business requires heavy foot traffic, you'll look for a location on a busy street. However, suppose your business is such that you can't expect to do very much daytime trade, but must depend on evening traffic. In these times, people tend to shun city streets in the evening. There are locations which are not on city streets, but which are the equivalent of busy shopping avenues: arcades, shopping centers, and malls. Many of the small stores which have all but disappeared from downtown locations are located in such areas.

You may need a location alongside related businesses. A women's shoe store may do worse than locate near a fashionable dress shop, since the customers of the dress shop are likely to be good prospects for shoes. In many cases, a street becomes known as "jeweler's row" or otherwise identified by having a great many businesses of a given type. Such a reputation draws customers seeking something in that particular line since the existence of a large number of emporiums offers an extensive selection and an opportunity for comparison shopping. Moreover, the fact that a large number of stores offering similar items can survive is good evidence of the basic viability of the location.

Knowing that a given location is good or bad for whatever business you plan is enough; it is not necessary to know *why*. What difference does it make that Bostonians don't like white eggs? As long as you know that that is the case, don't try to sell white eggs in Boston. Make it your business to learn the character of any given location.

The first order of business is, then, to decide what you need in the way of location characteristics—that is, will the location provide the right kind of customer prospects in the right quantity at the right times of day or days of the week?

The second order of business is to learn what is already known about the prospective location: What kinds of businesses are already succeeding there? What kinds have failed? How well are the existing businesses succeeding? What future new stores or new office buildings are planned for the neighborhood?

Inspect the location next. Study the traffic at different times of the day and on different days of the week. Take note of the kinds of people who shop there and what they buy. Talk to as many as possible.

You don't have to do this all on your own. The local Chamber of Commerce or businessmen's associations can often help with specific information. Old-timer local merchants will often give you an insight into the potential, as well as the history, of the location.

Don't play hunches. Hunches are unreliable. Trust specific information, and don't assume that your business idea is such a natural that it will succeed in the face of all odds. Few ideas succeed against the odds—especially if they are location-dependent and the location is wrong. You can't draw restaurant customers into a deserted industrial area or financial district after dark. You can't attract casual shoppers to an unlighted, run-down neighborhood after dark either. If common sense dictates that the location is questionable, check it out carefully and with great skepticism.

Let's have a look back at that businessman who tried to start an independent fast-food operation where a national chain had failed. Why is it a bad location, when another national fast-food chain operates successfully only a block or two away on the same street?

For one thing, the off-street parking is awkward to get to from the street, and is in poor condition. Moreover it's difficult to see the place before you happen upon it. It's on the right-hand side of a busy highway, and unless you announce your intention of leaving the road well in advance, traffic behind you will make it almost impossible to do so, without serious hazard.

A study of these conditions would have prevented a prudent investor from making such a mistake. Sound testing methods are suggested in the next chapter.

THE MOST IMPORTANT FACTOR IN EVALUATING AN IDEA

The single most important factor is, obviously, public perception. What you think is not important; what the public—your prospective clientele—thinks is all-important. But how do you know what people think or will think of your idea?

In suburban Washington, especially in the Maryland suburbs, many people complain rather bitterly that "there's no place to go" late at night, such as after a movie, when they'd like to have a sandwich or a plate of ice cream before trundling home. Every once in a while, some entrepreneur takes heed to these complaints and opens a restaurant or ice cream parlor with late hours. And after a few months he either gives it up or decides to stay open late only on weekends. For he finds that there simply aren't enough people who want to go out to a restaurant or ice cream parlor late at night.

Every survey specialist learns, soon enough, that what people say and what they really think or really do are not the same things. Polling is a difficult art, for this reason. And it is a most risky proposition to base an investment on the evidence of "what people say."

What does one do, then? Just take a deep breath and plunge in, hoping for the best? If you can't believe what people say, how can you judge the risk?

There is a way, and it is wise to take advantage of it—especially if you plan to try something quite new or different. Let's have a look at how some others go about hedging their bets before taking the deep plunge.

9

TESTING BEFORE PLUNGING

Take the temperature of the water first.

GUESSING IS NOT TESTING

Joe Cossman, one of those fellows who promotes one idea at a time until he's wrung it dry, prides himself on taking ideas others have been unable to promote successfully and putting them to work to make a profit. Cossman is a true entrepreneur, in that sense, and he is constantly alert for new ideas, or actively seeking new ones when he has completed a promotion.

Cossman reports that he will invest $500 and not more (or perhaps in these recent years of inflationary pressure he has raised that limit a bit) in testing a new idea. If he cannot convince himself that he has a winner by then, he drops the item and looks for the next one.

There are others who believe that a reliable test cannot be made for such a small sum of money. But Cossman has demonstrated enough success to make his own position credible. In any case, no one argues seriously with the concept of testing on a small scale before plunging, to limit the losses, if there are to be losses.

Madison Avenue advertising firms often try out their TV commercials in small theaters on live audiences before spending the client's millions on air time. Mail order firms make test mailings before committing large sums to mass mailings. A while ago McDonald's tried out fried chicken on its menu, testing it first by putting it into a few of their outlets. Apparently it didn't catch on very well, for it was dropped, and the public at large never learned that McDonald's was flirting with fried chicken.

People who write and self-publish books for mail order buyers often use a testing device too: they plan the book, but do not write it. Instead, they run a few ads and take advance orders. If the response is good enough, they buckle down and put the book together. If it is not, they return the money and advise the customers that the project has been abandoned.

FUND RAISING AS A BUSINESS

Every case is different, of course. Cossman limits the amount of money he will risk in trying out a new idea, while others have no fixed formula. However, Steve Savage of Randolph, Vermont, has actually worked out a formula for his line of business. In fact, his whole enterprise grew through continuous testing.

Steve started out to create a business for himself by seeking ideas which had to meet three criteria:

- Its profit potential had to be great (that is, high markup).
- It had to provide a product or service filling a need not being filled by anyone else.
- The product or service had to be "socially useful."

As a student, Steve had often been involved in fund raising, and he was well aware that fund raising was a necessary activity for all kinds of groups. He realized, also, that most of these groups really did not know how to go about raising funds and were often unsuccessful or only partially successful because they were learning by trial and error—a costly process. He began to formulate an idea of helping organizations in raising funds for their projects.

First, he sought out various groups and questioned them as to their problems. He found that many had no idea of how to raise money, while many others were offering cakes and candy, but were somewhat discouraged by the results. He discovered also that when a group participated in a fund-raising plan sponsored by a seller of goods, such as a candy company, the group had to buy some minimum quantity of merchandise and "eat" any leftovers.

"So I started experimenting with different products," says Savage. "Over a period of four years I developed different products, including giant silk-screened bulletin boards with various shapes, called 'Happy Hangups.' These sold very well, but they were so bulky that if a group did an outstanding job of selling, they often had to fill an entire bandroom with bulletin boards."

Savage kept experimenting with smaller, easier-to-handle products, but the students did not respond well to most of these. He tried out many products, including bath mats, huge waste baskets ("Colossal Containers"), and oversize stationery. All these products went well, but he still had the problem that they were too bulky for comfort.

Savage went at things somewhat differently than did most companies supplying merchandise for fund raising. First of all, he provided brochures with order forms, and had the students take advance orders, using these. Second, he placed no minimum requirements on the students, making it no-risk for them.

Savage discovered also that most candy drives for fund raising lasted for at least a month, and that the students had long since become bored to death with the work, while the teachers were growing weary of pushing the students to keep at it. So Savage began to test how long it really took to put a fund drive over. To his surprise (and delight), he discovered that the fund raisers could sell as much in three days as they did in three weeks, if properly organized.

Finally, he found the product that best satisfied the needs: jewelry. Until now he had stuck with low-priced items—$2 to $3—so he started with low-priced jewelry items too. In addition to earning approximately one-third of the retail price on the item, the student could win prizes for meeting sales quotas—records, stereo players, watches, calculators, and the like. But it wasn't long before his student salesmen began asking for "real" jewelry, and that was the signal to begin up-grading the line to more expensive items. Ultimately, he handled jewelry items retailing for as much as $40 each.

As you can see, Savage worked with high-school groups originally, but soon he was helping church groups and other organizations raise hundreds and even thousands of dollars with his merchandise and plans.

So selling jewelry to fund raisers has become a mainstay of Steve's business, and many organizations come to him year after year for their annual fund drives. But Steve Savage is exceptionally alert: he recognized, soon enough, that fund raisers could buy jewelry and other products from many other wholesale sources. He realized, too, that one of the reasons for his success was that he gave fund raisers many kinds of valuable counsel and guidance, as well as merchandise on good terms, with return privileges for unsold merchandise. He realized, that is, that he was selling information—guidance—as well as merchandise. So he wrote a book.

A FORTUNE IN FUND RAISING

It's a small book, less than 100 pages, neatly typeset and bound in a sturdy cardstock cover. Title: *A Fortune in Fundraising,* with a subtitle, "Make Money . . . Helping Others Make Money." Here's what Savage says in the opening chapter about the business of fund raising:

This is a "Mom and Pop" operation.

Or a single person operation—man or woman.

Really, the smaller the better. Big companies have so many layers of management and such huge administrative expenses, they can't afford to sell products to groups at reasonable cost. They can't provide fast and personal service. You can.

My wife and I have run our business from our basement and have made all the money we wanted. Occasionally, we have used part-time help for packing and shipping, but that has been a minor expense. Basically, no overhead.

We did not get rich quick. But we made enough money in

our second month of fund raising to pay all our bills. We have grown ever since. . . .

The book then goes on to explain the whole business of fund raising and what makes for success, including the following thoughts:

Some people think success is based on *luck.* They envy those who are *"lucky"* and spend their lives wishing that they had been "lucky" also.

The simple fact is that *"luck"* in business is spelled *"work."* Those who are *tough-minded* enough to *work* instead of *wish* are successful.

The book is a complete how-to-do-it manual for fund raisers, recounting Savage's own experiences, his methods for keeping records, and all the other details of how to do what he has done. And here is what he says about testing:

Do not make a big investment in inventory until you test your product. You may have to pay more per unit when you buy small quantities. That's OK. That's better than being stuck with stuff you can't sell.

Have at least five groups sell your product before you make a judgment about it.

Suppose your first five groups average selling 200 products per group. That's 1,000 products at $3 per product. You have sold $3,000 and are wild with excitement.

Caution!

I've always found that there's only one safe way to make sales projections:

Divide your most pessimistic *sales* projection in half.

Multiply your most pessimistic *cost* projection by two.

If you can do that exercise and still see a profit, then it's safe to proceed.

Note the highly conservative approach Steve Savage takes in testing. He urges that you cut your most pessimistic (lowest) sales projection in half and double your most pessimistic (highest) cost projection before you decide, even after making a sales trial. That may be part of what accounts for Savage's own great success.

Obviously, however, this formula is not going to apply to every situation. Not all businesses are based on a high markup, for example, and this formula, if used in some other cases, would prevent you from ever starting a business!

WHAT SHOULD YOU TEST?

Those Madison Avenue people who test their copy in small theaters usually address their tests to the effectiveness of their communication—to whether the audience is getting the message that was sent. In what is perhaps a classic story of how important such testing can be, one agency was reported to have tested a commercial for Kool cigarettes. The commercial showed a package of Kool cigarettes, across the front of which was stretched a chain. The camera zoomed in, giving the effect of the cigarette package rushing forward against the chain, accompanied by the voice over: "Break the hot-smoking habit!" And as the verbal message was completed, the chain burst asunder, and the Kool cigarette package swept forward, unencumbered.

Audience-reaction cards were distributed, and the audience advised the agency people, through these cards, as to what the commercial had said to them. To the dismay and horror of the advertising executives, they learned that the message received by most of the audience was this: "Stop chain smoking!" It was hardly the message intended.

But communication is only one facet that may be tested. In testing your own proposition, you are interested primarily in *appeal:* Is your advertising or other sales promotion producing orders—"pulling?" If so, why? And if not, why not? To get these answers, most people test the copy per se: they test the wording, the prices, and many other things. Especially if the promotion is a direct-mail promotion.

Among the many things which various people have tested are the color and the grade of the paper used in the literature, the color of the printing (for example, does two-color printing pull better than one-color printing?), the effectiveness of return envelopes, the effectiveness of prepaid return envelopes, the influence of bonus gifts, and others. Most of these tests are futile. For one thing, many of them test the trivia instead of the important factors. (Later, in a chapter on mail order, you'll learn just how test mailings are carried out.) Probably the most important things to test are these:

The offer itself—are people *interested at all* in the offer?
The medium—either the publication or the mailing lists.
The copy—*what* your literature says or *how* it says it.

These are the key factors that spell success or failure. The others have some bearing—perhaps a yellow brochure is slightly more effective than a brown one—but they are of minor importance, compared with the above factors.

Probably *the* most important factor is the offer itself: Does your basic proposition have any appeal—that is, does it address a need? To put this into simpler terms, aside from price and other considerations, are your prospects conscious of a need for what you offer? Have you struck a nerve? Is it what the customer wants?

My own experience in selling a newsletter (mentioned earlier) is a good example. For a long time, I had indications that not enough people wanted my newsletter—at least, not enough of the people I wanted to reach. I was faced with either settling for what I had been able to get, up to that point, or finding the way to the hearts of those I wanted to reach—of finding out, that is, what those prospects really wanted.

My next tests, therefore, were a bit different from most tests. I was not trying to discover the best copy or the best mailing lists; I was testing to find out what my prospects perceived as their needs.

ASK THE CUSTOMER WHAT HE WANTS

We established earlier that the only viewpoint that counts is the customer's. What I set out to do was to ask the customer to tell me what he wanted, what he perceived as his need, with

regard to the newsletter I published. To do that, I first assembled a mailing list of the prospects I was most immediately
concerned with: medium-size to large companies engaged in
government contracting. I had no need to test my earlier copy.
I had already tested that half to death. What I needed was fresh
copy, copy which would give me the feedback I needed, the
feedback from my prospects, telling me what they wanted.

First, I devised several different sales pieces, all similar in
many respects, but each focused on a different main appeal. I
did this by trying to put myself in the place of my prospects
and asking, "If I were marketing manager of a company such
as these are, what would be my major problems? What would
give me greatest concern? What would I see as being of the
greatest aid to me in winning government contracts?"

I came up with several ideas, and narrowed those down to
three, for my test: (1) help with understanding the procurement systems and procedures, (2) help with writing top-notch
proposals, and (3) detailed information on contracting trends.

I divided my mailing list into three parts and sent out my
literature, one-third with a major appeal to understanding procurement systems, one-third appealing to interest in proposal-
writing lore, and one-third geared to offering monthly analy-
ses of contracting trends. That is, these are what I stressed my
newsletter would cover each month.

It was in this manner that I began to verify a growing suspicion that my prospects were more concerned about the proposal-writing abilities of their staffs than about any other factor. And having verified this to my satisfaction, I added to
"Government Marketing News" the subtitle "The Journal of
Proposal Writing."

My customers had told me what they wanted, and I proceeded to deliver what they wanted.

This is testing your copy, of course, but not the way most
people test copy. Most people test different headlines, different
appeals, different strategies in the copy, *but always addressed to
the same need they believe their offer is geared to satisfy*. Testing in
the way just described is different in that it tests your basic

premise of what the customer perceives as a need, in effect asking the customer to verify your premise or invalidate it. This is carrying positioning to a logical extreme.

It can be made to work with virtually any product. It can be used to learn, scientifically, what otherwise might have escaped you. There is the case of the cosmetic manufacturer who brought out a new low-priced hair spray, soon after the first such product was introduced to the marketplace. The acceptance of the original hair spray was established, and the manufacturer referred to here reasoned that there must be a large number of people who would welcome the product in a lower-priced version.

But the low-priced spray did not sell well at all, and the manufacturer called in a marketing consultant. After studying the market, the consultant decided that the product was probably priced too low, so that prospects were skeptical of its quality. He advised the manufacturer to increase the price to more than double its introductory price. And as soon as that was done, the new hair spray began to sell well! Obviously, the customers had need for confidence that they were entrusting their hair to a good-quality product, and price was the only factor by which they could judge quality. Advance testing of the product market at two or three different prices would have established that from the beginning.

Suppose you are offering a new sport watch. Do your customers have a need for something new and different? For the latest style? For the most versatile timepiece? For the most handsome timepiece? For the most rugged timepiece? And the list goes on.

Review all the possible needs the customers are likely to perceive, select a manageable number (say, three), and *test.* After you find out what your customer wants, you can test for the other factors—the most convincing evidence, the most attractive literature, the best inducement to order without delay, or whatever.

10

SOME OF THE MOST BASIC BASICS OF BUSINESS

War is far too important a matter to be left to the generals.

—Bismarck

A FEW QUESTIONS THAT WILL OCCUR TO YOU—SOONER OR LATER

Retail bookstores usually mark up 40 percent—that is, they buy their stock at a discount of 40 percent below the listed selling price. Many hard goods, such as household appliances, are sold on similar markups. On the other hand, supermarkets work on a much smaller markup—a typical net profit is 1.5 percent.

There are other businesses where the markup is as high as 90 percent—that is, the dealer is selling the item for ten times what it cost him. And even higher markups are possible in many businesses.

Why this enormous difference? Why should one merchant work for such a small profit, when another gets such a huge profit? Or why should one merchant be entitled to get so much larger a profit than another? Why bother with businesses offering small markups, when there are businesses offering large markups?

To get at answers to these and many other related questions, you have to first understand the nature of various types of businesses, the different kinds of problems and expenses businesses of different kinds encounter, and the several ways in which to launch a business. First, let's have a look at basic business costs.

YOU MUST KNOW ABOUT COSTS

If you've been listening at all, you've heard others say, probably many times, "It takes money to make money." What that means, of course, is that there is expense—cost—involved in any business. The business person must invest something, no matter how little. Even to run the simplest service business—and service businesses usually require relatively little investment—requires some money "up front."

Suppose you are selling your technical or mechanical skills—installing garage doors, perhaps. At the least, you need your tools and a vehicle. If you happen to have these already—and most mechanics usually own at least some personal tools—you may not have to invest any more money at first. And if you have been getting business by word of mouth because many people know you as a good and dependable mechanic, you may not even be spending anything for advertising. (This is why so many people start with a small service business: in probably the majority of cases, capital investment needs are almost nil, and if you can get business without expensive advertising, you can make the business self-supporting from the beginning.) Even so, although you have not had to produce some ready cash at the moment you decide to become an independent businessman, you still have some investment, which you made when you bought your tools and your vehicle.

On the other hand, if you are in retailing, you have to invest in a place of business and pay rent plus, probably, spend something to equip your place of business with signs, fixtures, partitions, office equipment, and so forth. You may find it necessary to put an ad in the telephone book and/or in the local newspaper or radio/TV stations. And if you need help, you may have to meet a small payroll. All this before you have taken in the first penny!

Many thousands of small businesses go bankrupt every year. The two causes most commonly cited for this high casualty rate are undercapitalization (not enough working capital—

money) and poor accounting. Let's defer the problem of insufficient working capital for the moment and talk about the sad effects of inadequate accounting.

There are many different kinds of expenses connected with running a business. In addition to those we just mentioned, there are taxes and insurance, supplies and materials, printing, shipping or delivery, repairs, leasehold improvements, inventory shrinkage, and your own personal salary or draw from the business.

Accounting is the way you keep score. It's the way you tell whether you are making a *net* profit or not. Let's digress, for a moment, and make sure you understand that.

PROFIT, GROSS AND NET

Different accountants and different business people mean slightly different things when they use certain common terms, such as "gross profit," "net profit," or "pretax profit." No matter—we'll use them here in the most commonsensical way we can.

If an item costs you $2 and you sell it for $3, you have $1 gross profit on the item. *Gross* profit. Not *net* profit. Gross profit is the difference between what you paid for the item (or the cost of the materials and labor to manufacture it, if you are a manufacturer) and what you sold it for.

Net profit is what you are able to keep for yourself (for your business) after you deduct all the other expenses—rent, heat, light, telephone, advertising, salaries, and so on.

Your gross profit may easily be 80 percent, and yet your net profit may well be 5 percent, or even less. Why? Perhaps your other costs are "eating up the profits," or your overall sales volume is not great enough.

The problem with far too many businesses is that the proprietor does not even know what all the costs are and is unknowingly losing money. And in far too many cases, by the time the truth comes to light, the business is in such sad condition that no solution is possible except liquidation.

The purpose of accounting is to keep you informed at all times of all aspects of your business—costs, profits, losses. All these factors must be so organized that you know exactly what and where all costs are, what specific items are selling best or most poorly, which items are turning the best profit, and so on. In short, a good accounting system provides a complete profile of your business, enabling you to manage things for your own best interests and warning you of problems before they can become overwhelming. And the most important area is cost—cost accounting.

But don't make the mistake of leaving everything to the accountants. You should have an accountant or, at least, an accounting system (we'll clarify this in a moment), but *you must understand the accounts* if they are to be helpful. Accounting data are *management* information. It is extremely unlikely that you can do a good job of managing your business without both knowing and using those data.

TWO KINDS OF COSTS

If you sell books and you get a consistent 40 percent discount from the publisher, you know exactly what each book costs you—for example, a $10 book costs you $6, and you have a $4 markup or gross profit on it. It never changes, unless the publisher changes the list price: *every* copy of that book costs you $6 (unless it is "remaindered" or you somehow get a special buy).

That kind of cost is easy, because it's fixed against a list selling price. But what about the other kinds of cost? How much of that $4 markup goes to pay the other costs of doing business? Or, to put it another and more significant way, how much of those other costs must you add to that $6 basic cost before you know what your true (net) profit is on that book?

Some people refer to these assorted other costs as "hidden costs." If that's true—if they are indeed hidden from you— you have a problem. You must know what those other costs are. A better, or less ominous, name for those other costs is *in-*

direct costs. The book itself cost you $6 directly—the price you paid the publisher. That was the *direct* cost. The other costs are the costs of storing, displaying, and selling it, often referred to as "overhead costs."

So we are referring to two kinds of costs most businesses have: *direct* and *indirect,* which almost all small businesses call "overhead."

The problem, and the reason accounting information is so important, is that the direct costs are usually fixed (at least between price increases) and easily ascertainable, whereas overhead varies a great deal, according to sales volume and other factors. Here's why.

Let's suppose you are selling everything at 40 percent markup and doing $6,000 a month through January, February, March. With $18,000 in sales at 40 percent, your gross profit was $2,400 per month, or $7,200 for the quarter.

Now let us suppose that rent, heat, light, advertising, and so on cost you $1,000 per month, and you are paying yourself $1,000 per month. Your figures for the quarter are as follows:

Sales:	$18,000
Direct costs:	10,800
Overhead:	6,000
Total costs:	$16,800
Net Profit	$1,200

To break this down further, with total overhead of $6,000, divided among the $10,800 worth of books you've sold, your overhead *rate* is 6,000/10,800 = 0.5555 or 56 percent. That is, you have to add 56 percent of your cost to each book to recover your overhead costs and turn a profit:

$10,800 (direct cost of books) × 0.56 (overhead) = $6,048

Thus your *total cost rate* is $16,800 (total cost)/$18,000 (total sales) = 0.9333 or 93 percent of selling, leaving 7 percent net profit.

So far so good. But now we get into April, May, June, the second quarter, and we find sales are off somewhat, although our expenses—overhead—haven't changed. Instead of $18,000 for the quarter, we manage to do only $12,000.

Total sales:	$12,000
Direct costs:	7,200
Overhead:	6,000
Total costs:	$13,200
Loss:	$1,200

Even though you still mark up 40 percent on each sale, the total gross profit doesn't cover the overhead, and you are operating at a loss. Your overhead for this quarter is $6,000/7,200 = 0.8333 = 83$ percent.

In the first quarter, your total cost was 93 percent of the selling price, leaving you 7 percent net profit. In this quarter, your total cost rate is $13,200/12,000 = 1.1 = 110$ percent! It costs you $1.10 to make each $1 of sales, a pretty obvious loss.

The minimum volume you can do under these conditions, without actually losing money, is $15,000 per month ($15,000 × 0.40 = $6,000). If you continue to do $18,000 per month sales, but your overhead goes up, you are still on thin ice, with only 7 percent margin for error. Hence the preoccupation many business people have with overhead: it often makes the difference between profit and loss.

Incidentally, you may find that the "total costs" shown in these examples are referred to by your accountant as "costs of sales." Some accountants use that term, but it means the same thing—*all* the costs connected with the sale.

HOW DO YOU KNOW YOUR TOTAL COST RATE?

A logical question, and one which is often asked by newcomers to the above information, is, "How can I tell what my rate is going to be?"

In the beginning, you can only estimate, on the basis of what you know your overhead will probably be and what you estimate your sales volume will be. After you have been doing business for a while, you can begin to use your own sales history—if you have been keeping up your accounting records and studying them carefully—to know exactly what your rate has been and is likely to be.

One question which may occur to you now is this: If I am stuck with a fixed selling price and a fixed discount, what good is knowing the overhead rate going to do me? For one thing, if you make a good estimate of your probable rate when you start your enterprise, you'll be able to determine quite readily what volume of sales you must do as a minimum. That's important information.

But suppose you are about to enter a business which you can start at home. Immediately, you have reduced your overhead rate because you don't have to rent a separate establishment. And suppose you are going to begin part-time or, at least, are in a position where you do not have to draw a salary from the business right away. By forgoing your own salary and/or working at home, you can afford to start with a modest sales volume, and still begin to accumulate some net profits.

Or suppose you do a bit of testing and discover that if you operate a discount book store and sell at 20 percent below the list prices, you can quadruple your volume. Let's see what happens to your original operation:

Total sales, first quarter:	$72,000
Direct costs:	54,000
Overhead:	6,000
Total costs:	$60,000
Profit:	$12,000

Your overhead rate has gone down quite enormously, due to the greatly expanded volume: 6,000/54,000 = 0.11 or 11 percent!

In the actual case, your overhead costs would probably go up a little—for example, you might need a sales clerk, or have heavier shipping charges, and so on. But the increase in overhead would be relatively slight compared with the increase in sales.

There are further benefits, too: once your volume reaches higher levels, you begin to acquire some "buying power"— that is, because you buy in larger quantities, you begin getting better terms, such as an additional 5 percent discount, which puts you into a better competitive position than ever.

Moral: overhead rates are relative to sales volume, and overhead *dollars* are not as significant as the overhead *rate*— overhead dollars as a factor of sales dollars. That's the basis for all discount operations—a volume of sales great enough to keep the overhead rate low.

SOME OTHER SIGNIFICANT COST FIGURES

Most accounting systems separate all overhead costs out by category to help you (and the IRS!) understand what is happening. Philosophically, overhead costs are of two classes: fixed and variable.

Rent is usually a fixed cost. While it may go up from time to time, it remains stable until such time as it is raised. Unless you move your business or are especially persuasive with your landlord, you can't do much about your rent except pay it every month. Unless you do a great deal of telephoning in connection with your business, your telephone bill is likely to remain pretty much the same every month, as are your heat and light bills. For practical purposes, these can be considered fixed costs also, along with taxes and insurance.

On the other hand, advertising (except for Yellow Pages) is highly variable, according to how much you choose to use, and so are many other overhead costs. To put it differently, you have a degree of control over them: you can increase or decrease them, as business conditions dictate.

For purposes of managing your business, certain costs are far more significant to you than are others. For example, if your sales are highly dependent on the kind and amount of advertising you do, you'll be paying close attention to advertising costs and comparing them with sales figures to find out how effective your advertising is.

Selling cost

Almost everything in your business depends on your sales figures—how effectively you are selling your products or services. It therefore becomes important to determine what it costs you to get each sale—selling costs (not the same as "cost of sales" cited earlier). These selling costs can vary enormously from one business to another, which accounts to a large degree for the differences in markup.

Bear this single factor in mind (strange as it may seem, some neophyte business people do not seem to understand this): to stay in business, you must recover *all* costs, no matter what names we give them, including the cost of getting the sale. And that subject alone merits a discussion, which will help you greatly to understand the problems of how much markup is needed.

The cost of getting a new customer is always high. If $10,000 worth of advertising produces 500 sales, it has cost you $20 each to win those 500 customers. If your average sale to those customers was only $25 each, you may have lost money on the proposition overall. However, that's not necessarily the case. In some businesses, where the markup is high enough, it is possible to turn a profit under these circumstances. For one thing, suppose the item cost you only $2. You may have turned a small profit. Or suppose most of those customers were good for repeat business. In that case, you could probably afford to break even on the first transaction.

That is why a supermarket can afford to work on such a small margin: for the most part, supermarkets sell to the same customers every week of the year. It costs them something to bring that customer in for the first time, but if they manage to satisfy the customer, they will be doing business with her or him for a long, long time, with no further selling cost as far as that customer is concerned. By contrast, the customer who buys an automobile or dishwasher is not likely to be back for another year or perhaps several. The dealer must make enough profit on the first transaction with a new customer to have made the cost of getting that customer a worthwhile investment. Ergo, the much higher markups than in the food business.

On the other hand, there are many dealers who do business by mail. Now this eliminates the need for a high-cost retail establishment, of course. But experience shows that mail is often an expensive means for winning customers, and the mail order dealer must be prepared to pay as much as one-half the selling price to make the sale. Therefore, conventional wisdom in mail order is that it is highly risky to offer anything by mail at less than a 3:1 markup—that is, the item should not cost more than one-third the selling price, at an absolute maximum. But there are exceptions to this, too, and many successful mail order operations have been conducted on narrower profit margins than these.

Some less obvious costs

There are many ways of classifying costs, some more appropriate to one business than to another. In a retail establishment on a busy avenue, for example, it's pretty difficult to isolate selling cost, and any such figures would have to be regarded with great suspicion.

In an establishment that must keep a great deal of inventory on hand, the inventory itself represents a cost—the cost of keeping money tied up in stock rather than using it to earn more money. In many cases, where the business has had to borrow heavily for the inventory, slow-moving inventory also represents the interest on the borrowed capital.

There is such a thing as inventory shrinkage—perishable items which remain in stock loo long must be scrapped. But even hardware items in stock too long may become obsolete and be worthless. For example, auto parts have less and less value as time goes on and fewer and fewer models they fit remain on the streets. A cost factor is therefore involved in "shelf life" of items which are not returnable for credit.

Your accountant will also want to set up a depreciation schedule to retire the costs of furniture, fixtures, and equipment. Ordinarily, you do not charge the total cost of such items against the business in the year you buy them, but you "depreciate" them, which means you charge a portion of their cost off every year, until the end of their presumed useful life. For furniture and fixtures, this is perhaps ten years. For accounting purposes, the furniture and fixtures have been depreciated or used up in ten years, although you may go on using them for many years more, of course.

DO YOU NEED A PROFESSIONAL ACCOUNTANT?

Although this chapter has stressed the urgent need for accurate and thorough accounting systems—systems which provide timely data on which to base your management judgment—this doesn't necessarily mean you must either hire an accountant as an employee or retain the services of a public accountant.

There are at least three ways to handle your accounting needs. One, you can hire a full-time employee as an accountant. Two, you can have a public accountant set up your books and keep them for you. (The accountant will usually provide you with instructions for recording information, collecting receipts, and the like.) As an alternative to this, some people have an accountant set up the books, but the business proprietor keeps the books—makes the entries, per instructions—and the accountant does the taxes at each quarter and year-end. Three, you can use a standard bookkeeping/accounting system, which is usually available at your office supplier's establishment, in a single, easy-to-use volume.

For a small business, the last solution is often entirely adequate and satisfactory, at least until the business grows considerably in size.

Basically, most accounting systems have a daily journal, in which you record every transaction (large systems may have several daily journals), and a set of ledgers, which are so organized as to group various items and provide the output data you need to manage your business successfully. The reason for the daily journal is, primarily, to get the item entered or logged immediately. Later, perhaps once a week, you transfer the items from the journal to their proper pages and columns in the ledgers.

A typical small-business system contains all of this in one volume, which acts as both your daily journal and your ledgers. Usually, such a volume includes a great deal of related, useful information, as well as instructions for using the system—for example, important tax dates and lists of deductible items.

The Dome Simplified Weekly Bookkeeping Record (No. 600, by Nicholas Picchione, CPA, The Dome Building, Providence, RI), for example, is organized to be kept on a weekly basis. A journal sheet is provided for each business week of the year on the left-hand page. Here, you "journalize" by recording all payouts, listing the item, the date, the payee, the check number, the amount, and the category number. (See Figure 1a.)

On the facing right-hand page are listed 32 categories of deductible business expenses, such as telephone, advertising, and postage, with blanks to add any more you want. (See Figure 1b.) Once a week, you total the items from the left-hand page for each category and record the result under "Total This Week." The next column is "Total up to Last Week," and the third column is "Total to Date." By adding the first two columns, you have the figure for the third column, which is then transferred to "Total up to Last Week" on the next right-hand page. You know at all times exactly how much you have spent, total, for each category of cost and for all categories together.

Figure 1a. The Dome Simplified Weekly Bookkeeping Record: weekly expenditures.

DETAIL OF WEEKLY EXPENDITURES

MDSE. AND MATERIALS PAID BY CASH AND CHECKS				OTHER EXPENDITURES BY CHECKS AND CASH					
DAY	TO WHOM PAID	CHECK NO.	AMOUNT	DAY	TO WHOM PAID	CHECK NO.	ACCT. NO.	AMOUNT	
TOTAL THIS WEEK				TOTAL THIS WEEK					

Figure 1b. The Dome Simplified Weekly Bookkeeping Record: weekly summary.

WEEK ENDED					19			
TOTAL RECEIPTS FROM BUSINESS OR PROFESSION				**EXPENDITURES**				
DAY			AMOUNT	ACCT. NO.	ACCOUNT	TOTAL THIS WEEK	TOTAL UP TO LAST WEEK	TOTAL TO DATE
SUN.					DEDUCTIBLE			
MON.				1	MDSE.-MATERIALS			
TUES.				2	ACCOUNTING			
				3	ADVERTISING			
WED.				4	AUTO EXPENSE			
THUR.				5	CARTONS, ETC.			
				6	CONTRIBUTIONS			
FRI.				7	DELIVERY EXP.			
SAT.				8	ELECTRICITY			
				9	ENTERTAINMENT			
TOTAL THIS WEEK				10	FREIGHT & EXPR.			
				11	HEAT			
TOTAL UP TO LAST WEEK				12	INSURANCE			
				13	INTEREST			
TOTAL TO DATE				14	LAUNDRY			
MEMO				15	LEGAL EXPENSE			
				16	LICENSES			
				17	MISC. EXP.			
				18	OFFICE EXP.			
				19	POSTAGE			
				20	RENT			
				21	REPAIRS			
				22	SHOP EXP.			
				23	TAX — SOC. SEC.			
				24	TAX — STATE U. I.			
				25	TAX — OTHER			
				26	SELLING EXP.			
				27	SUPPLIES			
				28	TELEPHONE			
				29	TRADE DUES, ETC.			
				30	TRAVELING EXP.			
PAYROLL				31	WAGES & COMM.			
				32	WATER			
EMPLOYEE	TOTAL WAGES	DEDUCTIONS (SOC. SEC. / FED. INC. TAX)	NET PAID	33				
				34				
				35				
					SUB-TOTAL			
					NON-DEDUCTIBLE			
				51	NOTES PAYABLE			
				52	FEDERAL INC. TAX			
				53	LOANS PAYABLE			
				54	LOANS RECEIV.			
				55	PERSONAL			
				56	FIXED ASSETS			
				57				
					TOTAL THIS WEEK			
					TOT. UP TO LAST WK.			
					TOTAL TO DATE			

COPYRIGHT DOME ENTERPRISES

The right-hand page also has space to enter receipts for the week, payroll costs (if you have employees), and nondeductible expenses, such as personal draws, loans, or any other costs which cannot be deducted from your taxes. This section, too, provides columns for receipts this week, total up to last week, and total to date. So you can tell, almost at a glance, how you are doing, what expenses are getting out of hand, if any, whether sales are going up or down (or holding steady), and just about anything you need to know about how your business is doing.

There are also forms at the end of the volume for year-end summations, such as a statement of net worth and figures for your tax adviser. And, of course, you can simply turn the whole volume over to an outside accountant to do your year-end and/or quarterly taxes, if you wish.

All in all, it's an eminently satisfactory system for many beginning small businesses. Not only is it economical, but it makes it extremely easy to keep track of what's happening, since everything up to the moment you are inspecting is laid out before you on two facing pages. Instead of relying on your accountant for reports, you can check for yourself, directly, whenever and as often as you wish.

DIFFERENT BUSINESS BASES

As you can see from all this, there are many different bases for a business. Some are based on low markups, with a high volume of repeat business, while others are based on low markups with high volume, although not necessarily repeat trade. But there are also businesses based on high markups, with low or relatively low volume.

For example, many—perhaps most—manufacturers distribute their products to consumers through a chain of jobbers or wholesalers, who in turn distribute the products to retailers, who then sell them to the ultimate consumers. There are therefore several levels of pricing between the original manufacturer and the final purchaser. Both the manufacturer and the jobbers or wholesalers ordinarily take a relatively small markup, because they deal in large volumes of merchandise. The retailer deals in much smaller volumes, of course, and must usually take a much larger markup, consequently.

But there are other methods of distributing products than selling them and reselling them through a distributor/jobber/retailer chain. Some original producers of products sell directly to the consumer public, either through mail order or through direct salespeople. For example, Amway uses a pyramid chain of dealers—that is, dealers who are technically independent but function basically as an Amway sales force. Fuller Brush and Avon are also examples of this method of distribution.

Distributing in this manner combines several advantages of both the direct and indirect distribution methods. With fewer levels of distribution, the original manufacturer can usually command a somewhat higher price (higher share of the established retail price, that is) for himself, while still affording the dealers an ample margin of profit. Also, distributing through aggressive, direct-selling dealers/salespeople requires relatively little expensive advertising, further reducing the manufacturer's cost.

If you produce your own product, therefore, you have the options of selling it to a general jobber or wholesaler, hiring your own sales force for direct sale to the public, or setting up a dealer/salesperson force that works on either commissions or discounts. Even in the last method, there are several options. Three commonly used methods are door-to-door sales dealers (à la Fuller Brush and Avon), "parties" held in people's homes (à la Tupperware), and pyramidal chains of dealers and subdealers (à la Amway). In all these cases, whether the dealer must constantly seek new customers or can build a following of repeat customers depends primarily on the nature of the product. Fuller Brush, Amway, and Avon products are, by their nature, consumable, and dealers can build steady repeat customers. Household utensils (for example, heavy aluminum pots and pans), on the other hand, are difficult to sell to the same customers again, except at rather long intervals of time.

You can, of course, also be your own distributor, especially through the U.S. mails, as many small-business people are. Here, too, you can be a dealer in others' merchandise or sell a product you manufacture. There are pros and cons to both, of course. Let's look at some of the advantages first.

Selling other people's merchandise offers the advantage of immediate acceptability, if it is a brand name which people recognize. In any case, it offers you the advantage of allowing you to concentrate solely on selling. In many cases, the company will drop-ship for you: you receive the order, keep your commission or discount portion of the sale, and send the supplier your own shipping label, with the customer's name typed on it, together with the money to pay for it. The merchandise is then shipped out with your return address, so that the customer comes back to you for reorders.

On the other hand, if you manufacture the product yourself, you can keep the entire profit yourself, although you charge a retail price. You also control the product, because you are the source and not at someone else's mercy or depending on someone else's ability and willingness to provide prompt service to your customers.

There are disadvantages too. Selling someone else's merchandise, especially by drop-ship methods, rarely gives you that minimum 3:1 markup ratio you probably need if you are to turn a profit. More often, your discount is 40 percent or, at best, 50 percent. Moreover, it is difficult to be sure that your source will always ship promptly, accept your orders, maintain the price you have advertised, and so on. You are simply not in full control of your business when you are dealing in someone else's products, which you have advertised for mail distribution. (In a retail store you can offer a substitute, but that's rather difficult to do in the mail order situation.)

Offering your own product has fewer disadvantages, but it does have the one major disadvantage that your product and your young company do not enjoy a reputation yet, making it more difficult to close the sale.

YOU CAN'T HAVE IT BOTH WAYS

There is one final basic which is most important to learn: you can't have it both ways in business, any more than you can in any other aspect of life. That is, you can't attract both the "quality" trade and the "bargain counter" trade at the same time and with the same offers—you can't be both Macy's and Bloomingdale's at the same time.

Inevitably, your business will develop a reputation of some sort, and that reputation will attract a certain class of customers. If they are customers who customarily buy quality merchandise, offering them bargains will turn them away from you. Conversely, if you attract those who seek bargains, they will turn to other sources when you start offering them quality goods. You have to decide in advance what kind of trade you seek and position your business accordingly.

This is not entirely a matter of price, either. Even those whom you might characterize as "quality" trade are not averse to a bargain—they are often even seekers after bargains, as long as they believe that they are getting a bargain on quality merchandise. And those who stay away from what they believe to be the high-priced establishments will pay high prices for what they think is worth the price, as long as they don't think it overpriced or beyond their means. That is, a certain class of buyers would never patronize Bailey, Banks & Biddle simply because they think it is a store "out of their reach," but they may well pay the same prices in another establishment. This is largely a matter of customer psychology, and it is important to understand your customers and how they think—or how they react emotionally, to be more exact!

A discount rug and carpet dealer in my area runs a "big sale" every week, and advertises it, almost in the same words, every week. Logic would suggest that he must have worn his welcome and his message out a long time ago: customers should by now have become completely skeptical of his "bargains" and perpetual "sales." But obviously they haven't, since he continues to promote his merchandise this way year after year, and remains in business—is growing by adding branch stores, in fact. Still, there are many who will not patronize him, but will go to the prestigious department stores in the area and buy their carpets and rugs there, although they may be paying a bit more. Some people are completely suspicious of any bargain. For the latter type of customer, offering sales and bargains is the kiss of death; they will simply stay away in droves.

Department stores attempt to have it both ways by operating "bargain basements," in which they offer merchandise at lower prices than in the fancier showrooms on the upper levels. They succeed to some extent because they have compartmentalized their businesses, as a large corporation does when it sets up different divisions to pursue different kinds of customers with different products. But this is hardly appropriate for a small business, at least in the early growth stages.

The decision as to which kind of customer you will pursue affects everything you do—your advertising, your merchandising, your image in general. In fact, in many large-scale advertising and promotion campaigns, especially those involving the use of Madison Avenue professionals, "demographics" becomes an intricate art/science, and goes far beyond the rough classifications touched on here. In those cases, positioning products entails drawing up detailed profiles of the prospective customers by such characteristics as ages, sex, income, types of occupation, neighborhoods of residence, geographic location, and other such factors.

11

WHAT ABOUT CAPITAL?

Give me a firm place to stand, and I will move the earth.
—Archimedes, on the lever

In engineering it is considered the essence of wisdom to observe that anything can be designed and built, given unlimited time and money, but that the true art of engineering is to design and build it without enough time or money. Very much the same is true for management—any manager can get the job done with ample resources, but the true test of management is to be able to get it done with inadequate resources.

While the Small Business Administration and others are fond of observing that undercapitalization—lack of money—is a major reason for small-business failures, again and again entrepreneurs prove that money is not the vital ingredient, valuable though it may be. Resourceful people find ways to raise capital and ways to manage with extremely little capital—sometimes with none at all.

Jim Ling started what eventually became a huge corporate conglomerate by peddling shares in his one-man electrical contracting business. He went from door to door selling his shares. Jim Straw began with a weekly unemployment compensation check, starting a modest mail order business from his kitchen table. Tony Imbesi took on the Seven-Up bottling franchise in Philadelphia when no one wanted it, and he too went from door to door selling shares in what was eventually the distributorship for most of the East Coast, building a fortune in excess of $65 million. Willard Marriott, Sr., started the

111

now famous Hot Shoppe/Marriott chain (grossing over $1 billion a year today) with a hole-in-the-wall soft drink stand (R&W Root Beer).

None of these fellows had any capital. They raised a few dollars through selling shares, or they started on such a tiny scale that one week's paycheck was almost enough to put them into business.

In business, as in engineering and management, anyone can make money with enough starting capital. But most businesses start with little or no capital, and it is the one who can make do nevertheless who is the true entrepeneur.

ABOUT LOANS

The obvious place to raise capital, if you are contemplating business which simply cannot be started without at least a bit of capital (and there are indeed some businesses which absolutely require capital to start) is the commercial banks. It's their business to lend money to business people.

It's widely believed that a bank will lend you money as soon as you can prove that you don't need it—that is, as soon as you can provide collateral to guarantee the loan, such as a piece of property the banker can foreclose, if need be, stocks and bonds, savings account passbooks, or other tangible assets. If you have such assets, you need read no farther; any bank will gladly advance you a loan to the limit of those assets.

Unfortunately, most people starting a business do not have such assets, or at least not enough of them to cover a capitalization loan. So most people starting a business must seek other means.

One source is the personal loan or signature loan, as it is often called. Such loans are offered to people with good credit records and a means for demonstrating their ability to repay the loan—usually, a job. Such loans are generally available for $3,000 to $5,000, depending on the local laws.

It is possible, too, to make more than one such loan at the same time. But a job is virtually a must. If you are not working at the time you ask for the loan, it is not likely that you will be approved.

There are other sources. One of the best known is the Small Business Administration, which supports SBICs—Small Business Investment Corporations—and also guarantees bank loans to those who are not able to get the bank loan on their own merits. But it isn't exactly automatic: many beginning entrepreneurs do get loans, with SBA guarantees, but many do not.

To get any business loan which is not completely secured with collateral, whether backed by SBA or not, certain preconditions must be met. For one thing, you must show that you have made or will make a substantial investment of your own capital. Rarely will the lending institution advance all the capital, and rarely will the SBA guarantee a loan if you are not making an investment of at least some capital of your own. Also, you must make out a rather lengthy application, revealing all details of your personal affairs, property you and your spouse own, and so on. The rules require that you be of good character, with a good credit standing in your community. The rules require also, however, that you show the probable ability to repay and the precise uses to which the borrowed money will be put. You must therefore produce a "business plan."

The business plan is a detailed plan of the business, existing or proposed, showing exactly what is involved, how it will be run, the basis for expected success, the projections of sales and profits, the plan for paying off the loan, and every other pertinent detail.

Both SBA and commercial financial people report that by far the majority of turndowns of applicants for business loans are due to improperly prepared "loan packages" (applications), and that the deficiency is usually one of an inadequate business plan.

WHAT IS A SMALL BUSINESS?

The SBA defines a small business, generically, as one which is "independently owned and operated and which is not dominant in its field of operation." In practice, SBA sets size standards for the various industries to decide specifically whether a business is small or not. The smallest size standard, at present, is gross sales not in excess of $2 million per year, averaged over the previous three years. Size standards vary greatly, however, and may run to not more than $5 million per year, not over 500 employees, or other criteria, depending on the industry. If you have any doubts about whether you qualify as a small business under SBA standards, a telephone call to the nearest SBA office will probably get you an answer to that question. Once you verify that you do qualify as a small business, you may apply to SBA for assistance in getting a loan.

WHAT SBA DOES ABOUT LOANS

The principal SBA financial assistance is to help you get a loan from a private lending institution—for example, commercial bank—by guaranteeing the loan (90 percent of the principal). In a few cases, when the applicant is pursuing a relatively small loan which few banks care to handle because it is small and involves only a limited amount of interest, SBA may be able to make the loan directly, using government funds. However, SBA has a limited amount of money with which to do this, and would much prefer to guarantee your loan from a commercial source.

The law says that SBA cannot help you with a loan if you can get it from commercial sources, such as banks. Therefore, you must have been turned down by two banks before applying to SBA. (That's not too hard to arrange!)

A third alternative is a participating loan, in which SBA and the bank both put up part of the money, with SBA guaranteeing the bank's portion.

THE "LOAN PACKAGE"

Whether you apply to SBA or to some commercial lending institution, a properly prepared "loan package" or application is a must, as I mentioned earlier. Here are some of the things the bank and/or SBA want to know or see in that package of information (some of these things will apply only if you are already established, rather than seeking funding to get started):

- Recent P&L (profit and loss) statement and balance sheet.
- Brochures, booklets, or other information about nature of your business (just what you do, manufacture, or plan to do/manufacture).
- Exact plans for money requested—detailed projections of investments, sales, and profits for at least next year.
- Personal financial statement for yourself and partners, if any, and spouse. (Show all assets and liabilities, and net worth.)
- Business history (sales, profits, and so on), if loan is for existing business.
- If loan is for business to be started, show personal background and qualifications for running proposed business successfully.
- If new business, show exactly what your own direct investment is to be.

Remember through all this that your main goal in all this is to provide some evidence that the loan will be wisely invested and almost certainly will earn the money to enable you to repay it. If you already have a business and are borrowing for expansion, show the success of the past and the wisdom of the expansion; if the loan is for a new business, provide as much evidence as possible of your personal abilities and experience which qualify you to make a success of this business.

Bear in mind, too, throughout this, that sweeping generalizations are never very convincing, because anyone can make sweeping generalizations. Details, carefully assembled facts, and ample documentation are most convincing, however, and the more of these you have in your business plan, the more likely you are to get the loan without difficulty. The anecdote of how Don Dible persuaded a large printing house to extend credit to him illustrates this.

Dible wrote *Up Your OWN Organization,* which he planned to publish himself, as his first independent business venture. He completed the manuscript, organized Entrepreneur Press, and went seeking a printer-binder to typeset, print, and bind his book in quantity. He had no capital, but he visited a large printing house in Michigan, explained his plan, and asked the printer for credit.

The printer rejected his request flatly. He simply wouldn't consider it at all. But Dible would not be put off so easily. He had prepared a thoroughly detailed business plan—he hadn't undertaken this venture without a great deal of thought and careful analysis—and he pleaded with the printer to hear him out. The printer was not really interested; he knew he was not about to grant the credit to an utter stranger. But Dible pressed on, pleading that he had traveled to Michigan from California at his personal expense. Finally, the printer relented and agreed to listen to Dible's plan.

Dible went over his business plan in great detail. The printer listened intently, with increasing interest. He had never heard or read a business plan prepared so thoroughly.

When Dible finished, the printer made him a proposition: if Dible would remain overnight and make that same presentation to the printer's own sales staff, he would get the credit he had asked for!

Small wonder that poor loan packages is given as the most common reason both banks and SBA turn down applications for loans. Few people even plan their business ventures in adequate detail, much less document their plans completely. Would *you* lend money to an applicant who seemed vague about how he was going to use the money or how he planned to be able to repay the loan?

OTHER GOVERNMENT SOURCES
OF HELP

In addition to SBA and the SBA SBICs—Small Business Investment Corporations—there are the Veterans Administration, if you happen to be a qualified veteran, and the Department of Commerce. The VA also guarantees loans for veterans wishing to start a business, under much the same conditions as SBA. But the Department of Commerce has three other sources.

- EDA—the Economic Development Administration— makes loans and loan guarantees to businesses in economically distressed areas (listed in the Labor Department's quarterly listing of "Labor Surplus" areas). EDA's mission is to alleviate unemployment; to be justified, loan guarantees must demonstrate that they will either create new jobs or save threatened jobs.
- EDA has been establishing revolving loan funds with grants, ranging from a few hundred thousand dollars to several million dollars each, in various economically distressed areas, to make small business loans to local businesses.
- MBDA—Minority Business Development Administration (formerly the Office of Minority Business Enterprise)—is a Commerce Department agency established to help minority entrepreneurs get started. (Minorities are generally defined as black, American Indian, Hispanic, Oriental, and Alaskan natives, but not confined to these.) MBDA supports some 300 organizations throughout the United States to help minority entrepreneurs with loans and other assistance.

A visit to the nearest Commerce Department/EDA or MBDA office will bring you details. (Offices are listed in the last chapter.)

SBA, too, has special programs for minority entrepreneurs,

and has recently started loan programs to assist women proprietors, along much the same lines as the help offered minorities. Minority-owned small businesses or entrepreneurs wishing to start a business may apply to SBA's special offices set up for the purpose and/or to SBA's MESBICs—Minority Enterprise Small Business Investment Corporations.

OTHER WAYS TO FINANCE YOUR BUSINESS

Factoring. Factors are lenders who lend money against your receivables—that is, they help you "carry" your accounts. Typically, a factor will sit down with you every week or every month, go over your accounts receivable and advance you money against all receivables he considers to be good risks, and collect for those he factored earlier and which you have been paid for in the meanwhile. Or he may actually buy your receivables from you, at a discounted rate, in which case he does the billing and collecting, and takes the risks of slow payers (although he usually does the credit checking, too, and refuses to accept those he considers to be poor risks).

Selling your receivables to a bank. Banks, too, advance money against receivables or actually buy your receivables and collect them in your place. By discounting these to the banks, you are paying them interest. For example, suppose you have a 6 percent discount rate. The bank will pay you $94 for every $100 worth of receivables it buys, billing the $100, of course, and earning $6 for its trouble and use of its money. This is, in fact, the same as factoring, but usually carries a smaller discount rate. The factor usually will take risks the banks will not take, very much as a small loan company will take risks the bank will not take. And, like the small loan company, the factor wants a higher rate of interest—that is, a larger discount.

Usually, when you make such an arrangement with a bank, the bank establishes a "line of credit," which is the maximum amount of "paper" it will "buy" from you. However, if the bank is satisfied—if it collects the accounts without trouble and earns profits on the transaction—it will not resist your application to raise the ceiling on your credit line.

You may have already experienced this: if you bought a house, you signed papers with the mortgage company. But soon after, you probably got a letter and payment book from some bank, advising you that you were to make payments to the bank, in the future. The mortgage company sold the mortgage to the bank! This practice is also sometimes referred to as "assigning" your receivables. That means, simply, that you have assigned payment to the bank and authorized it to collect the bill.

Large retail chains, such as Sears and Montgomery Ward, handle their charge accounts this way, with all payments being sent to the bank, which runs daily balances on the store's account and charges interest on a daily basis. It's a well-established and accepted way of financing your receivables.

THE BEST WAY TO FINANCE YOUR BUSINESS

The very best way to finance your business is not to finance it at all—that is, to not require credit at all. And in many businesses, it is possible to run your business strictly on a cash basis, with no accounts to carry. In fact, there are even some situations in which you can get all your money in advance of delivery. And to take this even further, there are some cases in which you can get your customers to help finance your operation. Here is an example, showing how I and others have done this successfully:

In publishing my first self-published book, which explained how to win government contracts, I planned the book in detail and announced its publication to be. I accepted advance orders, promising the customers the first copies and a bonus. (The bonus was a free three-month subscription to a new newsletter on the same subject.) Before I had finished writing the book, I had taken in nearly $5,000 worth of advance orders, all prepaid!

Here is what Ralph did, starting a profitable small business with only $10. Ralph was an expert mechanic. He installed sliding glass doors, the types used to enclose showers and bathtubs. He worked for a Florida manufacturer of such doors, installing most of them in new houses.

One day he was approached by the salesman for a rival manufacturer. The salesman said to Ralph, "I hear you're pretty good at putting these things in."

Ralph nodded. "So I'm told," he said.

The salesman explained: "I'm with the _____ Shower Door Manufacturing Company. We don't have our own installers. We contract the installation out, but the guy we're using isn't any good, and we got rid of him. We need somebody good to do it on contract. We've got enough to keep a man busy full-time. Interested?"

Ralph was interested, and that night he met the salesman and the owner of the company to talk. They offered him an exclusive contract at $5 per unit. Ralph knew that he could do quite well at that rate. He agreed to start the following week.

Ralph had absolutely no capital, but he did have his own hand tools. That Friday evening, he bought a used truck for $10 down. Saturday he visited the construction sites he had worked on and begged enough scrap lumber from the builders to build the racks on his truck that weekend. And Monday morning he was all set to go to work, with only $10 out of his pocket! He was in business for himself, and his earnings doubled immediately!

Eventually, he had three trucks and several employees, as he discovered that there were other manufacturers who preferred to contract installation out to someone who was dependable and capable.

Being a small businessman, Ralph explained to various dealers for whom he did work (one of them the big Sears store in Fort Lauderdale) that he managed to keep his installation rates low because he did a cash business, and would want to collect either directly from the customer on the job (in the case of retail sales) or every Friday from the dealer or builder, in the case of sales in new construction. He had no trouble doing this, and was thus able to avoid being forced to carry accounts and borrow against his receivables.

If you are thinking about starting a business with limited capital but are still not quite sure what kind of business, you may wish to consider only those businesses which require neither a great deal of starting capital nor a great deal of operating capital—either because you can run a strictly-cash business or because you can get your wholesaler to carry you long enough for you to collect your own accounts. That is what is known as "trade credit," and not every case requires the salesmanship Don Dible had to employ to get trade credit.

TRADE CREDIT

In some businesses—either because they're highly competitive or for some other reason—it is relatively easy to get credit from the manufacturer or wholesaler of the goods you're handling. It is even possible, in some cases, to get merchandise on a consignment basis—that is, the supplier stocks your store and calls on you to check your stock every month. You pay for what you have sold, which he replaces in stock, and you never pay for the unsold merchandise on your shelves until it is sold. That was a common practice in the paint business, for example, and although they're not as common as they once were, such arrangements are still possible in many cases.

BEWARE THIS HAZARD

There are numerous "loan brokers" or "financial consultants," as many call themselves. They act as agents for lending institutions, seeking out clients and collecting fees, ordinarily from the borrower. If they are truly good at their work, they know how to prepare the loan package. The problem is that there are a great many neophytes working at this calling, and there are more than a few charlatans. Using such people is an approach to be undertaken with extreme caution.

Many of these people demand a substantial fee in advance—several hundred dollars. The true professional does not, and usually insists that you should be highly suspicious of any financial broker or consultant who does demand a fee up front. A number of these people are interested only in the up-front fee and never complete a loan for anyone. Only if the broker or consultant undertakes to arrange a loan for you without a front fee—that is, if his fee is based on a percentage of the loan itself—can you feel that he is at least reputable. (Percentages will vary, generally from about 0.5 to 3 percent, depending on the size of the loan.)

THINK ABOUT THIS TOO

It is not always an advantage to start a business with ample capital. In fact, quite the contrary: it is often an advantage to start with desperately little money! Here's why.

Unless you are already well-experienced in the business you are about to undertake, you have a spread of learning experiences ahead of you. And often, even when you have had previous experience, a new business does not always go according to conventional wisdom.

When I started in mail order—one of my ventures—a few years ago, I first invested a sum of money in buying a virtual library of books instructing me on all the various phases and all the inside tips and tricks of the trade. These books were all written by those who had had experience and were successful at mail order. On top of that, I became acquainted with many successful mail order operators via long-distance telephone, and invested a good bit of my sparse capital with the telephone company, talking to all the experts and getting their good advice.

My first efforts bombed pretty badly. Fortunately, they were modest efforts—they had to be, for I didn't have enough capital to "do things up right." I went back to my mentors, and received all kinds of good advice:

Don't try to sell more than one item at a time.
Give the prospects many items to choose from.
Keep expenses pared to the bone.
Use high-grade paper and envelopes.
Use return envelopes, postage paid.
Have your copy typeset.
Hire professional copywriters.
Run many test mailings.
Rent cheap lists.
Rent expensive lists.
Etc., etc.

Of course, it would have been impossible to follow everyone's advice, although I tried out many of the suggestions made, some of them at considerable expense. But I also experimented with many ideas as a result of my own experience.

I discovered, after a while, that one man's meat is another man's poison: what worked well for somebody else would not work for me, and what someone else said was a deadly error paid off well for me. Example: I let a friend write the first advertising copy for one of my early offerings, and it laid an egg, although he was an expert. (At least, he was making money.) I then wrote my own copy and had it printed, which he condemned immediately, after seeing it. "Awful!" he pronounced, sending my spirits into the sub-basement. But I had printed the literature, so I figured I might as well gamble the postage on it.

Yes, indeed, you guessed it: it worked very well for me, bringing in a stream of $89.95 orders for weeks.

I learned primarily from my own mistakes. And I soon realized that I would have made those mistakes in any event. But because I did not have a great deal of capital, the lessons were relatively cheap.

You can learn as much from a $50 mistake as you can from a $5,000 mistake. That was the biggest lesson I learned. It was a blessing to have started with little capital. I could have and would have made much more costly mistakes—the *same* mistakes, but on a much larger scale.

For the reason just explained, I do not assure you that this will work and that won't work. I tell you what my experience has been, and what others' experience has been. But you should venture cautiously, with little capital, no matter how much you have, and make your first mistakes *cheap* ones. There's time enough to put in more money when you are reasonably sure that you know what works for you and what does not work for you.

12

MARKETING AND SALES PROMOTION

A TV comic—one of those homespun country types—brought down the house as he described a not too bright acquaintance by remarking, "It ain't that he don't *know* nuthin'; he don't even *suspect* nuthin'!"

Paraphrasing, it isn't so much that many business people don't know the difference between marketing and sales; many don't even know that there *is* a difference. Even executives bearing the titles "Director of Marketing" often believe with all their heart that their job is to go knocking on doors, asking for orders.

Don Dible (*Up Your OWN Organization*) puts it this way in his seminars: "Marketing is the identification of a need or want for a product or service, which can be sold at a profit, using available resources. Sales is the conversion of existing inventory and/or service capability into cash."

Those definitions are as good as any I've ever heard, and they do establish clearly the difference between marketing and sales, as well as a good working definition of each.

Here's another way to put it, not nearly so definitive as Dible's definitions, but perhaps more memorable:

"Sales" is the business of getting orders, while "marketing" is the business of determining what orders to get.

Marketing, notes Dible, is *identifying* that need or want which we have talked about earlier in these pages. Moreover, it must be a need or want you can satisfy with what you have *available* in resources.

Sales, then, is converting those available resources into

125

money—getting orders for those available resources you are going to utilize.

Anyone who has ever worked with the typical sales force has heard the laments of some of the salespeople, as they explain—alibi—their failure to sell: the product/service line is all wrong for the market. It's priced too high. The territory is bad. And so on. Anyone who has had such experience also has seen the salesman who brings in orders the company can't fill. He can always sell what you don't have.

"Sales" is simply getting orders. Marketing involves the entire company—what the company has to offer, what it can do, how and where to seek orders, how to get leads, and a variety of other factors which *lead* to orders.

Advertising, for example, is part of marketing, as is market research (determining what the needs are and where the sales prospects are to be found), packaging, and many other facets of the business, all of which *precede and lead up to* sales activity—prescribe the sales effort, in fact.

BASIC MARKETING ACTIVITY

Whether you are already in business or about to enter into business, marketing should start with identifying what the business is—what you have to sell, *from the prospective customer's viewpoint.* Your own viewpoint is really of little importance, as this book has explained earlier. (If the concepts about to be touched on here seem to be familiar and possibly even redundant in the light of things you have already read in these pages, it's no accident; all of that earlier information was leading up to this most important matter of marketing.) Remember Dible's definition of marketing: the *identification* of a need or want for a product or service" which the customer will buy, at a profit to you, and which you can sell "using *available* resources."

If you are not yet ready to start a business, but are still studying the possibilities—trying to decide what business you want to enter—your study should begin along similar lines.

What can you offer, or what sort of things do you wish to offer? What natural assets do you happen to have? Special training or skills? Special knowledge of something a large number of people ought to want? A hobby which can be turned into a business?

One friend is an amateur lapidary: he cuts and polishes precious and semiprecious stones, then mounts them into settings as rings, brooches, necklaces, and other jewelry. It's a hobby, and he enjoys spending his spare time at it. But he got so good at it, and he created so much more jewelry than he could use as gifts and for personal use, that he began to sell off his surplus to make his hobby self-supporting. But soon he realized that he was almost giving his products away, and he began to charge something closer to the market price. And almost without realizing it, he had a spare-time business which was bringing him more income than his full-time job. He's stuck with the job because he has many years in and wants his retirement pension, but he has his second-career business already well under way!

Similar stories may be found among the ranks of stamp collectors, coin collectors, wood workers, and many other hobbyists. However, note this carefully: for the most part, these hobbyists do what amuses them, without thought to whether anyone else would be interested in buying their products or services. But if they decide to convert their hobbies to businesses, and they truly desire to be as successful as possible in the businesses, they must begin to discover just what the customers want, and begin to cater to the customer's wants.

One amateur woodworker, for example, with a garage full of equipment which enables him to turn out highly professional products, dotes on designing and making small boxes and chests of many kinds. Pretty soon, after he had reached the point of accumulating more finished goods than he could possibly use himself or give away as gifts, he began to participate in arts and crafts shows which are held regularly in shopping malls. And he began to discover, also, that while many people liked his handmade wooden boxes and chests, there were many who wanted end tables, lamps, book ends, and other objects to enrich the furnishings of their homes. At this point, Walt had to decide whether he was going to make what the public wanted or what he wanted. The choice was between frustration and success in his spare-time business. And he discovered that although he didn't like to make book ends as much as he liked making little jewelry chests, he got a great deal of satisfaction (as well as profit) out of satisfying the customer's wants. It wasn't long before he began to enjoy making book ends and other objects he hadn't made before.

It is totally self-defeating to try to force on the public what you wish to offer, without regard to what the public wants to buy.

MARKET RESEARCH

Market research has become a high art, even a science, in many quarters. When it is conducted on a large scale, formally trained people, usually mathematicians, are employed to survey and analyze demographics and other statistical data. Many learned volumes, including those published by U.S. government agencies, deal with the subject of market research.

However, such ambitious and costly researches are far beyond the means or even the need of the small-business person. There are far simpler and far more practical methods available for the small business.

Market research has two main objectives: (1) to discover what the market wants—what people will buy (as related to what you can offer) and (2) to discover where those people who are your prospects are. There are other, subordinate objectives, which can be reached only after those first two objectives have been reached. In particular, you need to know how to reach those prospects, or if you can reach them, and how to appeal to them. Some other secondary objectives relate perhaps more to selling than to marketing. But in any case, you must first get the answers to your two main questions—what does the market want, and where are your prospects?

Steve Savage, the gentleman who aids fund raisers, discovered through trial and error that his customers wanted merchandise that was light and easy to handle. *His* customers, mind you, not the ultimate consumers. The ultimate consumers, those people to whom his customers sold, were perfectly happy to buy those bulky, clumsy items Savage offered at first, but his customers were not the ultimate consumers. His customers were the students and others who had to go out and sell the items. Once Savage realized that bulky items were a problem to his customers, he began to seek lighter, smaller items, and he finally settled on jewelry.

Actually, Savage had a double analysis to make: he had to find out what his customers' customers wanted—what his customers could sell—as well as what was convenient to handle. But he was never confused as to which class of customers he had to appeal to and satisfy.

Gary Dahl's venture (Pet Rocks) was pure speculation: there was no way to determine in advance whether the public would be at all interested—whether the want could be created. But he accomplished his market research by the inexpensive expedient of showing his Pet Rocks at a trade show, which cost him a modest $25 for a booth. Had he flopped there, he would probably have dropped the idea entirely.

On the other hand, it is often possible to determine what the market is for a given item simply by studying what is already happening in that market—that is, by taking John D. Rockefeller's advice to study what some other successful person is selling!

Take the subject of publishing a newsletter, for example. It's quite easy to hunt up a list of newsletters already existent in that field, as a first indicator of the want for such a newsletter. If there are none or only one in that field, that is a good first indication that the market is pretty limited. On the other hand, if there are a dozen or more, that suggests that the market is pretty good (it appears to be supporting a dozen newsletters). But the danger exists, too, that the market is saturated, and you are going up against heavy competition if you enter it.

On the other hand, you can (and probably should) get a

sample copy of each of these newsletters and study them to see whether you can offer something they do not—something you think the public would like to have, something people want enough to induce them to subscribe. The conventional wisdom in this field is that if there are about five newsletters on the subject, there is probably room for another one—a good one. Fewer than five suggests a limited market, and more than five suggests entrenched competition that will be hard to beat. But conventional wisdom is often wrong, and you should investigate further, if the market looks good to you.

So far, that's general information—that a market exists. But a market is *people*. Who are they? Individual consumers? Corporate executives? Small-business owners? Government officials? Housewives? Automobile owners? Home owners? Jewelers? Food merchants? Stock brokers? Lawyers? Investors?

That kind of identification, while still somewhat general, is the beginning of zeroing in on your potential market. It's important that you make the most precise definition possible, in terms of what you wish to offer.

In publishing the *Government Marketing News*, for example, I finally discovered that my best "target population" (prospects) was individuals responsible for selling *custom* goods or services to federal agencies. They were the most interested in getting all the help they could in writing proposals, because it is necessary to write proposals for such contracts, and it is necessary to write the *best* proposals to win against the competition for those contracts.

Still, that wasn't enough. There are all kinds of businesses and other organizations that sell to the government, including nonprofit corporations and local government agencies, as well as business firms. Moreover, the *individual* in the organization who was the right target for me was not necessarily identified as the director of marketing or the chief of the proposal-preparation group. He might be a proprietor, president, publications manager, or any of several others. Moreover, some *kinds* of organizations responded better than others.

Over a period of time, I discovered that technical/professional organizations (for example, engineering firms and consultant firms) responded best, and that among these, software-development firms were *the* best responders. At the same time, some types of nonprofit firms also responded well.

To reach the right *individual* in the organization, I developed a special strategy: I addressed the mailing piece to the director of marketing, but I put a small routing box at the head of the letter, suggesting to the recipient that he should forward this to the right party, if he were not the right party to consider the offer.

One point that should be made here is that market research is not a one-time effort but should be continuous, always seeking to refine and sharpen the identification of your customer so as to constantly improve your sales effort. Every sales promotion, whether it is an advertisement, a direct-mail piece, or a special sale, should be part of your research, and results should be carefully tabulated and analyzed to enable you to add to your knowledge of your customers and their wants. In the case of my *Government Marketing News,* doing this has slowly but steadily raised the response rate to a point well beyond what the most optimistic book on the subject of selling by mail suggests you are likely to achieve.

Your first market research, therefore, probably cannot give you all the answers you want and need, but should tell you whether there is an adequate market—enough people who will want what you offer. You may remember the cases described earlier of entrepreneurs who advertised their new product before actually creating it, accepting advance offers. They consider this to be "testing" the market, but it is also basic market research to determine whether it is worthwhile to go ahead with the project. A negative result, however, is not necessarily the death knell: it may well be that your basic idea is a sound one, but your appeal is not right or your target population is not right. Let's go back to the *Government Marketing News* again for an explanation:

In the beginning, the results were not what I wanted them to be, and I almost abandoned the project. My initial appeal was wrong in both ways: it offered general news on government purchasing, and it was addressed to "opportunity seekers" and to very small businesses whose proprietors, for the most part, knew nothing of federal procurement. In fact, initially I found it necessary to give complimentary subscriptions to purchasers of my first book on the subject.

I then developed another idea: I had three volumes of information on government markets by this time, as well as the newsletter. I therefore offered all three, plus a one-year subscription to the newsletter, in a package deal—that is, for one overall price that was less than the sum of all if purchased separately.

I managed to sell enough of these to encourage me that the proposition was worthwhile, as a business enterprise, but still I wasn't getting the results which I felt I should get, with a potential market of about 250,000 organizations that sell to the U.S. government agencies.

It wasn't until my appeal began to stress the proposal-writing help offered by the newsletter and books that I began to make the breakthroughs I had been seeking for several years. But I could not have reached that point had I not carefully analyzed the accumulating results of several years' marketing effort with this package. My market research continues to this day, always seeking to get a better "profile" of the customer and what the customer wants.

"Sales" can address only what you have to offer, but "marketing" can (and should) address what you *should be* offering—what the customer wants, who the customer is, how to reach the customer, how to appeal to the customer. However, "sales" should also be feeding information back to marketing to improve the store of market information. There is no better source of market intelligence than the sales efforts themselves and the results they achieve or do not achieve.

By now you are beginning to see, perhaps, why so many are confused by the two terms, "marketing" and "sales," and why they have so much trouble discriminating between them. They are closely related, of course, and the objective of all marketing activity is to prepare the way to make sales by establishing a firm understanding of what business you are in (or plan to enter), what (who) your market is, and how to reach your market.

That latter, how to reach your market, is largely a responsibility of the sales effort, but can only result from the marketing effort. Quibbling over this is of no importance; the answer must be gotten, no matter how.

REACHING MARKETS

Reaching your market or making the sales appeal to those whom you have selected as your targets can be done in several ways:

General advertising.
Direct-mail solicitation.
Employee salespeople.
Dealers/distributors.
Combinations of the above.

"General advertising" refers to "print ads" in newspapers and magazines, commercials on radio and TV, billboards, and other ads which are broadcast—aimed at everyone—with the hope and expectation that in directing your appeals at everyone you will automatically reach those who are your targets. However, even general advertising can be directed, to some extent, by running print ads in those special periodicals read by each industry, but not by the general public.

For direct-mail solicitations, you must somehow gain access to the right mailing lists, unless your message is intended for everyday consumers.

Salespeople may be on your own salaried staff or may be dealers/salespeople, as in the case of Avon, Fuller Brush, or Amway.

Dealers/distributors include wholesalers, jobbers, retailers, and others who are, in a sense, actually the customers you are trying to reach, since you *sell to them*. But in many cases, they either have return privileges for merchandise they do not sell, or they order only what they have got advance orders for. Hence, even in these cases, you need to address sales messages to the target population.

Combinations of these methods are used by many large firms. Advertising and direct-mail solicitations are used to persuade you to call on your dealer and provide him the opportunity to close the sale. Most TV commercial advertising is broadcast in this philosophy. For most small businesses, however, the process of reaching the prospects must be far more selective and lower in costs than those large sales/advertising campaigns mounted by large corporations.

The key question is simply, how can you reach the prospects you have selected—your target population—at a cost per resulting sale that lets you turn a reasonable profit? If you are not yet sure who your prospects are, you must also design the initial efforts as tests or market surveys to help you refine your sales efforts and marketing strategies until you are getting enough sales per advertising/promotion/sales dollar invested.

Take note, now, that mail is one way of reaching customers. That is, "mail order" is not something different in the way of a business, but is a *medium* for communicating with prospects and trading—exchanging goods or services for money. Unfortunately, many people think of "mail order" as a business per se, rather than as one *means* of doing business, just as a retail store or a wholesale showroom is a means. It's true, of course, that some businesses lend themselves better to mail order as a medium than do others, despite the claim that anything can be sold by mail. (That may be a literal truth, but it would be pretty difficult to sell automobiles and a number of other items that way.) But within the limitations of what can be sold *effectively* by mail, the business principles are the same.

So, rather than deciding that you want to "go into mail order," you should decide what you want to offer, to whom you are going to offer it, and how you can best reach those prospects. Mail is one way to be considered.

This is not to say that you may not have first established certain constraints which make it necessary or highly desirable that you conduct your business by mail. It may be, especially if you wish to operate your business as a spare-time enterprise or, for some other reason, have decided in advance you want to operate a mail order enterprise. If so, one of your considerations is going to be, of course, what can be sold effectively by mail. But that does not change any of the basic business principles. It's simply a matter of where you start from, and you may be starting from any of a large number of basic positions and/or basic constraints:

A basic idea for a product or service.
A basic idea for a marketing/merchandising method.
A set of skills or special knowledge to offer.
A "connection" for some commodity at a special low price—say, access to a bankruptcy selloff.
A connection for some hard-to-find item(s).
Access to some special market, for which you are seeking something to offer.
A property which happens to be a good retail location.

Any of these may also entail some special requirements, such as the hours you can make available or the capital you can provide. These are the constraints which you must take into account, the *conditions* which must be accommodated in your business planning. Ergo, these affect your entire approach to marketing and sales. That is, what you offer, how you offer it, how you reach prospects, how you make the trade of money for goods or services must be subject to these preconditions, and the entire business plan must be structured to work within these constraints. It would be futile, for example, to advertise in Burma or Alaska if you are unable to make delivery to these destinations or if delivery is too expensive to make selling to prospects in these places profitable. Likewise, it would be unwise to undertake a business which by its nature requires salespeople making calls if you cannot find a way to place salespeople on the street with your line. All this may seem pretty obvious, but it is surprising how many people commit themselves to investments and great efforts without thinking such matters out in their early planning stages.

One essential element in marketing/sales, after you have decided what you have to offer that you believe people will buy, is how to let them know about it—how to make the offer. It's part of the sales activity, but it's called advertising.

WHAT IS "ADVERTISING"?

Before the days of high-speed turnpikes, every motorist had his day lightened by Burma Shave signs along the road. Usually, there were four in a sequence, spelling out four rhyming lines in a kind of jingle. Very soft sell. The objective was to make the name "Burma Shave" so familiar as to cause customers to ask for Burma Shave in the drug stores almost automatically. In those days, too, it was a rare barn standing alongside a well-traveled road which did not bear the words "Chew Mail Pouch Tobacco." That was a soft sell, too. No pressure at all on the customer; just repetition of the message.

The general approach to advertising in those days seemed to involve little more than making the product name familiar. That is, the concept was that if the name was repeated often enough, customers would buy the product.

Today, that concept has almost disappeared, except for what is sometimes referred to as "institutional advertising," in which no effort is made to ask the customer to buy anything specific, but just to appreciate the company's standing in our society.

Most of today's advertising contains specific sales arguments—exhorting the reader/viewer/listener to buy the product or service, and offering reasons for buying. Consequently, the principles of advertising preached by the experts in the field are almost exactly the same as the principles of salesmanship. And for that reason, it is my belief that advertising ought to be considered to be nothing more or less than written salesmanship.

Of course, the principles of each are adapted to the medium—to its limitations and opportunities—as we'll soon see. But the underlying principles are the same:

1. Get attention, arouse interest.
2. Generate desire.
3. Create credibility.
4. Ask for the order.

Getting attention

In "print media" (advertisements appearing in print), getting attention is usually accomplished through the headline, with or without the aid of art work, such as a photo or drawing. Most printed advertisements feature a large headline.

A headline can draw attention to itself through its own graphic impact, through what it says, or through both. Here is an example that shows how to do both: the headline is large enough to command the page, but it also delivers the basic message—the offer itself.

**Receive 26 weeks
of Investor's Digest
for $29**

Even so, the copywriter lost an opportunity to pack still another message in the headline by failing to use the word "only," to wit: "Receive 26 Weeks of INVESTOR'S DIGEST for *only* $29." This would have added the implicit message that the offer was a special bargain. The headline as it stands may suggest that in a quite subtle fashion, to the discerning reader, but the probability is that few readers will gather that part of the message.

It would be an important part of the message. The offer of a bargain—getting in on a special sale or special offer and *saving money*—never loses its appeal. Here are a few words and ideas which are generally deemed to be sure-fire attention-getters and interest-arousers:

Free	*Special offer*
New	*Sale*
Exclusive	*Save*
Be the first (to own one)	*Trial*

These and derivations of them never go out of style. Everyone wants to "get in" on things, be up to date, save money, get something for nothing, try new things. These words appeal to buyers' basic interests, and even in this sophisticated age, when we snort skeptically at "free" and "new," many still succumb to such appeals. Here's why:

The human animal tends strongly to believe what he or she *wants* to believe. All selling and advertising depends heavily on this characteristic. We'd like to believe that it is possible to become wealthy overnight, if only we could learn the carefully guarded secret of wealthy individuals. So we send for that $10 book or even the magic amulet we are offered by someone who claims that it worked wonderfully well for him. We'd like to believe that if we drink Floogle's Beer we're going to laugh it up at the tavern or on the beach with a lot of beautiful girls and handsome guys. And if we smoke Emphysema Cigarettes we are automatically rugged outdoors types to whom people look up. We're all Walter Mittys—we want to be healthy, handsome, or beautiful, highly respected, loved, rich, and it's mighty hard to turn down offers to make us so.

Of course, advertising is a numbers game: not everyone wants to smell good. Or, at least, not everyone is willing to switch from the perfume or after-shave cologne she or he is presently using. Therefore, the advertising message has to reach enough people to make up for the fact that perhaps only 1 or 2 percent of the readers will respond.

Evaluating the response

In all advertising, there are two major factors which concern the advertiser: how many people are reached by the advertising message, and how many people "respond"—order or ask for more information.

In so-called "institutional" advertising—that's the general advertisement extolling General Electric products or IBM computers—there is no way to judge response with any precision. Who can say how many people were inspired to order GE light bulbs or refrigerators as a result of the advertising message? But in advertising that asks the reader to order the product or send in a coupon for more information, it's quite easy to calculate the response rate. You know how many people were exposed to the message from the circulation of the periodical or the number of sales letters mailed, and it is easy to determine what percentage of that "population" is represented by the orders or inquiries you receive. That's referred to as the "response rate."

Keying your ads

Advertisers often put on entire campaigns, running the same advertisement in several periodicals, and perhaps even on TV. Because that costs money—a good bit of money—you want to know the response rate of *each* appearance of your ad so that you can discover where to spend your ad dollars for greatest results. To do this, you "key" your ad, using a different key for each publication. (Some will use a different key for each month to detect seasonal variations, too.)

There are a number of ways to key an ad. One common way is put the key on the order form or ask readers to send their orders to "Dept. AK-2" or "Drawer 13." That's the code that tells you where and possibly when the ad ran. Before long you can judge which periodical or medium works best for you, and even what months of the year are best for your offer.

Another way keying is used is in testing advertising copy or sales letters. (This is used widely in direct mail, about which more later.) Suppose you have several different ideas about what your ad should say, and you want to try them all out. You can use a different key for each version and calculate which version works best for you.

Some people key their ads by adding a letter to the post office box number: "P.O. Box 727-A." This is ignored by the postmaster, who puts your mail in Box 727 no matter what letter follows the number.

Still another simple way is to vary the spelling of your name for each run. If you are James T. Green, you might become James W. Green, James T. Greene, J. T. Green, J. Thomas Green, etc. You can make up dozens of keys this way, and variations in spelling your name or your company name on checks won't give you any problem at your bank, as long as you endorse the check the way it's made out.

THE MATTER OF MEDIA

The vehicle you use to get your advertising message to your prospects is the medium. If you advertise in periodicals—magazines and newspapers—you are using the "print media," for example. If you advertise or sell by mailing out sales literature to prospects, you are using the "direct mail" medium. And if you go to radio or TV, you are in the broadcast media.

But suppose you call on prospects or send your salespeople to call? Then you are into what is referred to as "direct sales," not to be confused with direct mail, although that, too, is a manner of making direct sales.

Each medium has its own pros and cons, as do most things. Let's look at a few.

The print media

Advertising in periodicals is generally expensive, especially if you use periodicals which have large circulation. Advertising rates are dependent on circulation figures: the larger the circulation, the higher the rates. Therefore, an ad in a local paper or a magazine with only a few hundred thousand circulation costs far less than would the same ad in a big city newspaper or a magazine with a circulation in the millions.

A full page in any large-circulation publication runs into thousands of dollars. Even in a periodical with a few hundred thousand circulation, a full page is likely to run into several thousands of dollars. There are therefore several things to think about when deciding on where and how to advertise.

Who reads the periodical? Are they the kind of people you want to reach—the right *prospects,* that is? (Now you'll begin to see why it is so important to know whom you are trying to reach—to *profile* your prospects.)

If you are offering a newsletter for investors, *The Wall Street Journal* may be just right for you. Business people read it. But if you are trying to induce prospects to order your new chocolate-cake recipe, "WSJ" is probably all wrong for your appeal, and you would waste your advertising dollars there. Or if you are offering a new pocket calculator, at least some of the *Journal's* readership might be right for you—but how much of it?

Remember that when you pay the periodical's advertising rate, you are paying for the presumed benefits of reaching all the readers. But suppose your message is likely to be of interest to only 10 percent of the readers? Then you are getting only 10 percent of the value you pay for. Ninety percent of your advertising dollars are wasted.

There are other considerations too, of course. One of them is this: your ad in a daily newspaper is good for only one day, whereas your ad in a monthly magazine is read and, presumably, "pulls" for the entire month (until the next issue comes out)—except for the "drag," a phenomenon discussed earlier.

For some reason, many readers will save an advertisement for many months, and then order. That is, months after the ad has run or the sales letters are mailed out, and after the main response has been satisfied, individual orders will straggle in, one by one. If the ad has run for a long time, it may continue to pull orders up to a full year after it has stopped running. Even on "special offers . . . good this month only," customers will order months later. I have found, in fact, orders resulting as much as two years after appeals were made.

But you can't and shouldn't depend on that phenomenon, for it is entirely uncertain and can't really be calculated. You must consider whether the publication is a daily, weekly, bi-weekly, monthly, or whatever; what its circulation is; and to what kinds of people it circulates. The fact is that your ad in a circulation of 200,000 of the right prospects may well pull more orders than it would in a periodical of 2 million *general* circulation.

Special-interest publications

There are many publications written to appeal to a limited group of readers with a special interest, such as these:

Supermarket Shopper—for housewives trying to save money on the shopping bill. (Circulation: 10,000)

Bon Appétit—"for affluent young men and women, interested in the good things of life." (Circulation: 1 million)

The Family Food Garden—"for food gardeners." (Circulation: 250,000)

Auto Laundry News—for carwash operators. (Circulation: 18,000)

Men's Wear—for those interested in retail apparel. (Circulation: 26,700)

That's a tiny sampling. There are thousands of publications, many of them so-called "trade journals" written for people in specific trades, many others for the average citizen with special interests or hobbies.

One excellent place to find out about these is the annual *Writer's Market,* published every year by *Writer's Digest* and listing thousands of different kinds of publications and related matters. But there are other such directories, too, most of which you can find in your public library.

"P.O." and "P.I." advertising

If you watch carefully, you may see advertisements which list the publisher's own address as the place to send your orders for the item advertised. In most such cases, these are

"P.O."—per order—advertisements. The supplier of the product has struck a deal with the publisher to have his ad run free of charge, with the publisher getting a commission on each sale. When the publisher receives the orders, he deducts his own commission—usually on the order of 50 percent—and sends the rest on to the supplier, who then "drop ships" the order to the customer.

Most publishers do not like it known that they will accept P.O. advertising. They fear that if it gets around, they will be bombarded with such offers, and they'd rather just sell the space. But most publishers do accept such offers from time to time (Remember Hubert Simon, whom you met in the first chapter?), especially when they are short of advertising orders for the month or have some page space that needs filling, or when the advertiser is enough of a salesman to convince the publisher that he will make a good profit on the thing.

Some advertisers do not ask for orders in their ads, but invite the prospect to send for more details or a free demonstration. This is referred to as "inquiry" advertising, and some publishers will accept "P.I." or per-inquiry ads. (For example, many of the occasional listings in *Parade,* the Sunday newspaper magazine supplement, require you to send your inquiry to *Parade*.) In these cases, the publisher sends the inquiry on to the supplier, who pays a flat fee to the publisher for each inquiry (for example, $2 each, but often far less).

Why "inquiry" advertising?

This probably raises the question in your mind, Why invite inquiries at all? Why not ask for the order? Here's why.

The size of the advertisement you run to a large extent determines how large an order you can ask for and get. A small, classified advertisement will bring in $1, $2, and $3 orders, but it's difficult to be persuasive enough in a small classified ad to get more than that. If you want to persuade the reader to order a $10 or $15 item, you must have a larger advertisement, called a "display" or "space" ad. But even a space ad can't sell a really "big tag" item, such as a refrigerator or a fur coat. To sell that, you have to get the prospect into the showroom. Or if you are somewhere in between these extremes—say you are offering a $250 item—you need to send the reader enough sales copy to close the sale—perhaps an entire brochure and a multipage sales letter. Ergo, you don't try to get the order in the ad, but only to persuade enough readers to become interested and send you their names so that you can go to direct mail with them. In short, you want to compile a mailing list, but you want a mailing list of interested prospects who are at least going to read your literature instead of discarding it immediately.

In fact, because for some of these propositions the mailing package is quite expensive—some cost several dollars apiece—you may even want to "qualify" the prospect, to screen out the idle curiosity seekers who wouldn't buy in any event. To do that, you may ask them to answer a couple of questions, to help you determine whether they are good enough prospects to be worth a $2 or $3 investment in an expensive brochure, or you may even ask them to send a dollar or two (which you promise to refund if they subsequently order) as "earnest money," again to screen out the idly curious.

In that regard, it is interesting that experiments show that asking for some nominal sum often *increases* the response because it adds value and makes the offer more credible.

That has another interesting aspect, which shows just how important credibility is. One acquaintance ran a small classified ad asking for $2, in return for which he would send the customer a special report and a free sample issue of his newsletter. The response was rather good, so he thought he would increase it by dropping the price to $1. To his dismay, the price reduction had the opposite effect: the response fell off. The reason for the fall-off was simply that the readers found they could believe the special report was worth $2, but they didn't think they would get anything of value for $1! This experience has been shared by many advertisers.

Direct mail

In spite of increasing postal rates and increasing printing costs, direct mail continues to be a favored way of reaching prospects. The typical direct-mail package consists of these items:

A sales letter introducing the offer.

Descriptive literature—flyers, circulars, brochures, and so on.

An order form, sometimes part of the literature, often a separate piece.

A return envelope, often prepaid, under postal permit. (Not everyone includes a return envelope, but it is a favored item, and many enclose one.)

The sales letter is generally addressed "Dear reader" or something along the same lines, but often has a headline above the salutation. It's a message addressed directly to the reader, usually telling the reader about the terrific offer enclosed, often with words circled or underlined and handwritten notations in the margin. Most copywriters try to make the sales letter a kind of heart-to-heart, between-you-and-me appeal. The general effect they are trying to achieve is one of a personal message.

The descriptive literature may be almost anything—circulars, elaborate brochures, testimonials, photos, and whatever else the advertiser believes will persuade the prospect.

Usually, some sort of order form is enclosed, often with a "special offer," if the reader "acts promptly." And by far the majority of such appeals include a return envelope, often with a prepaid indicia so that the reader does not have to find a stamp but may send in the order at once. In many cases, the customer may use any of several major credit cards, also, to speed things up or postpone paying for the item.

Those who use direct mail and put on sizable campaigns must mail many thousands of letters. At 15 cents each, this can mount swiftly into a great deal of money. To reduce this cost, the advertiser can get a special bulk-mail permit from the post office, which permits him to mail out his pieces for only slightly more than one-half the first-class postage rates. To do this, however, the mailer must sort the mail first into separate batches, by Zip codes, and bundle them, then take the mail to the post office and either pay for it then or charge a deposit account he has set up earlier.

There are at least two ways to affix the "postage" on bulk mail: you can use a special, precanceled bulk-mail stamp or your postage meter set for the bulk-mail rate, or you can print indicia, specifying the permit number, where the stamp would ordinarily go. The problem with this latter method is that the preprinted indicia are a dead giveaway that the envelope is pure advertising matter, which is an inducement to the recipient not to respond to it or even read it. That is, many people view such material as "junk mail" and discard it immediately. On the other hand, many advertisers assume the respondent will do so anyhow, so they make up a package which is clearly advertising, by its very appearance.

Obviously, using a system such as this, you have to mail out a great many pieces and depend on probability statistics— that is, even assuming that only a small percentage of addresses will order, you must clear costs and make a profit. (Does it begin to become clear why a large markup is necessary for many business propositions?)

In my own mail order operations, I use a business envelope with a first-class stamp. The only clue the reader has that it may be advertising matter is that the address is on a small label. Other than that, it may well be a piece of personal or business correspondence. Bulk mail never worked well for me, although many do use it, with obvious success. In my own experiments and tests, I have also tried using return envelopes and have discarded the idea as an unnecessary cost. I could find no evidence that its inclusion ever accounted for one extra order or that its exclusion ever cost me an order.

Broadcast media

For radio commercials, which are relatively inexpensive, you need only provide the station a script or a tape (they may make a tape of it, anyhow), unless you want sound effects and the like, in which case you will have to produce or pay the station to produce a recorded tape. Rates will vary, according to time (higher rates for prime time), and according to how many times you want it run.

TV is along the same lines, but here a tape is usually a must, and you have the cost of audiovisual production, of course. Even if you run P.O. or P.I. ads—and everyone has seen this on late-night TV, plugging kitchen appliances and glass cutters—you will have to provide the videotape recording.

Here, too, you have to decide if radio or TV will reach the right people, and at what hours and on what kinds of shows you will reach the right prospects. For the most part, radio and TV advertising for the small business is best suited to products or services for the general consumer.

Pros and cons of print versus direct mail

There are many things to be said in favor of using print media—display or classified advertising—but there are perhaps as many arguments against it. The same can be said of direct mail however. Some propositions just lend themselves better to one than to the other—they virtually dictate the medium— while others can be handled either way. Here are some of the considerations which have entered into my own thinking and decisions in selecting media.

The pros for print media are (1) convenience: little work is required of you once your ad copy is all set; (2) you can reach a very wide audience, often into the millions; (3) you can keep your message going steadily, if it continues to pay, with nothing more than telephone calls or brief notes; and (4) it's a highly professional way, in appearance, of offering your product, which alone gives the customer some confidence, especially if you are advertising in some fairly prestigious publication.

The cons are these: (1) it usually takes two to three months (sometimes even longer) to run your ad, because periodicals (not newspapers, but magazines) book their advertising and "close their forms" for advertising at least one and often three months in advance; (2) if you want your ad to run consecutively for several months, you have to order it all at once, for the reasons just stated, and gamble that you will get results and will want the ad to continue (otherwise, you'll have to accept a break in your advertising); (3) if the proposition requires a large ad, it's difficult to run small samples as tests, especially since you have to test each publication as well as each version of the ad—not to mention the long time frames in making tests, because of the long lead time for space advertising.

By comparison, direct mail offers almost the opposite pros and cons. You can run small samples and even run them concurrently, and know the results within a few weeks. You can operate on a small scale, if need be, reducing the risk and the capital required. And the cost per customer is likely to be smaller, although that is not always the case.

However, direct mail is a lot of work, unless you have a mailing house do it for you. You also need mailing lists. You can rent them for from about $25 to $75 per 1,000 names, but rented lists may or may not work for you. (They never have worked well for me.) In that case, you must run inquiry ads to get names or compile your own lists from whatever sources you can find.

I have always objected to giving periodicals free use of my money for the two or three months I am waiting for the ad to run. They usually require payment in advance, or at least well before the ad runs; therefore, you are paying in advance of getting what you pay for, and I object to that on principle. But a built-in problem with print media is that you almost always pay for a lot of circulation which is of no value to you—that is, usually only a percentage of a periodical's readers are good prospects for you, but you are paying rates determined by its *total* circulation. I object to that also.

WHAT'S A SATISFACTORY RESPONSE RATE?

People in businesses that depend almost entirely on advertising are forever worrying about their response rate, and those in mail order seem to insist that you must get 3 to 5 percent to make a profit—that is, three to five orders for each 100 prospects reached by direct mail. (It's more difficult to tell, really, how many prospects you reach by print ads, and publishers of periodicals often claim much greater circulation than they have, on the assumption that three or four people read each copy they sell.) Let's see how much sense that makes.

Typically, a mailing will cost you about $250 per 1,000 pieces mailed out. (Obviously, it may run more or less, depending on what you enclose, but $250 is a fair average cost.) A 5 percent response is 50 orders per 1,000 mailed pieces.

Now let us suppose that you are selling an item that costs you $3 to buy or make, and you get $10 for it. It costs you about $1 to mail, however, so "fulfillment" (filling the order) costs you about $4 for each order. Here are the figures, per 1,000 pieces mailed, *not counting your labor:*

Mailing	$250 (printing and postage)
Mailing list rental	40
Fulfillment	200 (50 orders at $4 each)
Total costs	$490
Receipts	$500 (50 orders at $10 each)
Costs	490
Gross profit	$10

Ten dollars is not very much to show for all that labor, investment, and risk. And it doesn't count your labor. (The above figures assume that you have no help but do everything yourself.) In fact, it's only 2 percent profit, an unacceptably low figure. Yet, many people will go on insisting that 5 percent is a good response rate!

Let's look at another proposition, in which you get only a 2 percent response rate, which many would condemn immediately as unacceptably low and a sure road to ruin. Let's offer a $50 item, with the same mailing costs, and with a $10 fulfillment cost:

Mailing (including list rental)	$290
Fulfillment (10 orders)	100
Total costs	$390
Receipts (10 orders @ $50 each)	$500
All costs	390
Gross profit	$110

Still no fortune, but we now have a 22 percent profit margin, which is probably at least adequate if we have managed to keep our general operating costs to a reasonable level.

What was wrong with the first proposition was that the markup—the ratio of cost to selling price—was too small, despite the 5 percent response.

One person, working alone, could mail out at least 3,000 to 5,000 pieces a week, earning enough, at 22 percent, to pay for the labor and risk. Obviously, you couldn't earn enough at 2 percent to make the whole thing worthwhile, even with enough help to send out 20,000 pieces a week. In fact, the profit margin does not make the risk worth taking.

The fact is that there is really no such animal as a "satisfactory" response rate, except in the specific terms of a specific offer, taking into account the costs, the markup, and the volume. The true measure is *return on investment,* whether satisfying that requires a 1 percent or 10 percent response. It's the only measure that makes any sense. It is all but impossible to reduce mailing costs appreciably—you couldn't shave very much off either postage or printing, let alone mailing list rentals, so that cost is virtually fixed. The variables you have to work with are other costs and your selling price. You must have the markup—usually at least 3:1, with even that a bit on the thin side—and you must contain the other fulfillment costs.

You should, however, consider the cost of getting the order in relation to the selling price. In the first case we postulated here, it cost $290 to get 50 orders—$5.80 each, which was a bit more then one-half the selling price. In the second case, it cost $29 to get each order, still somewhat more than one-half the selling price, but at the higher markup, which made it tolerable. Overall, the return on investment for the first proposition was only 3.4 percent, or $10 on $290 invested in mailing. The second case showed $110 on the same $290 investment, or a 37.9 percent return.

SHOULD YOU RENT YOUR MAILING LISTS?

Renting mailing lists is a fairly popular business, with many entrepreneurs in that business. The cost of renting a list (and you are paying for a one-time use, with the list "salted" to catch you at it, if you violate the agreement and use it a second time without paying for the second use) varies according to its quality, supposed or real. A list of "opportunity seekers"—people who have sent in inquiries but never bought anything—may rent for as little as $20 to $25 per 1,000 names. But they are names without great value, because they are names of people who may or may not be buyers—that is, good prospects. A list of people who have all spent $10 for a book has higher value: you know that they are book buyers. And so on. So good lists—supposedly good lists—can run to $65 to $75 per 1,000 names quite easily.

Anybody whose name is on those lists and who buys from you is your customer, and his "name" belongs to you: you need pay no one to make further mailings to him. But names you acquire yourself, either through compilation from directories or through your own inquiry advertising, are also your property, and you need pay no one for their use. Hence the great use of inquiry advertising.

The best mailing list you can get is the list of your own customers—if you have an offer which is amenable to repeat business and you have satisfied your customers. But any "good list"—one which has produced a satisfactory return on investment—is a good list to use over and over. It so happens that second and third mailings to the same good list usually produce equally good results every time, if the mailings are not spaced too closely to each other. And in many cases, subsequent mailings raise the rate of return, as the respondents begin to recognize your name and your offer. This is again a good argument for developing your own mailing lists.

HOW TO BUILD YOUR OWN LISTS

Building mailing lists takes time, especially if you use inquiry advertising. Compilation of lists from directories is much faster, but many maintain that compiled lists are not usually very productive. In my own case, I have found that to be partially true, but not wholly true: some of my compiled lists did not work well, but some others worked very well. In any case, it will take time to build your lists, but there are ways—at least one good one—to accelerate the process.

First of all, you should segregate your lists. When someone sends you an order, you should take that name off your general list and add it to your customer list. And even your customer list may be subdivided into categories, by size of the order (say all $25 customers versus all $5 customers) or at least in terms of one-time customers versus repeat customers (preferred-customer list).

In time, you will become acquainted with others offering items to much the same kind of prospects you do. Many such indirect competitors will swap lists with you—customer lists for customer lists and prospect lists for prospect lists. In that manner, after building up only a few thousand names of my own, I rapidly expanded my lists to about 30,000!

BUT I'M NOT INTERESTED IN MAIL ORDER . . .

For some reason, perhaps because it *looks* so easy, an enormous number of people are attracted to mail order. It does offer a large number of advantages, as well as some disadvantages, and we'll have some more to say on the subject later. But not everyone is interested in mail order—some people prefer more direct ways of doing business, such as running a retail establishment or dealing strictly with local trade. Much of what has been said about mail order and mailing lists is not, however, peculiar to mail order, but works as well when applied to other means of doing business.

It's not as common today as it once was, probably because so many city dwellers have taken up life in the suburban countryside, leaving the crowded cities. But once it was an unusual week that did not see every householder receive a dozen circulars, distributed by hand from door to door. Today, it usually is the mailman who distributes those circulars, generally addressed to "Resident." The method is different, but the principle is the same. Professional mailing houses have long lists of every city and suburban residential district, with all the addresses, each preceded by the word "Resident."

If you wish to do business with local residents, you have your choice today of hiring youngsters to distribute circulars or having the mailman deliver them to "residents." But a variation that is often used, made possible by modern conditions, is to have youngsters distribute circulars in parking lots, putting them under the windshield wipers of thousands of automobiles. And if your business is appropriate to the class of prospects, you might distribute thousands of cards and circulars quickly in crowded office buildings.

The important thing is not how you distribute them; there are always many ways for the enterprising entrepeneur. The important thing is what you say—your message or appeal. If that is right, any method of distribution will work.

HOW TO GET FREE ADVERTISING

"Advertising pays." That's a slogan advertising people and publishers are fond of using. And it's no doubt true: it's a rare business that can survive without advertising. But advertising also *costs,* and some methods cost more than others. Some are even prohibitively expensive for the new or small business. But there are ways to get free advertising. One of them was already described—the "P.O." and "P.I." methods, in which you do not pay for the advertising per se, but pay large sales commissions. That is, you *pay* after all; you simply do not take the risk of your advertising ever representing a loss to you. But neither do you realize the full profits of your sales.

There is something called "publicity," which is virtually the same thing as advertising, except that it is in some ways even more effective than conventional advertising because it is editorial matter rather than advertising matter; hence, it is more credible to the reader who is your sales prospect.

The principal way to get these editorial write-ups of your offerings is through the press release, which you send out to newspapers, magazines, newsletters, and any other periodicals you think suitable. And "suitable" means that the readers of the periodical are people who would be interested and, hence, good prospects.

For example, you would not announce a new furniture polish to the readers of *Model Railroader* (unless you thought model-train hobbyists could use the product in their hobby, somehow). Instead, you would seek out those publications which are addressed to housewives and others who use furniture polish regularly—say, *Good Housekeeping.*

The advantage of such publicity, as noted, is that it appears as editorial matter—that is, impartial reporting rather than commercially motivated claims of excellence. Ergo, it is far more credible to the reader. On the other hand, it is relatively difficult to get the editorial space—editors know what your purpose is, of course, and won't give you the space for nothing—and you have no real control over what portion of your press release is used, if it is used at all. That is, your release must offer the editor some news value and thus give him some reason to use it. That's what *he* gets in the exchange. And make no mistake about it: you won't get the space if your press release does not offer the editor something. (In the next chapter, we'll talk about how to write the press release.)

One other way to get free publicity is through the publicity stunt. Anyone who has seen enough Hollywood movies is aware that there are many press agents, often euphemized as "public relations" firms, who specialize in winning their clients free newspaper and magazine space—publicity. However, the typical publicity stunt is not that sensational, super-costly, and wildly unlikely extravaganza that Hollywood is so fond of portraying! Here are some of the publicity "stunts" which are carried out every day to win attention from the press:

Contests. Contests are so common today that unless you are putting on something like a beauty pageant, you'll have to be satisfied to get press coverage only from some local newspapers and a few newsletters. The contest that draws the attention of the large newspapers must be something pretty large and extravagant—a major beauty contest, something offering a spectacularly large prize, or having some newsworthy characteristic, other than the mere fact that it is a contest.

Spectacular displays. Sometimes the local newspaper or a magazine will be interested in an unusual window display or in any aspect of your business which is photogenic. Newspapers love to "scoop" other newspapers on photo coverage, as well as on stories. In this, as well as in contests, if you can come up with something that offers an unusual opportunity for photography, you may be able to get at least a photo and caption in the press.

A novel idea. If your business is basically novel—for example, Pet Rocks—you should be able to get the press interested.

A crowd stopper. If you have something that attracts a large crowd, your local press—and sometimes even the national press—is likely to become interested. (Have you thought of renting a gorilla or an elephant from a circus?)

Getting yourself arrested. Joe Cossman did this when he had a truck dump a load of potatoes on a New York City street to publicize his "spud gun." The $50 fine was cheap, he thought, for the publicity he got. Cossman also relates that when his dog had an extraordinarily large litter and he persuaded the local press to come out and do a picture story, he lined the dog's box with circulars advertising his product, and made sure they were placed to show up in the photos the local newspaper ran. Cossman runs seminars on how to succeed in business—they deal largely with how to *promote* business—and he strongly advocates that all efforts be bent to getting publicity before investing a dime in paid advertising.

The principle is to be newsworthy—something we'll talk about in the next chapter.

13

HOW TO WRITE SALES COPY

The obvious—and wrong—thing to do in writing sales copy is to bore the reader with how great your product or service is, even though it may be. Even experienced copywriters often forget this and fall into the trap of extolling the product, instead of answering the question always in the customer's mind: "What's in it for me?" That's the $64 question. You must explain to the customer the benefits of buying, the need to buy what you offer, as explained earlier. Now let's talk about how to get that across and other specifics of how to do what I have been urging you to do.

Some years ago, a gentleman whom I know quite well started a TV-radio service business, working from a shop he set up in his own garage at home. That kind of business is a local business, of course, and he knew that he must advertise locally. He did not want customers to bring work to him, however, since he was not organized to receive customers; rather, he wanted to go to them. He knew then that his objective was to place his telephone number with the prospects and somehow persuade them to keep his number handy, for the time when their TV or radio needed servicing.

He resorted to a simple solution: he had a 4 × 6-inch card printed up, announcing his home service for TV sets and radios, stating that he serviced all makes and responded promptly to calls, day or evening, and featuring his telephone number prominently in the middle of the card. The chief sales device was the message he had printed in bold type across the top of the card:

157

SAVE THIS CARD. YOU'LL NEED IT SOME DAY.

He hired neighborhood kids to distribute the cards around all the neighborhoods he wished to service, and had them put the cards under doors and automobile windshield wipers in large parking lots at supermarkets and shopping centers.

He got a few calls almost immediately, but the results were not spectacular. Nevertheless, he repeated the distribution a week later, and again a week after that, and again the week after that. And every month after that, for several months, by which time he had so much work he was forced to stop distributing cards!

Sometimes he got calls from other neighborhoods, and he learned that some of the cards had been passed on to friends and relatives. And sometimes he heard such stories as, "Geez, I threw your card out the first time I got it, but after a while I decided to hang on to it. I'm sure glad I did."

Once in a while he'd be told: "I threw your card out because I didn't need any service, but just as my set quit and I was sorry I threw your card out, I got another one under the door." Or: "I threw your card out, I'm sorry to say, but I asked my neighbor, when my set broke down, and he saved your card."

Again and again he was assured by customers that his admonition to save the card was a good idea and had resulted in the call.

What was the reason this fellow gave his customers for calling him? Just this: convenience. If they heeded his advice and saved the card, his number was the easiest one to find, the most convenient one to call!

This idea should work well for any business in which the prospect is likely to need the service one day, if not immediately—a resume-writing service, for example. Or an automobile service. Or almost any other kind of service people need periodically—plumbing, wiring, carpentry, appliance repairs, and house painting, to name just a few.

It took me quite a while to find the best words to sell large companies subscriptions to my own *Government Marketing News* newsletter, even after I discovered that the best appeal was to their need for help in writing proposals. Focusing on that gave them a sound reason for subscribing all right, but I had also the problem of credibility. What would convince them that I *could* help them?

I was handicapped for a long time by a rather common reluctance to "sound my own horn." I found it difficult, as most people do, to extoll my own virtues as an expert. I was on the verge of hiring a professional copywriter because a stranger would not be so hung up. Yet, I felt that no one could do it quite as well as I. (After all, if I'm such a good proposal writer, I ought to be able to find the words to explain why, shouldn't I?)

I got around my problem finally by simply deciding to write out a brief history of my own proposal-writing *accomplishments* (not "experience"), to help myself get started. When I had finished explaining on paper the contracts my proposals had won and the history of how each came about (many against heavy odds), I found that I was simply reporting, not bragging, and that the facts were impressive enough, without any superlatives.

I then reduced each account to the briefest history possible, naming names wherever I could without violating ethics or confidences, and selected the most impressive of these. I then cast around for a headline which would get some attention and be motivating as well. This is the headline I wound up with to introduce my credentials:

MAYBE I'M JUST LUCKY . . .
OR MAYBE I KNOW SOMETHING THAT *YOU* SHOULD KNOW

Near the end of my copy I said that if it were just luck, it seemed to be rubbing off on my readers, for many were reporting greater success in winning contracts. And I wound up saying: "I believe it's the methods and procedures I teach which are helping my readers, but even if it's only luck, couldn't *you* use some of it?"

I'm happy to report that a large enough percentage of recipients of the mailing package found me credible enough to subscribe and make the mailings well worthwhile.

THE TWO MOST IMPORTANT FACTORS IN SALES COPY

Although many professional copywriters identify four elements in good sales or advertising copy—attention, interest, desire, and action (asking for the order)—my own experience indicates that the two most important are these: make the prospect want the benefit(s) you offer, and convince him that you can and will deliver these benefits. Interest and desire are really the same thing, or nearly so: if you can arouse the prospect's interest, you can fan that into a desire—for the benefits, not the product or service per se. But you can get the order only if you achieve credibility—persuade the customer to believe that you will deliver what you promise.

Actually, you can and should try to get attention and arouse interest in one step by identifying the reason a prospect should be interested right away. If the headline or some other feature of the copy—say, an amusing cartoon—gets attention without arousing interest, there is no inducement to actually read the copy, and many who pause to glance at your headline or cartoon will not read the copy. You'll have no chance to arouse interest or desire.

The best specialists on Madison Avenue have erred along these lines, and with expensive campaigns. Here are two examples.

The Alka Seltzer campaign of a few years ago, which concentrated on stomachs and was amusing—it was artfully done—didn't sell Alka Seltzer and was dropped. The writers became so wrapped up in getting the viewer's attention, they forgot to sell the product!

Volkswagen had the same experience—the commercials were skillfully done and highly amusing, and they did get and hold viewer attention, but they didn't sell the product, and they were also dropped.

That's just another way of saying that the two commercials generated interest and desire to see the commercials and be amused by them, but they failed to generate any desire to buy the product.

There are salespeople who sell, and there are those who merely take orders. Copy which is merely amusing or entertaining, but does not *sell,* is also merely "taking orders," and is most unlikely to take enough orders to even pay for the ad, let alone return a profit. You can't wait for it to occur to the reader of your ad that it might be nice to try your product; it won't happen often enough. You must explain to the reader why he needs what you are selling, and urge him to do something about it—like ordering your product right now.

Maxwell Sackheim, considered by many to be the dean of copywriters (at least for mail order campaigns), believes that the sale is made or lost in the headline, and other experts in the field appear to agree. They say that if the headline does the job it should do, the rest of the advertisement or sales message (body copy) is of far lesser importance. Conversely, they believe, if the headline falls down on the job, the body copy probably can't save the day, after all. In short (my own interpretation), sell it *up front.* Start selling with the first word, and don't quit until the last word.

ABOUT HEADLINES

The perfect headline, in my opinion, tells the whole story in a capsule: it explains the benefit, tells the reader what is being offered that will deliver the promised benefit, and urges the reader to buy it. Unfortunately, it is not always possible to get all of that into the headline. So, since we must often settle for only one or two of those elements in the headline, here is what I believe to be the rank order of importance of those three items, as far as getting them into the headline is concerned:

1. The benefit.
2. The product.
3. The urge to buy (or make further inquiry).

Let's look at a few headlines which have worked well and see how close these come to the ideals listed. First, some book titles which were good headlines and were used as such in advertising the books:

How to Form Your Own Corporation Without a Lawyer
for Under $50.00
The Lazy Man's Way to Riches
How to Prosper During the Coming Bad Years
Winning Through Intimidation
How I Turn Ordinary Complaints into Thousands of Dollars

In each case the title explained the benefit, did it not? None said specifically that the product offered was a book, although that was almost immediately apparent, nor did any of them directly urge the prospect to buy. But each of these books did well, and I strongly suspect that the titles had a great deal to do with their success. All were (and are) motivating enough to persuade the reader to read on and learn more. But let's analyze them just a bit more.

Each of these titles describes a benefit. Three make it clear that they will show the prospect how to do what the title says can be done, and a fourth broadly suggests that it is a "how to" also. All have the appeal to some kind of profit motive— always a strong appeal in itself—but two (*Winning Through Intimidation* and *How I Turn Ordinary Complaints into Thousands of Dollars*) appeal also to another benefit: satisfying consumer or "little man" frustrations. And one (*How to Prosper During the Coming Bad Years*) has the double appeal of both profit and fear, both strong motivations. It is perhaps no coincidence that that one became a best seller, outstripping the others, although all of them did well.

Maxwell Sackheim wrote an advertisement for Sherwin

Cody many years ago, offering a correspondence course in English. The headline was this:

DO YOU MAKE THESE MISTAKES IN ENGLISH?

That ad ran successfully, without change, for some 40 years! Perhaps it would not work as well today, although I suspect it would because its appeal was to fear—the fear of being embarrassed by an inability to use English properly.

Another enduring headline, this one by John Caples, another famous advertising man, was this:

THEY LAUGHED WHEN I SAT DOWN
AT THE PIANO
BUT WHEN I STARTED TO PLAY!—

It was another advertisement—and headline—that was to run for years without change, so successful was the advertisement. In fact, "They laughed when I sat down, but . . ." was to become a famous laugh line, used as a foil by many comics for years because it evoked laughs even before the punch line. It became as famous and widely used in its day as "Please, Mother, I'd rather do it myself" and "I can't believe I ate the whole thing" were to become later, all classics in advertising.

One of Sackheim's headlines which identified the product and the reason for buying it was this one:

WHY I OFFER YOU THIS NEW KIND OF PIPE FOR 25¢

This was a few years ago, of course, when 25 cents was considerably more money than it is today, but was still a small price to pay for even a cheap pipe. Note that this ad states specifically that it is an offer, names the product offered, names the price, which is an inducement in this case, and even uses the word "new," which is considered to be a highly motivating word.

John Caples had some good advice on writing headlines. He advocated using the word "announcing" or its equivalents (for example, "presenting") as often as possible, and he entirely endorsed the virtues of the word "new" in headlines.

Other words he found highly effective and advocated—usually as the *first* words in headlines—were "at last," and "now." And he thought that using dates in headlines was arresting, as was the news style ("NEW PIPE OFFERED FOR ONLY 25¢" for example).

Victor Schwab listed "100 Good Headlines" in his book, *How to Write a Good Advertisement* (Harper & Row, New York, 1962). Here are a few he found to be good examples of the copywriter's art (numbered for purposes of discussions):

1. HOW A NEW DISCOVERY MADE A PLAIN GIRL BEAUTIFUL
2. HOW TO WIN FRIENDS AND INFLUENCE PEOPLE
3. WHO ELSE WANTS A SCREEN STAR FIGURE?
4. YOU CAN LAUGH AT MONEY WORRIES—IF YOU FOLLOW THIS SIMPLE PLAN
5. HOW I IMPROVED MY MEMORY IN ONE EVENING
6. HOW I MADE A FORTUNE WITH A "FOOL IDEA"
7. HOW A "FOOL STUNT" MADE ME A STAR SALESMAN
8. DO *YOU* DO ANY OF THESE TEN EMBARRASSING THINGS?
9. HAVE *YOU* THESE SYMPTOMS OF NERVE EXHAUSTION?
10. TO PEOPLE WHO WANT TO WRITE—BUT CAN'T GET STARTED

Let's have a quick look at each of these and analyze them.

#1: Strong appeal to every woman who wants to be more beautiful (and which one does not? Even beautiful girls often think they are "plain!"). Uses "new," you'll notice, and "discovery," both strong words, and implies the revelation of how the reader can do likewise.

#2: Famous title of a book, as well as headline, and appeals to everyone's natural desire to have many friends and be influential. Also uses "how to," an excellent attention-getter and motivator.

#3: Like number 1, strong general appeal to almost every woman, even the one who fancies she's a few ounces overweight. But also has two other virtues: it asks a question and implies that the advertiser has already given many other women "a screen star figure."

#4: The word "you" is always a good one, expressed or implied. "You" is the most important word in the language, in this sense. The offer is specified—a *plan* to make lots of money, and it's a *simple* plan.

#5: Includes the "how to" and suggests a simple method, since it reports improvement in only one evening. Clear suggestion that reader can do same.

#6: The "fool idea" is a good touch. It helps command attention—who hasn't had an idea someone else thought was foolish?—but it has that great appeal of the promise of wealth.

#7: Very much the same as #6.

#8: Appeal to fear, and made very plain by using "you" and asking a question. Many successful ads have been written around the fear motive.

#9: Again, the "you" and the question, but this time very pointed: readers like to take quizzes and examine their own symptoms.

#10: An appeal to a great many people who want to write, addressing a common symptom they can readily identify with.

Note one thing about every headline cited so far: they are all written in simple language, easy to understand. That's a basic principle—keep it simple.

Note, too, that all the headlines cited as good ones steer clear of adjectives and adverbs as much as possible, and try to stick to active verbs and nouns—laugh, follow, have, made, win, and so on.

In a booklet which he calls "Seven Deadly Advertising Mistakes" (CA$HCO Publishing Co, Brooksville, Florida, 1979), Maxwell Sackheim says that by actual test, two advertisments which were identical, except for the headlines, produced totally different responses: one pulled twice as well as the other. That demonstrates the importance of the headline, of course. He believes that a headline which depends on curiosity of the reader to get attention is doomed to failure, as are those which are merely clever or bragging and *promise* nothing.

Hubert Simon, in his book *How to Write an Ad That Will Sell Anything!* (Hubert K. Simon, Yonkers, N.Y., 1974), puts it this way: "Catch them fast—in the headlines. No one will read the rest if he doesn't read the first part of your ad. So, a good ad headline, like a good news item, summarizes the story to follow."

Simon lists three purposes of the headline: (1) to attract the reader's attention, (2) to get him to react with interest, and (3) to make him want to read the rest of the ad. He goes on to estimate that 90 percent of the ads which fail do so because of poor headlines. And he diagnoses poor headlines as those which fail to address a legitimate interest of the reader, such as family, money, home, or health. He agrees that *you* is the most important word in the language, to the reader.

A FEW MISCELLANEOUS POINTS ABOUT HEADLINES

There is some common mythology that a good headline must be short. Some of the winners cited here should disprove that. A headline should be long enough to do the job of getting attention, summarizing the offer (in terms of the reader's interest), and, if possible, identifying the product, at least generically. If this can be done in a short headline, that's an advantage, but the principles of good headline writing should never be sacrificed for the sake of brevity.

One way to get around this problem is to so word the headline that the first few words catch the eye and capture the imagination, drawing the reader on to read the rest of the headline. Note some ways this is done in good headlines (attention-arresting lead words underlined in examples below):

DISCOVER THE FORTUNE THAT LIES HIDDEN IN YOUR SALARY

161 NEW WAYS TO A MAN'S HEART—IN THIS FASCINATING BOOK FOR COOKS

GREAT NEW DISCOVERY KILLS KITCHEN ODORS QUICK!— MAKES INDOOR AIR "COUNTRY FRESH"

A WONDERFUL TWO YEARS' TRIP AT FULL PAY—BUT ONLY
MEN WITH IMAGINATION CAN TAKE IT

THERE'S ANOTHER WOMAN WAITING FOR EVERY MAN—AND
SHE'S TOO SMART TO HAVE "MORNING MOUTH"

Another way to handle long headlines is to vary type styles,
type sizes, and layouts. The ad begins with the attention-getting lead alone on the first line, usually in larger or different
type than the rest of the headline, which follows on succeeding
lines.

Here's an example of that:

THE $100 BILLION MARKET:

How to Sell Anything to the Government

Or use a blurb:

STOP WASTING POSTAGE!

The new POSTARATER tells you *exactly* how much
postage, can be adjusted to all rate changes.

To illustrate the importance of the headline, Sackheim tells
the tale of a book originally titled *Five Acres*. It sold fairly
well, but not as well as the publisher thought it ought to. At
the publisher's request, Sackheim suggested a new name. He
thought *Five Acres* too vague, for one thing—it could be the
title of a work of fiction, in fact, although it was not. In fact,
Five Acres does not give even a hint of the book's nature. Sales
picked up briskly and went on for some years, eventually to
over 500,000 copies, after the book was retitled *Five Acres and
Independence*.

Don Kracke, author of *How to Turn Your Idea into a Million
Dollars* (Doubleday, New York, 1977), makes very much the
same point when he advises choosing a short name for your
product, but not so short that it doesn't give the reader a hint
of what the product is or what it's all about. Kracke invents
and markets his own products. He started with vinyl sticky-
backed flowers and decorative designs, which he named
"Rickie Tickie Stickies," a name which he admits is somewhat

absurd, but which didn't appear to hamper sales. At any rate, the "stickies" part of the name gave the consumer some idea of what the product was.

One final note: writing a headline is something like writing the introduction to a book. You can't really write it well until you've finished the book and *know* exactly what you are introducing. If your headline is to be at least a broad hint of what's in your advertisement—what your offer is and why the prospect ought to be interested—you'll have to have worked out the copy first. That's not to say that you can't begin by drafting a headline. But it should be understood to be strictly a draft headline, to be rewritten, polished, and improved upon after you've written your copy.

ABOUT THE BODY COPY

The body copy—that text which follows the headline, blurb, and illustration, if you use one—is your main story. It is in the body copy that you deliver on the promise made in the headline—explain your tempting proposition in full, elaborate on the benefits to the customer, and *prove your case.* That is, you must make your offer *credible* to convince the prospect that you will do what you say.

Let's understand one thing immediately, if it hasn't already been made clear in earlier pages: no one makes buying decisions *rationally,* with perhaps the occasional exception, which we'll disregard because it *is* the exception, if it exists at all. Buying decisions are *emotional* decisions, because the prospect *wants to believe* in the magnificent benefits you promise. The problem is that the prospect may and usually does have a great deal of difficulty in simply accepting your word for it, even if you're General Motors or Kellogg's Corn Flakes.

There are several reasons for this skepticism. For one thing, every adult has had a bad buying experience, now and then—products or services which did not live up to the promises made. And the newspapers and magazines are full of information warning consumers to beware—*caveat emptor* is a well-known Latin phrase. Also, we all have a degree of reluctance to part with what money we have. We have to be made to want the product or service more than we want the money in our pockets or bank accounts. Finally, almost all of us want more things than we can afford, so we have to establish our own priorities. Even if you offer something absolutely unique, you are still always competing with every other business for the consumer's dollars.

The result of all this is pressure on the consumer to resist your appeals and his or her own desire to believe in the benefits you promise. Therefore, the consumer, before converting that desire into a decision to buy—to give up dollars for what you offer—must *rationalize* that decision. That's where the logic in your sales arguments comes in, to help prospects persuade themselves that the buying decision is sound, wise, and entirely justified.

Most people who buy a luxury version of whatever automobile they finally buy probably have trouble affording a car at all, much less an extra thousand or two for special interiors and extra features, much as they desire the luxuries. The salesman must work at convincing the customer that the luxury model is really a better buy than the standard model. He may argue that he is allowing a larger trade-in or a greater discount on the luxury model, so that you are really not paying full price for those features. Yet, your car will be worth far more when you trade it in for the next model. Or he may try to show you that some of those features actually pay for themselves by saving gas. Or perhaps they are extra safety features, which do not require any justification beyond the allegation that the car is safer to drive or less likely to skid or get stuck in a snowbank.

The smart salesman knows that unless you are one of those fortunates who have so much money that they can afford to buy whatever strikes their fancy, he is going to have *sell* it to you with emotional appeals to generate the desire and logical arguments to soothe your conscience, which tells you to go slow and think about it. And that is the sequence, too: first the emotional appeals, to crank up some interest and fan it into desire, then the logical "proofs," to help the prospect rationalize and reach the buying decision.

But even that isn't enough. Even then, buyers tend to hesitate and postpone decision. Therefore, good advertising practice is to "ask for action"—instruct and urge the prospect to act now.

HOW TO ASK FOR ACTION OR "CLOSE"

"Closing" is a much misunderstood term in selling. Most newcomers to selling—and even those who ought to know better—go through life thinking that "closing" means getting the order, making the sale, having the customer sign the order form. Not so. Closing means *asking* for the order. Sales professionals call it closing, and advertising people call it asking for action, but they mean the same thing: ask the prospect for the order.

In face-to-face selling, a salesman must close many times during the course of the sales effort—that is, he *should* close many times, and failure to do so is one of the more common causes of failure among salespeople. The typical tyro at selling completes his or her sales message and then stares expectantly at the prospect, hoping the prospect will say, "I'll take it." It rarely happens. Or, at least, the salesperson who doesn't wait for it to happen is likely to far outperform the one who does. Customers must be urged to make the decision, and guided into it. Here are some of the ways a typical close may be made in face-to-face sales situations:

"Will you take it with you, or can we deliver it for you?"
"What color do you prefer?"
"What day of the week is most convenient for installation?"
"If you will just sign right here . . ."
"Would you like a service contract with your new TV?"

That is, the close is made indirectly. And if the customer demurs that she wants to think about it some more or offers other resistance, the effective salesperson says, "Of course. What questions do you have?" or somehow smoothly swings back to sell some more, and tries once again to close, when the time seems right. In sales training, that's often known as "handling objections." But you close by *assuming* the sale, as an indirect way of asking for the order.

In fact, closing is an excellent way of finding out what the customer's objections are, and it is well known that customers are often reluctant to tell you what is truly troubling them about your offer. The customer may hesitate to say that he or she can't afford it or needs financing, or hasn't enough for the normal down payment, or wants her husband's approval. Until you find out what the objection is, you can't very well cope with it.

It's often difficult to tell when you have "sold" enough and should stop talking. A great many sales are lost because salespeople keep talking beyond the point where the customer is ready to buy. They somehow say the wrong thing, causing the customer to reverse a buying decision already made. Therefore, closing is also an excellent way of testing the customer for readiness to make the decision and buy—for determining whether you have talked enough.

In advertising, the situation is somewhat different. You've no way of judging reactions and making many closes, but can close only once—at the end of your message. That's one reason many advertisers offer "free trials" and refund guarantees. However, good advertising should definitely make at least one strong close.

A basic principle in closing is to make it as easy as possible for the customer to say yes. If you glance back at those several typical ways of closing, you'll note that none of them call for a yes-or-no answer: all are different ways of saying "yes!" Make the customer *work* at saying no.

If you look at some typical advertisements that ask for the

order, you'll discover several ways in which the advertiser has made it as easy as possible for the customer to order:

An order form included, with dotted lines to show where to cut it.

A separate order card, which may be torn out along the perforated lines.

A self-mailer, postage paid by the advertiser; just drop it in the mail box.

Instructions to send no money—"we'll bill you."

A question: "Bill you or your company?"

Charges accepted; just fill in the numbers.

A guarantee to return your own check, if you are not satisfied: your check won't be deposited for 30 days.

WRITING THE COPY

Most of what has been said about headline writing applies to body copy. It should be simple, for one thing, easy to read and easy to understand, whether it's a print ad, a broadcast commercial, or a sales letter and brochure. *Reader's Digest* is often used as a reference or standard for writing to the public. It's about the right level, sophisticated enough to get any message across, but not difficult enough to give anyone trouble— any reasonably well-educated person, that is. Believe it or not, many college graduates can't read beyond high-school level, and any text which is written at a level judged to be higher than mid-high school will give many people, even well-educated ones, trouble.

Here are a few examples of advertising copy addressed to well-educated business executives:

The problem with small business computers isn't just getting the right hardware. It's getting the right software.

Dictaphone puts everything it knows about dictation right in the palm of your hand. Dictamite is the smallest dictating machine Dictaphone has ever made.

This year thousands of businesses will look for a secured loan. And many will find themselves uncertain about which of several alternatives is best for them.

Note the simplicity of the copy. Easy to read, smooth-flowing, no complex sentences, no unfamiliar words. And note, too, how each starts by referring to a problem. Nothing makes a salesman more welcome than an offer of help in solving problems. Nothing gets the ear of the reader or listener faster, either, whether it's a business executive with business problems, a housewife with budget problems, or a younger person with dating problems. Everyone has problems of one sort or another, and if what you offer is appropriate to solving people's problems, it's a good place to start.

One of the greatest problems is to get all the important information into a short message. The technique that works for most writers is to first write it all out, in all its trivial detail—that is, prepare a list of everything you think is important about the item you're offering. Pore over that until you believe that you have included every reason you can think of for the customer to buy—all the benefits, all the features, all the good qualities, all the credentials—*everything*. In this first step, don't worry about the length of the message, but only about its completeness.

Then start prioritizing your items—put them in rank order of importance, most important ones first. But sort them into classes: benefits, for one class; credibility facts (proofs), for another class; attention-getters for still another. Now start trimming out all those items which are either redundant (repeating what you've already listed), or trivial (not really adding any great strength). Finally, when you have reduced these lists to those items you believe are really essential to your purpose and will impress the reader, start drafting a final advertising message. Remember, you're *drafting*, not writing final copy.

Now start trimming off all the verbal fat—the unnecessary adjectives and window dressing which only slow the message down without adding strength—until you have a lean, hard-hitting message. Finally, shorten and polish the sentences themselves, seeking the words with the greatest impact, selecting out the best opening sentence, working on getting the essence of the message into a good headline.

It's a great deal of work, but for most of us it's the only way to end up with that smooth-flowing copy which appears to have been just dashed off.

"Short" and "long" messages are short or long only in relative terms, of course. If you're buying space in a popular magazine, your major constraint is probably money. But if you are using direct mail, you can mail thousands of words for the same cost as a few hundred words (except for the difference in printing cost, which is relatively small).

Seminars, for example, are generally sold by direct mail, using four- or six-page brochures, usually, that present a great deal of information about the seminar, the sponsors, the speakers, and the program itself. Often, such brochures include testimonials, and most include a form for advance registration.

Note the features of the first page of the brochure shown in Figure 2:

- The headline obviously offers to make the participant more effective at selling.
- The body copy describes the offer—an intensive seven-hour seminar—and provides some evidence of its worth (more than 250 programs presented to over 10,000 participants).
- The evidence continues by revealing the credentials of the seminar leader.
- Additional evidence is the listing of some past client companies, many of them well known.

This front page is a summary of the inside two pages, where more information about the seminar leader, Donald M. Dible, is presented, a detailed outline of the seminar program is provided, and testimonials of enthusiastic veterans of these seminars are reproduced.

Figure 2. Announcing a seminar.

**University of Phoenix
Department of Continuing Education
Announces**

FUNDAMENTALS OF PROFESSIONAL SELLING

An intensive seven-hour seminar based on the results of more than
250 programs presented to over 10,000 participants in the last five years.
Led by Donald M. Dible, nationally acclaimed sales trainer,
convention speaker and author of numerous articles and books including
the 100,000 copy bestseller, *Up Your OWN Organization!*

Doubletree Inn
Randolph Park
445 South Alvernon Way
Tucson

Doubletree Inn
Fashion Square
4710 North Scottsdale Road
Scottsdale

Monday, July 23, 1979
9:00 a.m.-5:00 p.m.

Tuesday, July 24, 1979
9:00 a.m.-5:00 p.m.

Partial list of companies that have sent participants to this seminar:

Cincinnati, Inc. • American Rental Association • Western International Hotels • Tektronix, Inc. • National Freight, Inc. • KBHK TV • Southern Pacific Communications • American Home Shield Insurance • Rolm Corporation • Sunset Magazine • Lloyd's Bank of California • Dean Witter Reynolds • The Hibernia Bank • California Federal Savings & Loan • Mead Johnson Laboratories • Honeywell Information Systems • Sperry-Rand • Swiss Bank Corporation • San Diego Federal Savings & Loan • Computer Sciences Corp. • Control Data Technotec • Home-Pack Transport, Inc. • Blue Cross • Cermetec Microelectronics • California Dental Service • Imperial Bank • Gallery of Homes • Wells Fargo Bank • Monroe Calculator Company • Edno-DuPont • Westinghouse Electric Corp. • New Jersey Monthly Magazine • American Solenoid Company • Dart Industries • Ford Motor Company • EG&G Instruments • National Freight, Inc. • Girl Scouts of America • 3M Business Products • Turbodyne Corporation • Hewlett-Packard Company • West Point Pepperell • Texas Instruments, Inc. • Bourns, Inc. • Venezuelan International Airlines • Combustion Engineering • Lockheed Electronics, Inc. • Frederick Gumm Chemical Company • Microwaves Magazine • Varian Associates • Beckman Instruments, Inc. • Allstate Insurance Company

The last page includes the registration form and instructions for registering. It also offers a discount for groups from the same organization, as an inducement, and mentions that the cost is tax-deductible as a business expense.

Many emotional messages—direct and indirect promises—are included. Study these promises closely. Would *you* like to learn how to accomplish some of these things?

You met Charles N. Aronson, founder of Aronson Machine Company, earlier in these pages. He now publishes a

Figure 3. A small advertisement for a newsletter.

The Time of Your Life!
"PEEPHOLE ON PEOPLE"
The monthly newsletter that is sure to save you money on things you have to have *and makes it fun to save and to poke a finger in the eye of politicians and promoters.* The only newsletter that always tells the truth and tells it beautifully. *Bound to make your life richer in both money & marvels.* **$12-a-year. Send $12 to:**
Chuck Aronson, Writer & Pub'r
RR1   Arcade NY   14009

newsletter, among other writing activities, in his "retirement." Figure 3 shows one of his ads for his newsletter. Aronson's ads are usually somewhat subdued because he has such scruples about honesty that he leans over backward to avoid making promises which he believes would stretch the truth even slightly. Still, he manages to promise that the reader will find money-saving ideas, as well as satisfaction, in reading *Peephole on People.*

For his mammoth book relating his business career almost blow by blow, Aronson uses here the copy written for him by another man, who is less inhibited in his enthusiasm about the book, which is truly an unusual and remarkably insightful work. Note that the ad follows all the rules—the immediate appeal in the headline, followed up by expansion of that appeal in the body copy. Then the proofs: the book is factual, fully documented, names names. Then it goes on to ask for action, with urging to order immediately. (See Figure 4.)

Figure 5 is a good example of an unusual, attention-getting idea. It was a left-hand page in a business magazine. The fac-

Figure 4. Full-page advertisement for a self-published book.

ARE YOU SEEKING SUCCESS?
Would you like to know how it really feels to achieve Success? And what it really takes to get there?

How-To-Succeed books are available to teach you the technique and principles of success, but each falls short of its mark.

WHY? — Because these techniques and principles are taken out of context and taught as separate procedures. In order to truly learn the techniques and principles of success you must learn them *in context*, as they actually happen and as they relate to each other within the structure of business and life.

Now you can learn:
*How success begins.
*How each level of success is achieved.
*How each principle of success relates to others.
*How the techniques of success are used to generate further success.

And all this can be learned *in context*, in the actual sequence in which the applications of the techniques and principles of success are used to achieve your goals.

"FREE ENTERPRISE" is the true, unabridged story of a man and his struggle for success.

Chapter 1 begins with the day this man's business came into existence. You will learn, step-by-step, happening-by-happening, how this small company became the leader in its field with a multi-million dollar value.

"FREE ENTERPRISE" reveals to you the actual, fully documented techniques and principles used to create a truly successful business. And each principle and technique is revealed in proper sequence, exactly as it happened.

"FREE ENTERPRISE" is the true story of Charles N. Aronson and his company, Aronson Machine Company. Every detail in the story is factual and fully documented. Actual names are used.

Through the book's pages you live the techniques and principles of success with its author, as actual events unfolded. There are NO THEORIES; only the cold, hard facts of life are revealed.

"FREE ENTERPRISE" is no small work. It has nearly 1700 pages! But unlike dry "how-to" books, each page is alive, filled with the author's zest for life and living. Once you start reading, you'll hate to put the book down until you finish it.

When you have finished reading "FREE ENTERPRISE," you will have *lived* the techniques and principles of success with the book's author, Charles N. Aronson.

You will know how each technique and principle of success is to be used. And how each relates to the other. You will have *lived* their uses as they actually happened, not as some theory to be proved or disproved.

It is said that "Experience is the best teacher." But why struggle to gain your own experience by trial and error when you can *live* these experiences with Charles N. Aronson as they happened in his life? — Then go and do likewise, use those experiences to create success in your own life.

Now, for the first time, you can learn the true techniques and principles of success as they can and should be applied within your own life.

Most 200-page how-to books sell for $10. At that rate, "FREE ENTERPRISE" with nearly 1700 pages should sell for $85 — but you can get your hardcover copy for only $25, or your paperback copy for only $18 (plus $2 p&h, hc or pb).

Don't delay. Order your copy today. Within weeks you can experience the full flavor of sweet success and be using these techniques and principles of success in your own life.

Use the Order Form today. You won't regret it.

Sincerely,   J F (Jim) Straw, Marketing Consultant

ORDER From: Charles N. Aronson, RR1, Arcade NY 14009
Please send me a hardcover ($25)..... or paperback ($18).... copy of "FREE ENTERPRISE." I enclose .... + $2 postage & hndlg.

Name, Address, Zip: _____

_____

Figure 5. An attention-getting use of white space.

WHY SHOULD YOU PAY
GOOD MONEY
FOR A FULL PAGE
OF ADVERTISING
AND THEN WASTE MOST
OF IT?

ing page was headlined: "Doesn't make much sense, does it?" followed by copy about an office copier and waste in office copying, the white space in the major headline dramatizing the idea of waste.

HOW LONG SHOULD THE COPY BE?

Someone—perhaps it was Voltaire—is reported to have written a lengthy letter to a friend with an apology for such a long letter. "I did not have the time to write a short letter," he wrote.

It is, of course, difficult to get your entire message into a piece of brief copy if you have to provide a great deal of description and lengthy sales arguments. That's why you can't sell a $25 item with a 100-word classified advertisement. The larger the price tag, the more selling is needed. At the same time, advertising space is costly, and should be conserved. Therefore, copy should be long enough to do the job, but not one fraction of an inch or one word more than is necessary for that.

That leaves you with the choice mentioned earlier: if you can afford only a small amount of space or you think your item and projected sales would not justify more than a small amount of space, you should do your selling through sales letters and brochures or face-to-face selling. If you use print media and can buy only a little space, use it for inquiry advertising—to get the reader to visit your establishment or send for more information. Don't waste advertising dollars by buying three inches of space, expecting to sell $50 items in that manner.

There may be exceptions. (There usually are.) Some kinds of items are so well known as to require no "consumer education"—description, that is. In general, you are faced with one of the following basic situations:

Familiar product or service—for example, TV service. In this case, you do not have to explain or describe your basic offer, except any special provisions—easy payment plans, charge cards accepted, special guarantees, discounts, and so forth. Since virtually everyone uses the type of service and products you sell, the appeal is to call you rather than a competitor.

Unfamiliar product or service—for example, a new type of carpet sweeper. Almost everyone is a *prospect,* but you'll have to show him or her why your product is better than the conventional machines most people use. And you'll probably not make the sale without demonstration and face-to-face selling, anyhow.

Low-priced item, used popularly or suitable for popular use because it solves a common problem or fits an everyday need— for example, tooth powder.

High-priced or luxury item—for example, a new LCD wristwatch.

The situation dictates the terms of the problem and the range of solutions. For a newsletter, such as Aronson's *Peephole on People,* the copy does not need to explain what a newsletter is, but only what it delivers. However, some business newsletters run to $200 and more a year for subscriptions, and it would be impossible to sell them effectively in even a full-page advertisement, let alone a small space ad. Therefore, almost every publisher of newsletters (and there are literally thousands of them) sells subscriptions by direct mail, using sales letters and brochures, many of which are quite elaborate.

Likewise, to sell a luxury watch or other such item, you usually have to send the customer elaborate brochures, in color, which is extraordinarily expensive.

Space ads, then, are usually boiled down to their essentials. Copywriters, all too aware of the high costs of advertising space, labor to eliminate every unnecessary word.

TECHNIQUES FOR SHORTENING COPY

There are many ways to make your copy brief without leaving out essential information. In fact, making the copy brief often makes it more vigorous and easier to read, which adds impact to the message. For example, here is one way to boil copy down:

NEW LCD WATCH

- Quartz-crystal accuracy
- Gold or silver case
- Built-in light
- Unconditional 1-year guarantee
- Famous make

Another way is by using telegraphic style—eliminating the unnecessary articles, verbs, and other words, without which the message is still plain enough. For example:

Original: To prevent employees from wasting time and money, the Horizon system lets you control which phones can make outside and long-distance calls, and which phones can't.

Shortened: Prevent loss of time and money. With Horizon system you control which phones go outside, which don't.

Not only is the second version one-half the length of the first (and one-half as expensive to run), but it's far more vigorous, being in the second person imperative.

Sometimes a simple illustration will take the place of many words and use less space than the words would. But don't use illustrations for the sake of using illustrations. Use them when they save words or add impact, or when words really can't paint the image you need—for jewelry, for example, or anything else which depends on visual impact to be sold.

A POPULAR MYTH ABOUT PRINT ADVERTISING

There is a popular belief that readers won't stop to read any advertisement which is all solid text or which does not have a lot of white space. But experience proves otherwise. There have been many successful advertisements which are solid pages of text, with no illustrations and with an absolute minimum of white space. Some of them ran uninterruptedly for many years.

The simple fact is that if you capture the reader's interest, and if your copy *holds* that interest, the reader will read almost any amount of text. The clever ad with catchy illustrations and lots of white space will do absolutely nothing for you if the advertisement does not catch and hold the reader's interest. The white space costs you just as much as the space full of text and illustrations. Use it. Give the reader a compelling *reason* to read on, and read on he will.

FREQUENCY VERSUS SIZE

Recall the story a few pages back about that TV service fellow who kept distributing his cards every week (at first) and, later, every month? The principle that worked for him works in print advertising and direct mail also: repetition of a message pays off, for several reasons. One, your name begins to become familiar and, hence, be remembered. Two, seeing your advertisement steadily, month after month, builds confidence in you and suggests that you are a well-established and reliable business. Finally, even the reader who never reads your advertisement begins to *recognize* it simply because he has seen it so many times.

You may recall, also, that I mentioned that you can use a good mailing list over and over, and if your appeal is a good one, you'll get as good a result each time. In fact, in many cases, the results get better and better, through the first five or six mailings, before they begin to level off.

Whatever budget you have established for your advertising or direct-mail campaign, you will usually be far better off to spend that money on continuous, repeat advertising than on one-time or occasional large splashes of advertising. Quite often, an ad does next to nothing the first time it appears, but after several appearances begins to work well. Plan to advertise frequently—on a small scale, if necessary, but frequently.

WHAT ARE YOU REALLY SELLING?

In many cases, there is no way the customer can verify that your product or service will actually produce the benefits you claim for it without actually buying the product. A customer can ask for a demonstration of a vacuum cleaner or a TV set, or thumb through a book in the bookstore, before buying. But how can the customer verify that your perfume will excite the guys or that your newsletter will help point out the road to true happiness?

Many people, for example, sell books that purportedly reveal the road to riches. Napoleon Hill's *Think and Grow Rich* is a classic of that kind. But even after buying the book, the buyer will have to wait a long time to discover whether the secret works for him or not.

Therefore, the point I made several times here—that people buy what things *do* for them, not what things *are*—is not entirely true. In a great many cases, people are buying what they *think* the product or service will do, what you have convinced them it will do. In short, the customer is buying your *promise* of benefits, rather than the benefits per se! You are selling promises.

Bear that in mind as you develop your sales copy. You are asking the customer to give you money in exchange for a promise.

Jim Straw, originator of the American Business Club and publisher of *Business Opportunities Digest* and *Business Intelligence Network,* uses full-page copy (see Figure 6) to sell memberships in his American Business Club, which is a novel idea he had. He uses this copy also in his direct-mail solicitations, along with a sales letter and other literature. This proposition is selling promises with a vengeance, because not only is it intangible, but the advertising copy is restricted by legal considerations, which prohibit it from even appearing to be a lending institution of any kind. Nevertheless, staying carefully within the legal bounds and weighing every word, Straw

Figure 6. Full-page advertisement for American Business Club.

TWO QUESTIONS

WHICH WILL AFFECT YOUR FINANCIAL FUTURE

1)CAN YOU BORROW up to $10,000 from your local banker on your Signature?

If your answer is YES, then read no further. Our Congratulations! You have made it!

But, if your answer is NO—

2) WOULD YOU CONTRIBUTE $25, $50, or $100 to your friend because he has a good solid business idea that should make money?

If your answer is NO, you are not our kind of people, but Thank You for being honest.

If your answer is YES, even with reservations (i.e. depending on the deal), then this is your invitation to join the AMERICAN BUSINESS CLUB.

The ***AMERICAN BUSINESS CLUB*** is an organization of independent business people who are dedicated to making money. People, like yourself, who know that it takes money to make money. Without money, a good idea is just that—a good idea. But, with money, that good idea can become a dream come true.

Every month, the ***AMERICAN BUSINESS CLUB*** makes Capital Concessions (Grants) to small business people.—Capital they use to expand or start their businesses.

Not many independent business people can readily qualify for a loan of $10,000; no matter how good their idea. Ideas, unfortunately, have no collateral value.

Now, if you had 1,000 good friends, who could each contribute $25, $50, or $100 for your venture, you could get the amount you need and start making your dream come true. BUT, very few of use have 1,000 friends and if we did; where would we get the time to talk to each one of them, explain the venture, and finally get them to put-up the money. Then again, how many of your friends have the insight to understand your idea.

As a member of the ***AMERICAN BUSINESS CLUB***, you will have at your disposal a multitude of business friends who are ready and willing to contribute to your Financing. They are business people who, like yourself, can understand and visualize ideas. They look for profits because profits pay for the many comforts of life.

The primary purpose of the club is to allow the members a fair and equal chance to raise the capital they need to do their business through a co-operative effort.

To accomplish this purpose, the members of the club pool their money in a central fund (much like a Credit Union). That money is then dispersed to those members requiring capital to do their business.

There are NO Securities Offered or traded, and NO Loans made or repaid, within the club. This means ***NO Loan Fees, NO Co-signers, NO Collateral Requirements,*** and ***NO Interest.*** Money dispersed from the club central fund is dispersed as Capital Concessions (Grants) from the members to you.

And, there is ***NO Waiting***, you may submit your Financing Proposal and request for Financing Assistance the day you receive your club membership kit.

The ***AMERICAN BUSINESS CLUB*** is the only organization of its kind in the world. The only place where small business people can pool their resources to rais the capital they need to do their business. It is established to do what conventional lending sources will not do for the small business community. The club is the most remarkable & revolutionary small business financing concept of the past 25 years.

Raise the capital you need. Join the ***AMERICAN BUSINESS CLUB.***

Your Financing Requirement is handled directly thru the club. (We do not send you lists of people to contact.)

You don't have to prepare a complicated and extensive Loan Package. (The club has a simple 4-page Financing Proposal form that includes all the information necessary.)

You fill-out onlyone Financing Proposal for each of your Financing Requirements. (Your Headquarters staff does the rest of the work.)

You receive the proceeds for your Financing Requirement directly from the Club's central fund. (You do not receive your capital in bits and pieces.)

You may request any amount that you require through your membership, as long as it is for a specific ***BUSINESS*** purpose. (No personal or non-profit making expenditures are even considered.)

You may"tap" the Club's central fund for subsequent Financing Requirements for as long as you are a member of the club.

Our organization is effective, because small business people stick together. As long as we stand together, no individual member need ever fail. So, as a participating member of the ***AMERICAN BUSINESS CLUB*** you can raise the capital you need to do your business.

If you don't believe it—you are not alone. Many people are just like you, but once they become a member of the club, their attitude soon changes. Our members do use the club to raise the capital they need, and they don't have to go begging conventional money sources for an even break.

Our Club dues are $100 per year.—No reduction in dues is ever offered.

Upon receipt of your Enrollment Card, with required dues, we will send you the complete ***AMERICAN BUSINESS CLUB*** Membership kit. Your kit will include everything you need to use the club effort to raise the Capital you need for your business.

Join the ***AMERICAN BUSINESS CLUB***, today, and start building for the future. NOW is the time to start making your dreams come true; return your Enrollment Card today!!

- WARRANTY -

If, within 10 days, after you receive your membership kit, you are not satisfied that association with our group will benefit you, simply return the kit, as received, and your club dues will be refunded in full.

- FOR THE RECORD -

Listed below are members of the ***AMERICAN BUSINESS CLUB*** who have received Capital Concessions (Grants) from the club's central fund.—As a member of the club, you could be one of them.

R.L.K. (Ashland, OH)—*$5,000*—to expand a Locksmith & Security Services business.

D.E.P. (Culver City, CA)—*$4,000*—to make the down-payment to acquire a Commercial Printing business.

G.R.B. (Jacksonville, AR)—*$3,591*—to start an Accounting, Bookkeeping, Income Tax Preparation, and Debt Collection business.

E.H.R. (New York, NY)—*$3,513*—to self-publish a series of Self-Help, Motivational Reports and Booklets.

R.J.S. (Mt. Laurel, NJ)—*$2,990*—to buy Vending Machines.

B.G. (Streator, IL)—*$3,437*—to expand a Country Store/Gas Station.

F.C.V. (ElDorado, KS)—*$2,200*—to start a Financing Brokerage.

E.J.D. (Roy, WA)—*$2,625*—to expand a Tire Salvage & Disposal business.

H.D.Y. (Bloomfield, IA)—*$2,000*—to patent a new invention.

F.M.G. (Houston, TX)—*$2,500*—to buy a Janitorial, Office Cleaning business.

AND . . . . there are many, many others. The list keeps growing month after month.

The ***AMERICAN BUSINESS CLUB*** means business. It can mean "money" for your business. To start. To build. To expand.

The primary purpose of the club is to allow you a fair and equal chance to raise the capital you need to do your business. The club is a well-organized, co-operative effort.

- IT WORKS!! -

AMERICAN BUSINESS CLUB
3110 Maple Dr. N.E. ● Suite 114 ● Atlanta, GA 30305

- TRIAL MEMBERSHIP ENROLLMENT CARD -

Please enroll me as a member of the ***AMERICAN BUSINESS CLUB*** for one year. I understand this is a *Trial Membership* only and that I may examine the membership, read it completely and then make my final decision.

If I decide that the Club is not for me—for any reason—I will return the membership kit *in the condition I received it* within ten days from receipt and you will return my $100 by return mail. There is *absolutely no risk* to me, at all.

I enclose **$100**:

☐ Check/MoneyOrder ☐ VISA/BankAmericard ☐ Mastercharge

Credit Card # ____________________ Expiration Date ____________

Signature ____________________________________

PLEASE PRINT:

Name ____________________________________

Address ____________________________________

City ____________________ State ________ Zip ________

Figure 7. Full-page advertisement for Hubert Simon's Rat Race
book.

Take the afternoon off . . . EVERY afternoon!

a surprisingly simple way to get

"Out of the Rat Race

(and into the chips!)"   by Hubert Simon

If I can, you can

Betty says I was never meant to be a businessman. My lawyer, accountant, analyst and son-in-law all agree (with unnecessary enthusiasm).

Nonetheless, we now own an air-conditioned split-level home and his-and-hers cars. We've been to Europe 14 times in eight years, and criss-crossed the Caribbean.

(Before all this, we'd go to New Hampshire in a beat-up old Plymouth, to sponge on the relatives.) Nowadays it's mink coat, wine cellar and gourmet dinners for 8 (including the relatives, thank you) without turning a hair.

All this, working HALF the time you wage slaves do. *(And enjoying it twice as much.)*

People who knew me 'when' whisper, *how did HE ever do it?*

Actually, I have no monopoly on the idea; others have struck the same little 'gold-mine'. (I'll tell you about some of them who put me to shame.)

Let me ask: do you equate 'escape' with 'sacrifice'? I don't! Not any more. *Once you are on track,* you realize that people glued to payrolls are just making it for somebody else.

You CAN start this without leaving your job. You CAN try it out before you burn any bridges. And you can ask those perceptive questions:

"How much capital would I need?"

In 1942, I was a rear-rank buck private at Ft. Monmouth, N. J., earning $21 a month, less deductions. I started this on my own time — nights and weekends. True, I had $200 in the sock, but that also had to cover cigars, beer, nylons — everything. (You don't need 'capital'.)

"Why are you giving away the keys to the kingdom? And if it's so simple, why isn't everybody rich?"

Betty swears I have more fun *writing* about this than doing it! (Writing about it is also profitable.) Actually, hundreds of others have discerned the same little secret and *are* doing it. I believe far more people could, should and would . . . if they just knew how.

"What exactly will you send me? I've 'had' all that inspirational malarkey."

So have I. Let's forget Horatio Alger and deal in specifics. For example:
• Can you do 3 days' work that will bring in $92,000? *(I did, and I'll show you how.)*
• My checklist of 5 essentials for a 'winner'.

• What I obtained for $37 that brought in $26,000 *(and how you can adapt the same procedure.)*
• Three key words that helped an Italian immigrant in Pelham, N.Y. amass $300,000.
• Why 92 out of 100 'amateurs' never get to first base, until . . .
• How to get STARTED (without that one little stumbling block).

Of course, it's not ALL peaches and cream. We make mistakes. Some days it rains. I can't *promise* that you'll be a rich man. (But you certainly can LIVE like one!)

And I *do* guarantee this: the *pleasure* will begin long before you kiss the boss goodbye. You won't be *bored.* The gratification of seeing your own 'flower' grow is half the fun. Not to mention the ease-up of *tension* . . . the freedom of working *when you feel like it.* (Once you have it, the Money becomes less Sacred.)

Nothing I ever did was so downright exciting as that flush of pure joy the first time I realized we were 'in'. That really hit home! Don't pass through without giving yourself a chance to experience that thrill.

How about it? Why not stop jumping every time the phone rings? Why not get old J.B.'s frown out of your nightmares? PAY THOSE *!#% DEBTS! Take the afternoon off . . . *every* afternoon!

Sounds too good? I've been doing it for 23 years. I'm betting you can, too. Why not let me prove it?

$1,000 worth . . . for only $5.95?

Perhaps you think this is just a "gimmick"? But it's not.

Actually, my fees for *personal* counsel are out of sight. If you want it straight from the horse's mouth, bring along $1,000 . . . plus travel expenses.

But why bother? *The identical information,* in an ordinary gray cover, is only $5.95. It won't win artistic awards, but if what's inside doesn't knock you out, return it within 30 days and get *your money back.* (No questions.)

Do You Qualify?

When people ask, "What training do you need?" I recall Somerset Maugham's story, "The Verger", about a janitor who used to clean St. Peter's Church until a young Vicar discovered that he was illiterate, and fired him.

Jobless, the man invested his meager savings in a tiny tobacco shop, where he prospered, bought another, expanded, and ended up with a chain worth $150,000.

One day his banker said, "You've done well for an illiterate, but where would you be if you could *read and write?*"

"Well," he said, "I'd be janitor of St. Peter's Church in Neville Square."

HERE'S MY 30-DAY GUARANTEE:

Get Your Money Back!

I won't consider this sale completed for 30 days. (Digest, appraise, TRY this. PROVE that it really can be.) Then, if you wish, just return it and get your $5.95 back by airmail.

Hubert Simon
1280 Saw Mill River Road
Yonkers, N.Y. 10710

All right, old scout, I'll take that bet. Send "Out of the Rat Race (and Into the Chips!")

If I bounce it back within 30 days, you'll return my remittance by *AIR-MAIL.* With that understanding, I enclose $5.95 as payment in full.

NAME . . . .

ADDRESS . . . .

CITY, STATE . . . . ZIP . . . .

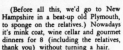

manages to make the promise plain and to persuade enough people to join every year to make the idea a viable one.

Hubert Simon is a master at the art of advertising and sales. Figure 7, his advertisement, is an excellent example of the art. Although the title of the book he sells is a good headline in itself, Hubert puts his blurb *over* the headline, rather than beneath it. Note the order form for the Yellow Pages advertising book keyed Dept. H in his full-page ad shown in Figure 8, and in his smaller ad in Figure 9.

Of course, advertising—teaching it to others, that is—is an important part of Hubert's business, as the ads following the one for his book reveal. All are good examples of what can be done with a bit of information. But note that all sell promises—secrets of success in business.

Elmer Wheeler, who was acclaimed as America's greatest salesman, summed it up neatly when he said, "Sell the sizzle, not the steak."

HOW TO ACHIEVE CREDIBILITY

It's easy to say, "Prove the case," as I indeed have admonished you to. But it's much harder to actually do so. The following discussion provides a few hints that will help you. (Go back and study some of the sample ads reproduced here, as you read this, and see these principles in practice.)

First, what will constitute "proof"? Or, at least, evidence? Is it the credentials of the individual, as in the case of Don Dible leading a seminar? Or pure logic? Or testimonials? Or case histories? Study the sample ads, and you will see that each of these have been used.

But there are other considerations, too. Examine the following two statements, and see which you find the more convincing:

Hundreds of thousands have been sold.
278,000 have been sold at this date.

Figure 8. Selling Yellow Pages advertising know-how.

How Much of YOUR Business Comes from Your Ad in the Yellow Pages?

ARE YOU GETTING RESULTS?

SALES

....from your Ad in the 'Phone Book?

If your answer is "LESS THAN 50%" ... you're missing a good bet.

Experiments by thousands of firms across the USA has lead to the development of techniques which can double ... and even TRIPLE ... your sales through optimum use of "YELLOW PAGES" advertising!

You doubt that? Well ....

— "Our new ad brought 50 calls in 45 days," says an outboard motor dealer in Akron, Ohio.
— "We now get 10 calls a night when it's cold," reports a fuel burner installer in Dayton.
— "Changing my ad brought me $3,000 in premiums," says an insurance agent in Rochester, Minn.
— "Saturday morning in here looks like a fire sale!" exclaims an Ohio building supply dealer.
— "This one change in our ad stimulated many sales," says a Pittsburgh paint dealer.
— "One job pays for the ad. Yet 60% come from it," says a construction company in Cincinnati.
— "We got 57 calls the first day this appeared!" says an auto dealer in Pennsylvania.

Our new manual — which you are welcome to try for one entire month, at our risk — is called YELLOW PAGES ADVERTISING: HOW TO ELECTRIFY RESPONSE!

It shows how dozens of others have done it ... gives you their comments!

It shows how YOU can do it ... actual ads for you to adapt.

● This manual contains 88 reproductions of "YELLOW PAGES" ads (from 62 different fields) that exemplify superior technique. Many of the headlines, competitive offers, copy blocks and illustrations are easily adaptable to your own purposes.

● These ideas can help you spark up your business ... gain an edge on competition ... create a warm, friendly feeling ... get RESULTS fast ... at very little cost!

● MAKE YOUR BUSINESS WELL-KNOWN AND ADMIRED FOR "EXTRA SERVICE," INTELLIGENCE, COURTESY, INTEGRITY, DEPENDABILITY.

REMINDER

● Get the customer coming to you FIRST. (The one who gets him first, often sells him.)

How does YOUR ad in the "Yellow Pages" measure up?

	YES	NO
Are you featuring at least 3 competitive advantages?		
Does your border make the ad "stand out"?		
Are you taking advantage of the one way in which "Yellow Page" ads differ from all other promotion?		
Will your Headline compel attention?		
Does your copy answer prospects' questions?		
Does your illustration catch the eye and help to sell?		
Do you invite "collect" calls?		
Is your slogan both powerful and clever?		
Does your ad contain a test "key"?		
Have you a closing line that calls for ACTION?		

If you can answer "YES" to all 10 questions, you do not need this manual. Otherwise your ad can (and should!) be improved to draw maximum response ....

H. K. Simon Co., Inc. Dept. H
1280 Saw Mill River Rd.,
Yonkers, N.Y. 10710

Kindly send "YELLOW PAGES" ADVERTISING: HOW TO ELECTRIFY RESPONSE". I enclose special price of $12.95 under money back guarantee of satisfaction.

NAME_____

ADDRESS_____

CITY_____

STATE_____ ZIP_____

Figure 9. A quarter-page advertisement for a book.

How To Write An Ad That Will Sell ANYTHING!

After all, it's the AD, more than any single factor, that pulls in prospects when you want to sell a house . . . a car . . . or merchandise.
Here in a fascinating manual, you will find a single technique that will enable you to write a great ad about ANYTHING in one day!
This in itself may be worth the entire price. But you will also find far more.
For example: WOULDN'T YOU LIKE TO KNOW—

- the ONE most important point in any ad?
- how to instill BELIEVABILITY?
- how to pick responsive media? (There's no point writing a good ad if you don't know where to run it!)
- the TRUTH about 'truth' statements?
- the mistake most people make in writing an ad?
- 27 examples of great ads?
- special considerations for small space copy and classifieds?
- what makes people respond?
- why some classifieds do better than display ads?
- a mental trick to improve any ad?
- and much, much more!

For 28 years Hubert Simon has owned an Advertising Agency and publishing firm that is rated by Dun & Bradstreet, listed by McKittrick's.

Priced at only $12.95, this is a genuine bargain: it relates, in 50 succinct pages, what it took Hubert Simon 28 years to learn . . . the treasure of a Master Copywriter's background distilled into one uniquely helpful manual. Satisfaction guaranteed. Try it for 60 days and then return for refund — if you can part with it!

H. K. Simon Co., Inc.
1280 Saw Mill River Rd., Dept. H
Yonkers, N.Y. 10710

60-day TRIAL

I accept! Please send "How To Write An Ad That Will Sell Anything." I enclose $12.95 which will be refunded within my 60-day trial.

Name ....

Address ....

City .... State .... Zip ....

"Hundreds of thousands," while not untrue, sounds too much like the fellow who says, "Oh, I've been through this thing a thousand times," when you know he really means about five or ten times. People are given to that kind of hyperbole, used for impact and not meant to be taken literally. "278,000" is in another class: it smacks of *reporting* rather than exaggeration. It will be accepted as fact because (1) it's quantified in specific, rather than general, terms, and (2) the number is not rounded off. Someone else might have written, "300,000 have been sold," and in so doing lost the persuasiveness of that more precise number.

Quantify as much as you can, and don't round numbers off. Use the closest numbers you can come up with. Even if you're estimating and your formula delivers an odd number, use that number.

Lay off the adjectives and adverbs, especially the superlatives. Use nouns and verbs, and use active voice. Used properly, they can be far more dramatic and impressive than the superlatives are. Example:

> Jones and Company is the largest firm in its industry, and has been in business over a half-century.

> versus:

> Jones and Company operates 73 outlets in 12 cities, grosses nearly $550 million annually, employs 6,800 people, was founded in 1927.

Which would you believe? Which is evidence and which is claim?

Do you believe the advertiser who claims "thousands of satisfied users," or are you more likely to believe the advertiser who reprints endorsements and testimonials and offers to produce the original letters on demand?

Of course, terms such as "free trial" and "money back guarantee" help also, and are widely used. In fact, I used them myself for a long time. However, I felt that they also had a possible harmful effect in that they suggested that my products *needed* a guarantee. That bothered me. If my credentials were good enough—and my personal credentials in my professional field are my chief asset and chief evidence of validity—they should be enough, without the negative and suggested self-doubting qualities of the guarantee and free trial. So eventually I eliminated those phrases from my advertising, while I laid even greater stress on the evidence that I could and would deliver on my promises. And, behold! I lost absolutely no business in so doing. If anything, the response actually improved. So I am not the greatest of believers in that free trial and money-back guarantee, unless you feel that your credibility is not good enough to get you by without them.

TED BATES AND THE "USP"

Some time ago (several chapters ago, in fact), you read about a crackerjack insurance salesman, Frank Bettger, who developed one superlative selling device: he rocked his prospect back on his heels by saying, "Mr. _____, I can do something for you that no one else in the world can do."

Ted Bates, an advertising executive and agency head, has built his campaigns on a concept very much along the same lines. He calls it the "USP," for Unique Selling Point.

Bates believes that the key to a successful advertising campaign is to find some unique point that will capture the prospect's attention and interest, at the least, and even be the clincher in many cases, He studies every advertising problem to find that USP, and usually he manages to come up with one.

Now the word "unique," as used in USP, does not necessarily mean that the item offered must itself have some unique feature. It means that the advertising must be able to *claim* something unique or somehow express some point which is unique, if only in that no one else has thought of it as a selling point.

In one campaign carried out to sell the product of a Milwaukee brewer, Bates built the campaign around the fact that the brewer cleaned and sterilized his bottles with live steam before filling them with his product. This was not unique in itself, but was the common practice in the industry. But the public obviously did not know that, and no other brewer had ever advertised it. So Bates utilized it as the USP for that campaign, along with dramatic illustrations of the sterilizing and cleaning process and an appropriate headline. And once he had used the concept, the brewer's competitors were barred from using it for fear of saying, "Me, too!"

As with most such ideas, Bates's USP has its uses, but I seriously doubt that it should become a religion. However, if you can find a true USP, *and* if it *fits* your campaign (I would never force-fit it), try it. Bear in mind, however, the inherent hazard in being *too* different, and the even greater hazard, perhaps, in falling so in love with the idea that you distort a good sales message because of it. Gimmicks do not sell merchandise. Only sound advertising and sound marketing can do that. In adopting some magic cure-all for advertising problems, there is a serious danger of simply getting clever or cute rather than producing an effective sales message in your ads.

HOW TO WRITE A PRESS RELEASE

The format for a press release or news release (both terms are used) is simple enough. Somewhere at the head of the form it should announce prominently that it is a press or news release. An individual should be identified as the "contact" or source for more information, on the assumption that an editor who is interested may want to call and get photos or more information. And, of course, the release should be written in a "news style." That, however, doesn't necessarily mean the journalistic "who, what, when, where, why" news lead, for many press releases are written in the style of newspaper feature stories, a more flexible and informal form.

By far the majority of such releases wind up in the "circular file." Newspaper and magazine editors are all but swamped with them every day, and few merit publication because few have been written to be worthy of publication. The editor will use those press releases which appear to offer something of interest to the reader of the editor's publication.

Consider Figures 10 through 13. Each of the samples appeals to a different type of reader and a different type of publication—not necessarily the daily newspaper, which appeals to

Figure 10. A typical association news release.

∩euur release

September 25, 1979   Contact: Eileen Torpey
FOR IMMEDIATE RELEASE   (703) 273-7200

Keynote speaker at the Second General Session of the National Audio-Visual
Association's 1980 Convention & Exhibit in Atlanta, Ga., January 9-14, 1980, will
be M. Mark Lee, vice president of the New York-based consulting firm, Standard
Research Consultants. The session is set for Sunday, January 13.

His presentation, "What Is Your Company Worth?" will take attendees through
the procedure to estimate the value of a company.

General Convention Chairman, Erwin Burke, Burke's Audio-Visual Center, Inc.,
South Bend, Ind., said that, "after attending this session and going through
Mr. Lee's step-by-step process, any business executive will be able to make a
rough determination of the value of his or her company."

In his work for Standard Research Consultants, Lee has prepared numerous
studies, including the valuation of an electronics company in preparation for
a public offering and the appraisal of closely-held bonds of a brokerage house.

The NAVA Convention & Exhibit is the major event of the year for members
of the A-V industry in the United States and brings together manufacturers,
producers, dealers, distributors and users from all over the world for one of
the largest and most important A-V marketplaces in the world.

For more information write: NAVA Convention, 3150 Spring Street, Fairfax,
VA 22031.

NAVA is the trade organization of the audio-visual industry, representing
A-V dealers, manufacturers, producers, non-theatrical entertainment and religious
film distributors, and education and trade publications.
4377-979   #   #   #

NATIONAL AUDIO-VISUAL ASSOCIATION, 3150 Spring Street, Fairfax, Virginia 22031 (703) 273-7200

Figure 11. News release used successfully to generate sales.

Government Marketing News
Box 6067   Wheaton, MD 20906

<u>FOR IMMEDIATE RELEASE</u>

Contact: Sherrie Holtz
301 460-1506

AN IDEA WHOSE TIME HAS COME?

Proposals are going to have to be better than ever, as Congress slashes procurement dollars for the coming year, if government contractors want to continue to win new contracts. And government marketing consultant Herman Holtz believes its time has come for his journal of proposal writing, the <u>Government Marketing News</u>.

Originally a newsletter for contractors, <u>Government Marketing News</u> began to change its style as editor-publisher Holtz discovered that most of his readers were more interested in learning some of his exclusive know-how in writing winning proposals than they were in news items. When he discovered that, <u>Government Marketing News</u> adopted the subtitle <u>THE JOURNAL OF PROPOSAL WRITING</u> and began to devote more and more of its space every month to providing readers such tips as how to <u>appear</u> to be the low bidder (when you are not), how to ensure getting a high technical point score, how to get special attention with your proposals, and dozens of other strategies and techniques that he calls "proposalmanship."

Holtz began to learn the craft of writing the winning proposals as an aerospace engineer, later as a general manager and director of government marketing. He became a consultant to other firms when others began to note his remarkable success in winning contracts with his proposals, while apparently violating all the "rules" of conventional wisdom. (His proposals have, to date, produced over $100 million in government contracts.)

"The fellows are already beginning to feel the pinch," he observes, "and they are starting to break down the door to learn how to write really outstanding 'props,' where they didn't think it was very important before."

His monthly journal is $95 a year, but he accepts new subscriptions on a first-time basis at $60 a year. It's GOVERNMENT MARKETING NEWS, BOX 6067, WHEATON, MD 20906.   ###

Figure 12. An IRS news release.

News Release

Department of the Treasury
Internal Revenue Service
Public Affairs Division
Washington, DC 20224

Media Contact: Tel. (202) 566-4024
Copies: Tel. (202) 566-4054

For Release: 11-5-79

IR-2175

Washington, D.C.--The Internal Revenue Service today announced that final regulations concerning excess business holdings of private foundations generally will allow an active corporation in which a foundation has excess stock held since May 26, 1969, to acquire new subsidiaries or assets without creating business holdings for the foundation.

This adopts the general approach taken in proposed regulations published in the Federal Register on January 3, 1973, rather than the approach in proposed regulations published on May 22, 1979.

Private foundations and their disqualified persons--primarily substantial contributors and family members or businesses related to contributors--generally are permitted to hold up to 20 percent of the voting stock of a corporation. The limit is 35 percent if someone other than the foundation and its disqualified persons has effective control of the corporation. The limit is also increased if the foundation and its disqualified persons have held more than 20 or 35 percent, respectively, since May 26, 1969.

Private foundations are subject to an excise tax on excess business holdings under section 4943 of the Internal Revenue Code. If the foundation and its disqualified persons hold more than permitted, the tax is five percent of the value of any stock held in excess of the limits. If the foundation does not dispose of the excess holdings within a correction period, there is an additional tax of 200 percent.

X   X   X

Figure 13. An SBA news release.

N E W S | **SMALL BUSINESS** ADMINISTRATION

Washington, D.C. 20416

Jean M. Nowak
(202) 653-6822

1441 "L" Street, N.W

SBA #79-65

FOR IMMEDIATE RELEASE
WEDNESDAY, OCTOBER 17, 1979

INTEREST RATE ON SBA'S DIRECT LOANS IS RAISED

WASHINGTON, D.C., OCTOBER 17 --- The interest rate on loans made directly to small businesses by the U.S. Small Business Administration (SBA) has been raised to 8¼ percent from 7-3/8 percent, according to SBA Administrator A. Vernon Weaver.

The direct loan interest rate is tied to the cost of money to the U.S. Treasury and is adjusted annually. The increase was effective October 9.

Involved in the increase are direct business loans made under Section 7(a) of the Small Business Act, development company loans made under Section 502 of the Small Business Investment Act and non-physical (economic injury) disaster loans.

Direct loan funds are limited and become available only after a borrower has been turned down by a bank and is unable to obtain funds under SBA's bank guaranty or immediate participation programs.

the general public. However, the daily newspaper contains a number of special sections, and when you send a release to a newspaper, be sure to send it to the attention of the proper editor—food, sports, business, news, or whatever.

The release should be typed double-spaced to permit the editor to make such changes as necessary, just as you would submit any manuscript double-spaced to an editor.

You may use a headline or not, as you see fit. However, my personal belief is that a headline is most helpful, and one should be used. It's tough enough as it is to get an editor's attention with a release, and a well-written headline helps.

In general, what is true for advertising copy generally is true for writing releases. You still have to get attention, arouse interest, develop buying desire, and make the close. But here, your sales prospect is the editor.

What Interests an Editor?

An editor has one prevailing interest: whatever will interest the readers of the editor's publication. Appeal to the readers, and you appeal to the editor. Therefore, begin by considering the ultimate reader: what will interest that reader?

But before we discuss that, let's consider what your immediate target population is. Who are the editors? Or, rather, what publications are they editors of?

Obviously, there are all the news media—newspapers, news services, news magazines, and news departments of radio and TV stations.

There are all the general-interest magazines, the kinds you find on your newsstands. (They are on the newsstands *because* they appeal to the public in general, or at least a broad segment of the general public.)

But then there are all the magazines appealing to special interests, the periodicals called "trade journals" and "house organs." Every business and every industry has at least one of these, and often several. Here are a few, just to give you an idea:

Automotive News—for people in the automobile industry.
Pacific Bakers News—for professional bakers.
Constructioneer—for construction contractors.

Obviously, you must select those editors whose readers would be interested, for reasons connected with their businesses or occupations, if what you want to advertise is suitable to some of these.

There are also several thousand newsletters, some of which are addressed to the general public, but many of which are addressed to narrow segments of business and industry and to various kinds of professionals. Most of these publications have a relatively limited circulation—as low as a few hundred subscribers in the case of some highly specialized newsletters. But in the aggregate, the total number of readers reached is quite high, and the probability is that you can have your news item picked up by a large number of small publications, if you have written it well.

Get Attention First

As in advertising copy, try to use the headline to tell your story in a phrase, if you can. But try to work a "hooker" into your headline—"new," for example, is almost always attention-getting, if you can back it up in some manner. Editors of periodicals are almost always interested in news, if it is legitimately *news*. Here are examples:

NEW CARBURETOR GUARANTEES MORE MILEAGE
SIGNIFICANT BREAKTHROUGH IN SOLAR ENERGY CELLS
VITAMIN PRICES CUT

The release must pick up directly from that headline and begin to prove it. Editors are weary people who are justifiably skeptical of claims, especially when they are headlines in the concealed advertising that most press releases obviously are. They'll stop reading your release immediately if they believe that you cannot support your headline and are simply making claims you can't back up.

Editors are likely to want novel information, too:

PUBLIC GOES CRAZY FOR PET ROCKS
MR. UGLY CONTEST ANNOUNCED
MINI-SKIRTS ARE BACK
MAILMAN BITES DOG

If you can tie your release into something of current interest or combine several features, you are likely to catch enough interest to merit a reading of your release:

REPORT EXPLAINS LOOPHOLES IN NEW TAX LAW
SEVEN NEW WAYS TO CUT ENERGY COSTS
BURGLAR-PROOF SECURITY LOCK INVENTED

In many cases, with a bit of writing skill, you can take some mundane, perhaps not even new or interesting information and make it appear fresh, new, and interesting. For example, in selling my own publications and services to help people learn how to win government contracts, one of my press releases began with an explanation of the fact that the federal government employs a large number of full-time purchasing specialists, and the headline read as follows:

U.S. GOVERNMENT EMPLOYS 130,000 FULL-TIME BIG
SPENDERS

Other releases I used for this same purpose stressed some of the government's more novel procurements:

FEDERAL GOVERNMENT RENTS MULES
FEDERAL AGENCIES HIRE GO-GO DANCERS

The copy must, of course, follow up immediately and lure the editor into reading further.

But There's Nothing Interesting about What I Sell . . .

Unfortunately, by far the overwhelming majority of press releases are dull and uninteresting. That's because most writers write with ME instead of YOU in mind. They seem to have some quaint notion that the editor is bursting to print their deathless prose, and of course the opposite is true. To write releases that have at least some chance of being picked up and used by editors, you must learn to analyze your proposition from the reader's viewpoint. What does the reader *care* about? What will amuse, excite, alarm, charm, startle, or otherwise catch the reader's attention? That is what will catch the *editor's* attention.

I'll concede that most products are of themselves not very

interesting. But an imaginative person can find something of interest, or *create* something of interest. Let's consider a couple of very dull products and see what we can do about them that would merit some free editorial space.

"How to Get a Year's Supply of Vitamins Free"—This headline could be used to announce a contest of sorts. Suppose you put some kind of token in one bottle of the vitamins you sell and announce that the lucky purchaser of that particular bottle will get one year's supply free. (Of course, this idea can be applied to almost any product.)

"Free Booklet on Vitamins Offered"—Suppose you prepare an interesting booklet on vitamins and offer it free with every order. If you can find some especially fascinating facts about vitamins—and enough research is almost certain to turn such facts up—you'll have excellent material for several good releases. This would also work for many other products.

"Does Good-Luck Amulet Really Work?" If you sell costume jewelry, it shouldn't be too difficult to carry some kind of good-luck charms or reproductions of some item considered to have a "curse" on it, even if you do so only to establish the basis for a good news release! Of course, many intriguing headlines and stories can be developed out of such items.

The point here is that if the item does not have some intrinsically interesting facet, *create* one. Combine the ideas of the publicity stunt with the press release.

New-Product News

Many consumer magazines carry a "new products" section, in which they tell readers about new items of interest. These sections are relatively easy to get your item into, if it is really new *or can be made to appear new* by stressing some new use for it or some new feature embodied in it. For example, if you sell hair-curl rollers made of some new material, that may itself justify coverage—if you can make it interesting enough in your write-up.

The possibility of getting your item described in these sections is greatly enhanced by supplying the editor with a good photograph, usually a black-and-white glossy. Editors tend to prefer 8 × 10 glossies, but today most will accept a good 4 × 5. Such prints are not too expensive, and a good photo will overcome many deficiencies in writing.

News Services

There are services that will distribute your press releases for you, for a smaller sum of money than the cost of postage. At this writing, the Washington News Service (National Press Building, Washington, D.C. 20045) will distribute 400 copies of your release for only $45. (I have used this service, with good results.)

YOUR OWN PROMOTIONAL NEWSLETTER

A promotional device used with great success by many small entrepreneurs is the "house organ" type of newsletter, distributed free of charge or at a nominal charge to anyone who appears to be a potential or actual customer.

Some entrepreneurs have used a variation of this: they prepared and mailed a free newsletter while getting their business started, and then began to make a small charge—say, $5 a year—after becoming established. The charge may be fairly represented as covering postage and printing only, because it does, so that the newsletter may be offered "free"—for cost only.

This is particularly useful if you are in some type of business which is either repetitive—that is, the customers are re-peat customers—or involves some kind of "big tag" item. By using such a regularly scheduled publication, you are, in effect, sending out a four- or eight-page news release regularly. For purposes of economy, such newsletters are usually quarterly—issued four times a year. They contain useful information, but are designed primarily as sales-promotion literature, of course.

By offering this kind of newsletter. free of charge, you can get names and addresses from small classified advertisements, and your mailing list—which is, of course, your customer and customer-prospect list—will grow steadily.

OFTEN-OVERLOOKED OPPORTUNITIES FOR FREE ADVERTISING

The next time you visit your local supermarket, search out the bulletin board inside the entrance and notice, among all the "bicycle for sale" and "baby sitting" notices, how many commercial notices are posted. Not too long ago I ordered my business cards printed by someone who had left his brochures (mass-printed by the source and rubber-stamped with the local dealer's name and address) stuffed into one of the pockets on the local A&P supermarket bulletin board. It was a mail-and-telephone transaction—we never met—and I was entirely pleased with the results. The only fly in the ointment was that the dealer failed to add my name to his mailing list, which cost him added business: I would have ordered some other things from him, had he had the wisdom to keep a customer list and solicit more business from that list!

Most people have at least a dozen supermarkets within easy reach. That's a dozen free "billboards" for you. But there are other free billboards: bulletin boards in community halls, university buildings, and public buildings of many sorts.

If you live in a small town, your local newspaper may be persuaded to run a story and perhaps even a photo of the newest businessperson in town, especially if the editor is having a "dull day" for news. A local chamber of commerce or other such organization may have a newsletter in which you can get a mention. And it's probably wise to join such organizations, too. You may be able to work out cooperative deals with other business people whose businesses complement yours. For example, if you write resumes, a local printer may be happy to refer customers to you, in return for which you refer your customers to him. Or you may be able to work out a similar mutual-reference service with an employment agency or two.

Think in terms of what related interests your own customers are likely to have, and you can conceive of many such arrangements. (Example: our own local printer keeps a bulletin board in front of his own front counter and permits customers to post their business cards or other notices there.)

Cossman recommends that you spend not one cent for paid advertising until you have exhausted all possible means for getting advertising/publicity free.

HOW TO CUT ADVERTISING COSTS BY 17 PERCENT

Advertising agencies write copy, shoot photographs, draw illustrations, produce videotapes, and buy advertising time and space for their clients, among other services. And, for large accounts—those which buy a great deal of time and/or space—they do not charge their clients one cent! Yet, the agency can make large profits on good accounts.

How do they do it? Simple: an advertising agency gets a 15 percent discount normally on all space and/or time it buys for clients, plus 2 percent additional for prompt payment. On $1 million worth of space/time, the agency can get as much as $170,000 discount. That, less the costs for preparing the client's advertisements and placing them, is the agency's profit.

Among those who buy a great deal of advertising—for example, mail order people—it is common practice for dealers to set up their own in-house advertising agencies and save 15 to 17 percent of their advertising costs. In fact, if you place advertising consistently with the same publications, the advertising manager is likely to suggest to you that he will be happy to give you the discount if you set up your own advertising agency.

Doing so is simplicity itself. You need only a name for

Figure 14. Typical insertion order for advertising space or time.

J. SMITH & CO.
1463 Main Street
Sioux Falls, South Dakota

INSERTION ORDER

TO: Men's Wear Daily
Advertising Department
171 Mary Lane
Sioux Falls, SD

Order No.___723___

Date_____11/26/80_____

Advertiser:_Apex Merchandise Co._

_____

ISSUE DATE:Mar, Apr, May 1981___ SPACE:_½ page_____

TIMES:_3_____ RATE:_$850_____

POSITION:___Above the fold_____

SPECIAL POSITION INSTRUCTIONS:_None_____

COPY & AD MATERIAL ATTACHED:_Yes_____

AMOUNT DUE:_$2,550_____

LESS 15% AGENCY COMMISSION:_$382.50_____

LESS 2% CASH DISCOUNT:_$43.35_____

NET AMOUNT DUE:_$2,124.15_____

_____
Joseph T. Smith (signed)

your private advertising agency, stationery, and insertion-order forms.

Let's suppose that you are the Apex Merchandise Company. Your name is Joe Smith. You can have letterheads and envelopes printed bearing the name "J. Smith & Co., Media Specialists." Or even plain "J. Smith & Co." You also have insertion-order forms printed, preferably, although not necessarily, in carbon sets.

Figure 14 shows a typical layout for an insertion order, filled in by J. Smith for his client, the Apex Merchandise Co. J. Smith & Co. will be billed for the space.

Of course, you may vary the form as you see fit, but the sample shown includes the kind of information you will have to supply.

14

NOT EVERYBODY WANTS TO BE A TRADER

We have been talking principally about ideas which can be the basis for a business, and about how to operate a business successfully. However, there are a number of enterprising people in the country who make a business of selling ideas themselves. And even this is accomplished in several ways: (1) outright cash sale of the idea, (2) sale of the idea on a royalty (percentage) basis, and (3) selling the information to a large number of people.

On what basis one should sell an idea depends largely on the idea itself: some ideas lend themselves to direct sale for cash and/or royalties, while some ideas cannot be sold this way but can be sold as information in books, newsletters, and other publications.

PATENTABLE IDEAS

If your idea involves the conception, design, and manufacture of a device of any sort, and if it can be patented so as to convey protection to you as the originator or inventor, you have a commodity which may be salable. *May* be? Yes, may be. May be, because although in issuing a patent the Patent Office acknowledges that the device is new and original and merits patent protection, that does not warrant that it has any commercial value. Many patents never return the cost of the patent procedures to the inventors. Practical commercial application and commercial value have nothing to do with patentability, and the Patent Office has no concern for these aspects of new devices.

205

In general, to be patentable, the device must be something new and different—use a new principle or have some original basis—and either a working model or a set of disclosure drawings must be produced. Inventors are characteristically almost paranoid in their fear that someone will steal their ideas, although patent thefts are really the exception. At the same time, it makes good sense to protect your design before attempting to sell it or market the item, if you decide to market it yourself.

Contrary to popular opinion, new patents do not necessarily involve complex scientific principles or Rube Goldbergian apparatuses (although there are plenty that do fit that characterization). Many patents are issued for relatively simple devices, such as the plastic egg carton which replaced the papier-mâché egg carton in many places. Patents are issued for store displays, potato peelers, and hair curlers. Some of these may be great improvements on existing devices, while others may be completely new ideas. The consuming public may accept some of these with great enthusiasm and reject others with cold indifference. Going to market with these is usually an out-and-out gamble.

Suppose you dream up a new toy or game, for example. Taking it to market yourself is both difficult and expensive. Here are just some of the things you have to do and problems you must overcome:

You have to have enough of the item manufactured to provide samples and to fill at least some initial orders. This may involve several thousand items and may require fairly expensive tooling and equipment.

You need packaging—cartons, display stands, posters, instruction booklets, and other related items.

You need a sales effort of some sort—direct sales representatives, advertising, or distribution through a jobber or wholesaler. The use of a jobber or wholesaler is likely to mean a much larger initial production run to provide initial stock for their inventory.

You need to price the item, which can be quite tricky: you

need to price it to cover all costs and give yourself a reasonable profit, yet keep the price low enough so that you don't doom it to failure in advance.

You need a physical distribution system (unless you have managed to get a jobber to handle distribution for you).

Aside from the capital and labor required to do all this, there is the risk element: after all the labor and capital investment, the item may not sell at all! Even the large corporations, with all their capital, physical resources, research efforts, and marketing skills, often guess wrong and have to write new items off by closing them out as quickly as possible. In fact, there are a number of entrepreneurs who specialize in buying up stocks of items which have failed in the marketplace and unloading them at flea markets, fairs, and auction sales.

On the other hand, you may not be able to get a major firm interested in marketing your new item, in which case you've little recourse except to abandon it or try to market it on your own. One heartening fact: the big corporations are run by fallible humans, and they guess wrong on both sides. They have at times turned away new items which have succeeded in someone else's hands.

Usually, when you do manage to sell your idea to a company such as Mattel, the deal will be on a royalty basis— perhaps 5 percent, perhaps more. Or less. Occasionally you may be able to get an advance, but it's not exactly a common practice.

IS THERE MONEY IN IDEAS?

Richard E. Paige is considered to be one of America's leading inventors and creators of new ideas, with many patents issued in his name. In his book, *Complete Guide to Making Money with Your Ideas and Inventions* (Prentice-Hall, Englewood Cliffs, N.J., 1973), Paige says that there is *no* money in creating new ideas and inventions, but only in *selling* them. And he offers this checklist of questions by which to evaluate the merits of your new idea or invention: Does it really work?

Is it new? Useful? Patentable? Practical to make at acceptable cost? Can it be sold? And that latter is the $64 question, of course, for if the answer to that is "no," the other answers don't really matter.

Perhaps the most commonly offered advice for spawning new ideas is to observe problems and try to think up solutions. Paige has a slightly different view, at least for some cases: see things with "different" eyes. What is a disadvantage to others can often be made an advantage to you.

Let me add another bit of philosophy to that: to increase the commercial possibilities of your idea or invention, try to find *simple* solutions to problems. In engineering I learned a long time ago that any fool can come up with a complex solution, and many do. (In fact, some solutions are so complex that I'd rather have the problem than the solution!) Real genius lies in finding simple solutions to problems. Therefore, you do not necessarily have to solve something which has never been solved before. Suppose you find a problem solution which appears fairly complex. Can you think up a simpler solution to the problem? If so, you may have a commercially valuable idea right there!

For example, one problem that always faces people in offices is that of holding together pages of reports or other sheaves of paper with a temporary binding that is easily applied and easily removed. There are many such devices, but which is the most popular? That's right, the simple paper clip. No one has yet been able to improve on it!

Truly great ideas, like truly great inventions, are usually simple and almost impossible to improve upon. Once conceived, they cause almost every observer so say, "Why didn't I think of that?"

Suppose you were the owner of a market, and you observed your customers struggling with increasingly heavier shopping bags as they selected items from your shelves. What would you do?

Sylvan Goldman, who owned not a store but two chains— the Humpty Dumpty Stores and the Standard Food Markets, in Oklahoma City—saw the difficulty growing as his stores grew larger and larger. His simple solution was the supermarket shopping cart, which he invented in 1937, revolutionizing shopping habits. In fact, its acceptance was so swift it caught other supermarket owners flat-footed, and for years Goldman sold his carts to other store owners at $7 each.

A solution such as that is almost obvious—or seems so, later. But not all problems are so apparent or solutions so obvious, unfortunately. Deliberate and sophisticated analysis is often necessary to find solutions. In fact, analysis is often necessary to identify or define the problem! It's quite easy to confuse the symptoms with the problem itself. And in our sophisticated and complex society, even problems with simple solutions become buried deeply in the system and must be first rooted out and exposed to the light before a solution can be found.

Analysis is therefore not necessarily aimed directly at solving problems, but often at finding the problems first—sifting the symptoms or results from the causes. And in a surprisingly large number of cases, once that is done, the solution is amazingly simple, yielding readily to the most basic logic. In fact, once the true root problem is properly identified and defined, the solution becomes obvious and suggests itself.

HOW TO ANALYZE A PROBLEM

Once it was my duty to take over management of an office that did work for NASA on a cost-plus contract. One of the many problems I encountered was that our monthly invoice almost invariably was returned by NASA as in error in many items. And they were right: every invoice was loaded with incorrect entries. Although I was no accountant, I felt it necessary to examine the accounting system.

I found that we had a rather complex system of recording labor hours and other expenses, designed by some high-priced accountant to follow his formal training in accounting systems. What troubled me about it was that the system required several stages of transfer of figures, from many records to a second set of records, then to a third set, and finally to a public voucher. There were so many possibilities for error in making these many transfers, it would have been a minor miracle had we been able to turn out perfect invoices every month.

I applied some rather conventional systems analysis to the problem. I started with the invoice, which was the major objective of the system, after all. The only other records we were legally obliged to maintain were individual time cards and copies of bills for outside services or subcontracts. It did not require much study to determine that only one step was required between these two sets of original records and the final invoice: collecting and integrating costs into final subtotals for reporting and billing. I therefore designed a simple worksheet expressly fashioned to transcribe to the invoice. This not only reduced the opportunities to make errors in transferring figures, but also gave us a simple means for checking and verifying our invoices before sending them out.

The point is that I did not know what the problem was when I started. Having so many errors in our bills to the government was a management problem, but when it came to analyzing the situation to find a solution, the first thing I had to face was that erroneous invoices were not the "problem," at this point; they were *symptoms*. The problem lay in making more transfers of figures than absolutely necessary. Once the problem was identified and defined, the solution was obvious: devise a system that eliminated unnecessary transfers—*simplify* the system.

Always, in symptom analysis and problem solving generally, if you want to go straight to the heart of the problem and find a *simple* solution, you must first be able to state the problem in simple terms so that there is no doubt whatsoever of what is wrong.

In attacking the problem described here, I knew that my quest was to answer two questions: Where are the errors occurring? Why (or how) are they occurring? Looking for "where" was simple enough: track down the items, step by step, on any erroneous invoice, to their source. "Why" and "how" were then pretty obvious.

In another, somewhat similar case, the shop was handling printing orders for the Government Printing Office. Billing was somewhat complicated by the need to specify on the invoice the number of plates, sides printed, number of impressions, number of sheets collated, number of staples, and so forth—as many as a dozen items and operations to be listed and priced separately, per our contract. Each time the shop turned over its job sheet to our accounting department, the accounting people had to select and transcribe all the information, and they could not really decipher all the shop jargon, let alone transcribe and bill it.

Again, the solution was simple enough, once we had decided what the true problem was. We devised a special worksheet for checking each job into the print shop. On the sheet was listed every operation, with the unit price for each. When the job came in, the print shop recorded the number of each (plates, staples, sheets, and so on) and checked them off as completed, as the job progressed. When every item was checked off and the job sent out, the sheet was duplicated and the duplicate sent to the accounting department. The accounting department then made up an invoice for the total amount and attached the duplicate of the worksheet as the detailed account the contract required.

Neither of these ideas had any value outside our own organization, but they were both invaluable to us in the organization. Both illustrate the principle of the simple solution, made possible by the simple definition of the problem itself. Accomplishing this requires independent thinking—never mind how anyone has done it before, but ask, "What am I trying to *accomplish?* What *end-result* do I want?" Frequently, that means working *backward*—starting with the end-result defined, then deciding what is needed to accomplish that end-result, what is needed to accomplish *that* preliminary to the end-result, and so forth.

In many cases, as in the case of preparing a proper public

voucher with which to bill NASA each month, we have both *ends* of the problem. We know what we want (an unfailingly correct public voucher, or invoice) and what we have to start with (time records and bills or receipts for whatever else is to be charged to the contract). Our problem is to get from one end to the other or to translate those time records and bills into a correct accounting. Or, as illustrated here, we can identify those two points as A and B, our objective then becoming to *find the shortest way from A to B.*

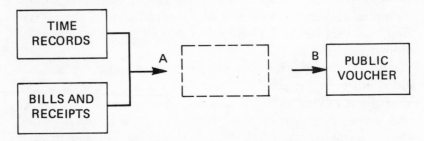

The single most important thing in the process is to remember always where we are going: our true objective. As an often-quoted Harvard professor, William Leavitt, remarked once, "If you don't know where you are going, any road will get you there." Only "there" may prove to be somewhere you later realize is not where you should have been headed at all.

Unfortunately, there are many who find all sorts of interesting byways to explore, and they sometimes lose sight of what they originally set out to do. And some others become so caught up in the intricacies of designing systems and procedures that they begin concentrating on the means rather than the end.

Fortunate, in this respect, are those we refer to as having "one-track minds." They do not permit themselves to be derailed. They never forget what they started out to do. When they set out to drain the swamp, they do not permit the waist-deep population of alligators to distract them, let alone interfere with draining the swamp.

This is what is known popularly as keeping your eye on

the ball. Decide in advance where you are going and never lose sight of that goal. Don't allow yourself to become infatuated with cleverness or inhibited by what has always been the "accepted" way—conventional wisdom. It takes *courage* to be creative, because creativity requires that you think *independently* and be able to smile indulgently and keep your cool when less imaginative people sneer and jeer at your "fool" ideas. There is, in fact, a method established for doing just this, and though it was designed to be used by a team of people, it can be readily adapted for use by a single individual with imagination. It's called value engineering or value analysis, and in some government offices it's also called value management. Without getting into all the details of how it works, here is the story.

ANYONE CAN BE A VALUE ENGINEER

World War II found the United States with enormous production demands for a wide variety of goods and, at the same time, with many of the usual sources of supply shut off. Even with rationing and the suspension of most nonmilitary manufacturing, raw materials were in short supply.

The usual remedy for such a situation is the substitution of other materials and acceptance of some degradation of quality and performance, and the United States was forced to accept those alternatives. When the desired raw material was not to be had, the best known substitute was used.

At the General Electric Company an engineering manager was struck by a curious fact during the war: not every substitution of raw materials resulted in lower quality or poorer performance of the final product. In fact, in quite a few cases the product was manufactured at lower cost more rapidly, was of better quality, or performed better than it would have with the material usually used—and sometimes the product had several of these characteristics! He found it intriguing, and he kept an eye on it, since he found that it happened rather often.

With the war finally won and over, he assigned one of the staff engineers, Lawrence Miles, to investigate this strange phenomenon and see if this kind of beneficial result could be made to happen on purpose rather than by accident or coincidence.

Larry Miles thus became the father of what is today known as value engineering, and spawned the Society of American Value Engineers (SAVE), which regularly certifies value engineers as CVS—Certified Value Specialists. Larry Miles came up with the first set of organized procedures to "value-engineer" products and deliberately seek out ways of getting better or at least equal results at lower costs.

Philosophically, value engineering is the first cousin of systems analysis. Both are concerned with function and simplicity—practicality of design. Both address the *result* desired and the most efficient way of producing that result. However, value engineering has tended to be hindsight redesign for many years, and has focused on engineered products. Only in recent years, the term "value management" has come into use and efforts have been made to utilize the method in other than engineered products and during initial design stages rather than after the fact.

Basically, the method revolves around the concept of *function,* and function is what something *does* rather than what it *is.* Yes, it makes good sense to examine this idea in light of marketing concepts: people buy things for what they do, rather than what they are, so value lies inescapably in what anything *does.* And if something can be made to do the same thing it always does, with the same or greater dependability and quality and at lower cost, it becomes more valuable: it's a better and less expensive product, without sacrifice or compromise to its quality and reliability.

Functions are on three levels: (1) the basic or primary function—what the thing is supposed to do overall; (2) the secondary or support functions—those which help the thing accomplish its main function; and (3) other functions which have no direct bearing on or interdependence with the main function.

There are certain rules which must be followed to maintain absolute objectivity. In particular, several questions must be asked: What is it? What does it do? What else does it do? How else could it be done? How much does it cost?

There are also rules for how functions must be defined: in only two words, a noun and a verb (for example, spins wheel, releases cam, protects check, punches holes). This part of the discipline is to ensure clear, unequivocal definitions.

In examining a device, every part or component is subjected to the scrutiny, and its function defined, so that it soon becomes clear whether any part fails to contribute—that is, whether there are any functions not necessary to the basic or main function. The analysis is conducted at several levels, so that each individual part is finally subjected to the questions of "What does it do?" and "How else could it be done?" And of course, the initial answer to the cost question is ultimately reexamined in light of the question "How else could it be done?" which leads to the question "What would *that* cost?" If the function can be accomplished in another way, at lower cost, by eliminating parts or unneeded functions and without sacrificing quality or dependability, an improvement has been made.

Value engineering may be applied to how parts are made, seeking a less costly way to make them. It may be applied to conserve something other than money, too: an equipment or system may be value-analyzed to conserve materials, energy, time, or any other variable involved. Instead of "What would *that* cost?" the question might be "How long would *that* take?" or "How much energy would *that* use?"

The value engineering team uses brainstorming techniques to arrive at its answers and its alternative ways for doing things, but the individual can use a similar discipline to develop new ideas or simplify methods and devices already in use. What is involved is asking yourself these same tough questions, and you can apply this to almost anything you find about you, from a mouse trap to a paperwork system.

Or the questions could be turned around. The fellow who discovered that useless plastic may have asked himself, "What could this be used for?" to come up with Silly Putty! Remember, value analysts are trying to improve products and reduce their costs, whereas you are trying to come up with ideas which will make you some money. Keep your eye on *that* ball. If you can't find the profit potential in your new idea, forget it! Before you spend your time analyzing some product or system to improve it, ask yourself whether a simplified product/system will have a good marketing potential. I simplified our internal accounting and invoicing methods, but there was no outside commercial potential in what I did, because the problem was peculiar to our own organization. I could not have found more than a handful of prospective customers for my system, had I bothered to prepare a package of forms and instructions.

If you look around, you can find all sorts of problems to be solved and things to be improved. If you can learn to identify basic functions accurately—and a surprisingly large number of people have difficulty doing that—you'll have no difficulty putting your finger on just what needs improvement. But it's not always obvious.

What, for example, is the basic function of a "check writer" machine? What does it *do?* If you answer "writes checks," your improvement quest must be fixed on a simpler and better way to write checks. But you've flunked the course. The machine exists to safeguard the check from being tampered with—from being "kited" or raised by a forger. The question should be, "What else will protect checks, and what would *that* cost?"

It's easy to fall into the trap of failing to see the true basic function of any device or system. Even the professional value engineers slip up occasionally. In one case, evaluating the functions of an overhead projector, the value engineers defined its basic function as "project image." It's true that the machine does do its job by projecting an image. But that isn't the *reason* the machine is used. The overhead projector is used to *present* an image large enough for everyone to see in a room. The instructor or lecturer doesn't really care *how* that enlarged image is created. So, if we allow ourselves to believe that "project image" is the true basic function—the reason for the existence of the machine—we shall bend efforts to find better ways to *project* an image, instead of seeking better ways to *present* a large image, whether the process involves projection or not.

Here is a simple example for you to try out yourself: What is the basic function of a secretary? If you answer that one, you'll do better than the professionals. In asking that question, I found few able to think out a good answer!

The reason? Because secretaries have been used and misused as typists and "go-fers" for so long that executives have forgotten that they hire secretaries to save their time by relieving them of many routine and semiroutine chores. The popular image of a secretary today is of an attractive female who types and files well, answers the telephone, and fetches coffee. That, of course, does not justify the salary differential between those classed as secretaries and those classed as typists and clerks. But a true secretary not only answers the telephone, but handles routine calls, opens the mail and answers much of it (subject to approval, of course), makes notations and digs out relevant files to help the executive respond to other correspondence, and anticipates many of the executives needs, such as travel reservations, screening unwelcome visitors, and so on. Unless a secretary does, in fact, save a significant portion of the executive's time, allowing the executive to concentrate on his or her primary duties and responsibilities, there is little point in having a secretary!

We often fall into the trap of becoming obsessed with the means rather than the end, and unnecessary frills begin to have a life of their own, giving rise to such long-term acceptance that any suggestion of change is met with a startled, "But we've *always* done it this way!" That's the syndrome which must be met and overcome: the security blanket of having "always done it this way." That's the excuse for not *thinking* and growing, and that's the tailor-made situation for the true "idea man" (or woman).

But it's not change for the sake of change, of course. It's

change for the sake of improvement. In the past few years, solid-state electronics has revolutionized technology. It began with transistors, starting circa 1960, and grew into today's tiny electronic chips, which have made pocket calculators and desktop computers possible, to mention just two major advances. But transistors—their principle, that is—are not really that new. Solid-state electronics existed, exemplified by simple and relatively crude devices, as far back as 1870. But no one attempted to develop the technology until after World War II.

The laser was conceived by a scientist sitting on a park bench in Baltimore and reflecting on the subject of coherent light. Perhaps he was aware of Edison's frequent remark that it took more thinking to know *what* to invent than *how* to invent it.

But not all inventions or new ideas have to be on such basic items as the laser or the electric light. Even minor improvements can bring rich rewards. The potato peeler, for example, was a minor invention, a simple device, but it found almost immediate acceptance because it was by far the best answer yet to the problem of an unpleasant household chore, and no one has yet made any basic improvement to the device, although many minor refinements have been made.

"Scotch" tape is a good example. The original sticky-backed cellophane tape had a glossy surface, which offered two problems: (1) one could not write on it, and (2) it yellowed and peeled, eventually. Although far more costly, the tape with a frosted surface is far more popular today, because one can write on it and it's virtually invisible when applied. Also, it has a better shelf life.

Art Newman, of Milwaukee, will buy and sell just about anything, if the price is right and it is a quantity deal. He stumbled into "surplus" or "closeout" merchandise almost by accident, after opening a retail store in 1951 with two TV sets as his entire stock. (That's all he had money to buy.) His first closeout buy was of several hundred $6.95 coffee makers, which had cost a neighboring dealer $3.50. The dealer was having trouble selling them, and offered them to Newman at

$2 each but, to Newman's surprise, accepted Newman's offer of $1 each.

Since then Newman has bought and sold outboard motors, lawn mowers, garden sprinklers, fishing equipment, golf bags, lock sets, camping equipment, tricycles, and hundreds of other items, all closeout lots which Newman could offer at bargain prices. (He sold those $6.95 coffee makers which cost him $1 each at $1.99 each.)

Art Newman has a standing offer to pay commissions if you can find him a good closeout lot. Or he will take one off your hands. Or work with you to sell one you've got. Or sell one to you. You can have it almost any way you want, as long as Newman can see a profit in it for both of you. (See the last chapter for Newman's address and more information.)

Several "go-fer" services have sprung up in major cities. For a fee, you can have someone do your grocery shopping, walk the dog, fetch the mail, or perform other such chores. Some young swains have been reported to use go-fer services to send proposals of marriage!

Obviously there are needs for such services, or such enterprises could not succeed. They are convenience services, of course. (One woman paid a go-fer $10 to get her a carton of cigarettes when she didn't want to brave the heavy rainstorm outside.)

The moral of this is: think of the things you dislike doing for yourself. Perhaps others also dislike these chores and will gladly pay to have them done.

SYSTEMS ANALYSIS AND FUNCTION

The most serious obstacle to creativity is the background all of us have in how things have "always been done." Over the years, we become chained to thinking in terms of the already familiar. A young executive, assigned his own secretary for the first time in his life, never stops to think about how his secretary can best help him in getting his job done, but only thinks how he can use this new convenience and status symbol. And he can look about and find an ample number of examples set by others who use secretaries as personal servants rather than as supportive coworkers.

Almost all significant progress is made by swimming upstream, by doing things differently. And to do that, you must unchain your mind from conventional logic, which is inevitably based on how things are presently being done.

The term "systems analysis" has been in vogue for some years, to the point where it is now a platitude. Unfortunately, many people who use that term do not have a true appreciation of what it means.

Value engineering is itself a form of systems analysis, and is built around the key to systems analysis: *function*. And function is the very idea which makes many—especially non-engineers and non-scientists—have difficulty in mastering the concept. But function is the key. Translating concepts into true functional terms is an excellent means for unchaining the imagination from conventional wisdom.

Let's suppose we want to invent a powered device for felling trees in the forest—something other than the manual ax and saw. Our first thought, unless we are otherwise trained and conditioned, is to cast about for some practical means for powering the traditional saw. After all, the saw is the most practical tool we know of for cutting trees down. All we have to do is link it to a power source.

Some of the elements are easy. We know that electric power is impractical, for we are going to be cutting trees in forests miles from electric power sources. Obviously, the power source must be some sort of internal-combustion engine—gasoline-powered. It's not too difficult to build a small gasoline engine, light enough for a hand-held tool.

If we are to use the conventional saw blade, we have to arrange a mechanism to convert the engine's basic power to a reciprocating—back and forth—motion, which is the way a saw is used.

That poses a few problems, but they're mechanical and not too difficult to solve, insofar as mechanical power trains and motion conversions are concerned. The design does give us a few problems with weight and reliability. Each reversal of direction results in some loss of power and creates a great deal of mechanical stress. If the tool is to have a reasonable degree of reliability—that is, not require too frequent repairs—we have to beef up some of the mechanisms, which then add weight.

But then we find a much more serious problem, as we proceed. The conventional saw blade, used in a carpenter's saw, is light, tough, and flexible. But it is designed for use at relatively slow speeds, as a manual tool. Under the high-speed conditions of this new tool, conventional saw blades just don't stand up. They overheat, they bend and buckle, and they even break off, with dangerous results.

Perhaps we could find a saw blade that can do this job. But perhaps we can find a better way, if we begin to think in terms of *function,* and not how it has always been done. Let's think about that.

First of all, let's forget about the idea "saw" entirely, and think about how to cut trees. We cut trees—all woods and even metals, for that matter—by making a large number of repetitive small notches in the wood with a series of small knives. In a conventional saw, we call these "teeth." Each makes a tiny cut, and over the course of thousands of such tiny cuts, the tree or board is finally cut through. Obviously, it is the little knives which cut the tree, not the blade which carries them.

Applying a value-engineering kind of functional analysis, we would ask ourselves, as soon as we find that the conventional saw blade won't serve our purpose, "What does it do?" And our answer would be, "Carries the knives." Our next question would be, therefore, "What else would carry the knives?"

With this kind of attack on the problem, we wouldn't be long in answering the latter question with, "A chain." And soon enough, we would realize that with a chain carrying the little knives, we no longer need the reciprocating action, with all its problems, but can use a rotating action, with the chain turning forever in the same direction, operating at high speeds and with relatively little danger of breaking, getting fouled in a hard knot, or causing any of the many problems involved in that conventional saw design we tried to adapt to this new tool.

This is the kind of thinking that creative people do. They dismiss conventional wisdom and how it's always been done. They question everything—what? how? why? what else? why not?

Today, most lumbering is being done with power saws—*chain* saws. Even the handyman can buy a small model, suitable for use by one person. Today, that series of small knives is still the best way we know to cut down a tree. But tomorrow, someone will come up with a better way—perhaps a laser device, which will probably be called the laser-saw so that users will recognize the need it serves, although it will not be a saw at all.

The microwave oven is a good example of this. It's not really an oven at all—the enclosure is to contain the radiation, not to build up a circulation of heated air. The underlying principle has been known for many years, and is almost as old as the radio. In fact, all electronics engineers, including those old-time "radio engineers" ("electronics" is a relatively new term for what began as "radio"), knew the dangers of "RF burns," a basic hazard of working with radio energy at high power levels. But it wasn't until recent years that someone began to think of converting this well-known effect into a useful device. In fact, the microwave oven was a practical possibility many years ago, but the public at large probably wasn't yet ready for such a device.

Innovation—creativity itself—is the combination of two or more already known concepts to create something new. Edison knew that an electrical conductor would heat and glow brightly enough to shed light, if enough current was applied. And he knew that the effect had to be accomplished in a vacuum to prevent the conductor from burning out immediately through chemical oxidation. His quest was to find a suitable material to use as the conductor.

SERENDIPITY IS THE MOTHER OF INVENTION, TOO

Serendipity is difficult to define. Some people have said it's finding something you didn't know you lost. But more accurately, it's accidental discovery—something that happens by chance and turns out to be of value. It can lead to a new product, a new marketing idea, or even to an opportunity you had previously overlooked.

Take the case of Jim Ryder, who had discovered that truck drivers made more money at what they were doing than he made as a mixer of cement. He therefore bought a second-hand truck, beefed up its carrying capacity with "helper springs," and began to deliver building materials. His business grew, as customers discovered that he always kept his promises and delivered on time, and he eventually added more trucks and expanded his business. But his real breakthrough came when one of his customers asked him to lease one of his trucks. Ryder developed a leasing plan, and thus was born the large truck-leasing business which bears his name.

Chance can create a product, as in the case of the forgetful workman who went off to lunch one day and forgot to turn off the mechanical "crutchers"—stirring rods used to mix the ingredients for soap. Returning from lunch, he noticed that the soap mixture had been thoroughly aerated—was perhaps far more full of air bubbles than usually—but no harm seemed to have been done, so he let it go to the frames. It was some time later, when customers began to call for more of "that soap that floats," that the soap manufacturer began to deliberately aerate what was to become later known as Ivory soap.

Many advances are made with chance as a key ingredient. Charles Goodyear discovered the secret of vulcanizing rubber through chance, and chance contributed to Madame Curie's discovery of radium and even to Pasteur's work. And it was Pasteur who observed that fortune favors "the prepared mind," by which he was merely saying that when something happens by chance, the creative person continues to ask "why?" and "what" instead of simply dismissing the phenomenon.

Way back, near the beginning of this book, I mentioned a mail order dealer who cashed in on people's desire for convenience by charging them 50¢ per item to order government giveaways in their name. How did he get that idea? He had noticed that in a magazine aimed at "opportunity seekers," the publisher listed for the reader all the brochures and literature offered by his advertisers and invited the reader to check off whatever he was interested in and send along 50¢ to cover handling. Thereupon, the publisher would order all the items listed for the reader. Our mail order dealer wondered what would happen if he charged 50¢ *per item* and offered to help the reader get something perhaps more valuable than advertising literature—books and other valuable items the government gives away without charge.

Two ex-GIs, Larry Deutsch and Lloyd Rigler, had that kind of curiosity when they were served tender and delicious steaks in an inexpensive restaurant, at prices far below what such steaks ought to cost. On investigation they found that the chef used cheaper meat cuts but treated them with *papain,* which softened the tough tissues. They negotiated with the chef and bought the recipe from him, along with the right to use his name, which was Adolph. They packaged the papaya extract, along with the salt and other flavorings Adolph used, and tested the salability of the product in a local department store, at 49¢ a bottle, launching the success story that Adolph's Meat Tenderizer became. What they paid for the formula and the name is unknown, and perhaps Adolph would have been much better off to have sold an interest in his idea rather than all rights to it. But it probably never occurred to Adolph that the product was useful to anyone else but operators of small, inexpensive restaurants. Deutsch and Rigler, on the other hand, had the imagination to perceive a market.

YOU SHOULD KNOW ABOUT COPYRIGHT, TOO

You can patent a device, whether it's as simple as a new type of cardboard display stand or as complex as a new kind of computer. In a sense, you can patent the *idea,* as long as the idea is original, works, and has been translated into either a working model or a set of design drawings.

When it comes to other kinds of creations, the type which are usually thought of as artistic creations—written works, musical compositions, and the like—there is another kind of legal protection which enables you to exercise ownership of your creations. It's called "copyright."

Obtaining a copyright is much simpler than obtaining a patent. In fact, to gain copyright protection for your published works, you need only place the copyright notice on the work when it is published. That means the word "copyright," the abbreviation "copr.," or the symbol ©, followed by the name in which the copyright is claimed and the year. That confers "statutory" copyright protection. You can of course register the copyright with the Copyright Office of the Library of Congress, if you wish to, for a fee of $10 for most written works, which will be necessary should you ever get into litigation—that is, sue someone for infringement. Full details and forms for registering copyrights are available by writing to: Copyright Office, Library of Congress, Washington, DC 20559.

Ordinarily, it is necessary to obtain a copyright only if you yourself are the publisher. If you sell a written work or other copyrightable property to a publisher, the publisher will apply for the copyright.

Neophyte writers and composers often express the fear that a publisher will steal their property when they offer it for sale. Perhaps such things have happened, but they are rare occurrences. No reputable publisher would think it in his interest to steal a literary work from the author.

One more point of confusion about copyright and what it protects: contrary to a common misunderstanding, copyright does not guarantee the copyright owner exclusive domain over the ideas or information contained in the copyrighted work. It *does* guarantee exclusive ownership of *that particular combination of words* in the property (or combination of notes in a musical composition, or combination of lines in a drawing, and so on). You cannot copyright ideas or information. Anyone may use the ideas and information you have published to create another publication, which itself may be copyrighted, if it is presented in a new and original combination of words.

There's an old joke that stealing material from one or two sources is plagiarism (which is copyright infringement, if the material is from copyrighted works), but stealing from 50 or 60 sources is research. It's amusing, but largely true. A great many written works are created in just that manner—by rewriting materials gained from many sources.

CAN YOU MAKE MONEY AT WRITING?

The word "writer," to many, conjures up images of the struggling novelist or playwright. Or perhaps of the successful novelist or playwright. But for every novelist and playwright, successful or otherwise, there are hundreds of others earning a living, if not a great deal of money, as writers of one sort or another. And a great many opportunities to earn money at writing do not require great literary talents or even great creativity. In fact, many who are not especially gifted with an ability to express themselves well in writing manage to earn substantial money through the printed word. Here are a few examples.

One writer compiles a miniature almanac every year (the information is not hard to come by) and sells the manuscript to a large banking chain. The bank adds its own advertising messages and prints the almanac as a free giveaway to its customers and prospects. It's an effective promotion device for the bank, and an every-year income for the writer.

A number of people write resumes for those in need of resumes, and that means almost everybody who seeks a job these days. True, many people write their own, but a great many will pay to have theirs written for them.

Many associations and companies that publish newsletters and even small magazines for their members and customers do not maintain their own publications staffs but pay free-lance writers and editors to assemble these publications and do whatever writing is necessary.

A writer with a camera and the ability to make first-class photos can earn a living doing commercial writings of various kinds. Good photos help greatly in selling manuscripts to trade journals and other commercial publications, and editors will often buy material they don't even like too well if there are good photos to be had with the stories.

Some writers-photographers are free-lance journalists. They equip their automobiles with telephones, CB radios, and police-band radios and cruise all day, picking up police calls and speeding to the scene of an event where they believe they can get good photos and a story—or even just good photos. Eventually, many of these become well known to local newspaper editors and are even hired by telephone to cover events coming up spontaneously on the police bands, when the newspaper can't get a staff person out in time. (For these fellows, the car telephone is a must!)

A good newspaper feature story can be sold over and over. Newspapers do not pay especially high rates for a story—perhaps as little as $25 for a fair-size feature. But the typical newspaper editor wants exclusive rights only in his own circulation area and has no objections to your selling the story to other newspapers in other cities or states. If you have a story that is appropriate to other cities, you may be able to sell the same story to as many as a half-dozen editors. And, of course, that applies to photos also.

If you are a photographer, you will ultimately build a large file of stock photos, and these become a valuable property, once it becomes known that you have a collection of stock photos and will sell prints.

There are several other ways you can earn money with your camera. For one, store owners often pay for photos of their own displays. Real estate agents and owners of homes up for sale will often pay to have a good photo or series of photos made of the properties. "Gala openings" of new stores, banks, and other businesses are often good for photo services. And if owners don't want the service, you may find some of the trade journal editors interested in buying photos of such events or of unusual sales promotion ideas, such as novel displays and novel sales.

If you want to pursue this path, start by doing whatever writing and/or photography jobs you can get. Soon enough, you'll find a field in writing/photography that fits you comfortably, and you'll begin to specialize, as many writers do eventually.

Peter Weaver is a Washington-area free-lancer who specializes in consumer information. He writes a syndicated column on the subject and does a few minutes on a Washington news program once every week, among other things. In his own book, *You, Inc.* (Doubleday, New York, 1973), Weaver describes a problem he had with a new station wagon which so upset him that he started looking into consumer problems about warranties and repairs, and branched out into consumer problems generally. He describes his book as "a detailed escape route to being your own boss"; in fact, that's the subtitle of the book. Originally a journalist, with experience on newspapers and news/business magazines, Weaver found himself vaguely uncontented with earning a living on someone's payroll, taking orders he often didn't agree with. He began to break out by starting a spare-time business column about Latin America, one of the foreign scenes he was familiar with, having worked in it as a correspondent. His little business, *Weaver Reports,* won a few subscribers, didn't show a great deal of profit, but gave him a psychological payoff he needed: it proved he could do something in his line of work on his own. Ultimately, when he decided to break out of being someone's employee, he went into his consumer column and from there branched into some related fields, such as how to start a small business. Which is how I happened to meet him, when he interviewed me for an article he had been commissioned to do for the new business magazine, *Successful Business*.

In introducing the reader to his book, Weaver comments that he'll "never go back" (to working for someone else), that he's made a lot of mistakes, but they're *his* mistakes, "not some other dummy's mistakes."

SOME PITFALLS TO BE WARY OF

Many large corporations require new employees to sign agreements to ensure the corporation's "shop rights," as they are referred to, if the corporation is in some technology or manufacturing business. These agreements generally mean that the company claims ownership of any bright new ideas or inventions you come up with while in their employ, *even if you developed the idea or device in your own spare time*. But even if you leave the corporation and start a business of your own, with a bright new idea or patent, your former employer may very well claim that you developed the idea or patent while in his employ.

There really is no good protection against this situation, except a sufficient lapse of time between the time you leave an employer and the time you file for patent or begin marketing your new idea. Otherwise, you may find yourself in a legal fight you cannot win, against the greater power of the corporation.

It is wise, when accepting a position which involves signing such agreements, to examine everything you sign most carefully, and be sure that you are willing to be bound in this manner.

If you are in the business of selling your ideas—and ideas

per se are not patentable or copyrightable—it is quite difficult to sell them without revealing them, of course, and in revealing them there is always the danger that you have already given away that which you have to sell. One way to afford yourself at least some protection is by the disclosure agreement. In this agreement, you will have described the essence of your idea and provided a contract form which binds the party to whom you have disclosed the idea to pay you royalties, or whatever compensation you have agreed on, if the other party utilizes your idea. This is not the most satisfactory protection in the world, but will at least give you a place to stand if the other party attempts to use your idea without compensating you. Of course, it would be wise to have a lawyer draw up the contract form for you to make it as binding as possible yet not obligate the other party should he not wish to buy your idea.

A trademark may be registered with the Patent Office, which confers sole rights to its use upon you. However, the law requires you to protect your own trademark by not permitting anyone to use it as a verb (a trademark is always a noun) or to print it without the symbol ® (for "Registered") or an asterisk and footnote which says "Registered Trademark" or "TM." "Cellophane" was once a registered trademark, but Du Pont lost the rights to it by permitting others to misuse it, and many other trademarks became common nouns and verbs through the same process. Should anyone utilize your trademark in an unauthorized way, you are required to protest immediately in order to discharge your obligations to protect your own trademark.

Although you may copyright any combination of words in a text of any kind, you cannot copyright titles. Anyone may "steal" your title, just as you may take anyone else's title, should it appeal to you. However, if you have a title for a periodical and you feel the need to protect it, you can probably register it as a trademark, which will then give you the exclusive rights to its use.

In general, do not rely on "gentleman's agreements,"

sealed with a handshake. Perhaps there was a time when this was a valid and reliable way to seal a business agreement, but if so, it no longer is. And that is not only because the other party may choose not to honor the agreement later, either. (Even a written agreement is of dubious value if the other party does not mean to fully honor it.) Memories are faulty, and it is most hazardous to trust to memory. Contracts are written to document and spell out the details of the agreement, as well as to bind each party legally. If the other party is unwilling to enter into *written* agreement with you, that itself is a danger sign. There is absolutely no sound reason for not entering into written agreement if two parties are dealing in good faith.

15

SOME IDEAS THAT HAVE WORKED

Making money by the barrel

Under federal law, whiskey must be aged in new, charred oak barrels. They cannot be used again, except for storing grain neutral spirits (for example, vodka) or for aging what must be called "corn whiskey," for which the market is rather limited. So these costly oak barrels are of little use to distillers after their first use.

A gentleman in Maryland happened to acquire a few of these used whiskey barrels and decided to see if he could sell them. He found they sold rather readily to stores, which wanted to use them for displays, and to individuals, who used them for storing things and moving. He soon found out, also, that the furniture manufacturers would take quite a few from him as frames for making barrel-shaped furniture.

He soon discovered, however, that many customers wanted half-barrels, which made fine planters. In fact, the demand for half-barrels was even brisker than the demand for whole barrels. He thereupon developed a power saw to cut the barrels into equal halves. (The design of that saw is a closely held secret.)

Today, his principal problem is finding enough barrels. He can sell all the used oak whiskey barrels he can get and still not entirely satisfy the demand.

Anxiety pays off

A student working his way through college came up with a novel idea: a "survival kit" for fellow students cramming for finals. In the kit were cookies, Alka Seltzer, instant coffee, and other necessities. He solicited other students' parents by mail and delivered the kits to the students at $10 each. During the semester he managed to earn $10,000.

Specialty publishing

That same student who sold "survival kits" for final examinations learned that most colleges lose money on alumni directories and don't particularly relish publishing them anyhow. After graduation, this student entered into the business of publishing such directories, and flourished almost from the start.

The more it changes . . .

The French have their own way of saying that there is nothing new under the sun: "the more it changes, the more it is the same." There's good evidence for it, too. In medieval times, few commoners were literate. Some of those who were became "public scribes." For a few coins, they would write letters or other documents for other commoners. A Chicago woman ran a small classified advertisement, offering to write letters for those who hate to do so—any kind of letter, from love notes to letters of rage and outrage. To her amazement, her telephone began to ring almost immediately and hasn't stopped since. She charged $2.50 per page, and the idea is catching on elsewhere. Lots of people hate to write letters at all, some fear they can't do it well, others are too timid to tell someone else off.

Perhaps the woman was inspired by a young fellow in Toledo who offered to make a tell-'em-off telephone call to anyone you care to name, at $5 each, plus tolls, of course, for toll calls. He reported having all the work he could handle. But a Florida woman with a good singing voice came up with still another wrinkle, patterned after the now defunct singing telegram, no doubt: for $7.50 (plus tolls, if appropriate), she'll call and sing greetings to your friends and loved ones.

Almost-ready-made correspondence courses

Education and training are booming these days, and a great many people are taking home-study (correspondence) courses in a variety of trades, from office skills to electronics. One enterprising man came up with a simple way to assemble correspondence courses. He buys well-detailed how-to-do-it books at wholesale and in quantity, takes them to his local printer and has the spines cut off, then assembles the chapters into individual lessons, to which he adds examinations he makes up.

Another man buys used correspondence courses from students who have completed their studies and resells them as used courses. He reports doing a brisk trade in these.

Arts and crafts

The surge of covered shopping malls has given great impetus to arts and craft shows. Most malls have several such events a year. Individual artisans offer their products, using folding tables. Most such shows are arranged through an entrepreneur who makes the deal for all the open space in the mall, then recruits the individual exhibitors. Among the products usually found are macrame, wooden ware, ceramics, glass, toys, clothing, coins, stamps, antiques, brass, imports, and a variety of other specialty items. For some, such shows are good for extra money, second incomes they earn moonlighting; for others, it's a full-time business, and they travel around the country from mall to mall. One woman who makes a full-time business of it sells coffee tables and lamps made of cypress slabs, which are finished with a hard plastic surface that is transparent and reveals the natural beauty of the wood. Another exhibitor is an artist who creates three-dimensional objects of burlap, which he stiffens with some substance and shades by charring slightly with a blowtorch. Those who make a full-time business of such shows usually have a van or panel truck and exhibit at flea markets, fairs, and other such places, as well as at shopping malls. Some entrepreneurs who rent the space and book the exhibitors have exhibits of their own.

Valet parking on city street

A group of college students in Washington are taking advantage of crowded city streets to earn a little money every weekend. They arrange with those hosting parties to provide a valet parking service for arriving guests. The host pays the students a fee, based on the number of guests expected. The students take the cars from the guests, issue tickets, and find legal parking spaces. When the guests leave, the students fetch the cars. No charge to the guests, although tips are accepted.

Consignment shops

Some entrepreneurs, taking advantage of the popularity of arts and crafts, start consignment shops. The artisans leave their goods with the merchant on consignment, the dealer sells them, pays the owner when the items are sold. Consignment shops work at discounts (wholesale) of 20 to 40 percent, depending on the type of item. Twenty percent is acceptable for fast-moving and repeat items; otherwise, it is difficult to turn a profit at less than 40 percent.

Custom writing service

Not only companies and other large organizations hire free-lance writers; many individuals have need for such help. In addition to their needs for resumes and letter writing, individual customers often have need for help with such writing chores as speeches, briefing papers for committees they serve on, presentations, and a variety of other things, often unexpected. Small, classified advertisements can bring a surprising number and variety of small writing assignments.

Printing brokerage

A little-known occupation is that of printing broker. It's a middleman business that provides a useful service to both the printer and the printing customer. Many individuals engage in this, but there are also some rather large firms in this business. The printing broker has a simple business: he or she sells printing to the customer at the normal retail price, orders it from the proper printer at the wholesale price, and keeps the difference. There are at least two ways to enter this business, neither requiring any front-end capital investment.

There are several large printing firms that operate on a national basis and do all their selling through dealers or brokers. They will furnish you with a sales kit, with all the samples and selling prices listed, and you then represent the firm as a sales representative.

However, you can also make arrangements with local printers, working out your retail and wholesale prices. But you will probably need to make arrangements with several printers, because few printers, if any, do all kinds of work. Some firms will print only brochures, manuals, circulars, and other everyday work, and will not handle "fancy" work, such as engraved wedding invitations or embossed business cards. This is, for most printers, "specialty" printing, and even when one of their regular customers requests business cards, they pass the order on to a printer who does such work (usually one of the out-of-town, large firms) and earn a discount. (That is, they act as printing brokers themselves, in these cases.) Then, too, there is printing work that requires special equipment to be done efficiently—snap-out business forms are a good example of this.

For the printer, using a broker has the advantage of providing him with a commission salesman, in effect. But, even better, he does not have to do all the billing and keep track of all those accounts: you pay him and bill your customers.

The customer benefits, too, in that you call on him and, unless the order is being shipped to him from an out-of-town plant, you generally deliver the work. He has the convenience of your service, and does not even have to pay extra for that convenience.

In practice, some printing brokers are even able to bid competitively on large printing jobs (such as government jobs) and win them.

Garage sales

If you've never gone to a garage sale or yard sale, take the time to visit one. Most are miniature flea markets: a variety of items are displayed there, some quite useful, others appearing to be worth more as scrap metal or scrap paper than as useful objects. Yet, a surprisingly large number of people will pay out crisp dollars for things which you might have thrown away as used up or no longer of interest to anyone.

Most people who hold garage sales or yard sales are cleaning out their long-stored, accumulated "junk." About to throw things out, they are prompted somehow to stop and consider whether they might recover a fraction of the original acquisiton cost by holding a public sale.

Many people have discovered to their delight that they can get more than they thought they could, and they can sell many things they considered worthless—an old console radio that no longer works, some tarnished old flatware, a collection of wide—or narrow—neckties, grandmother's old shawl, old-fashioned kitchen chairs. Some have been so successful at their first sale that they have made a business of garage sales. Having sold out all their own old stuff and gotten some idea of what old junk will bring, they begin to hunt down and buy others' old possessions and accumulate enough for another sale.

If you do not have a yard or garage, such an enterprise is still available to you: almost every area today has at least one nearby flea market, usually held on Saturdays or Sundays, sometimes in an open field, sometimes in a covered mall of some sort. The entrepreneur who arranges such flea markets rents space to the individual exhibitors, usually at such small prices as $5 or $10.

Collection services

In these days of booming inflation and buying on credit, the need for collection services has grown steadily, as have government regulations controlling collection practices. Collection agencies are usually assigned accounts to collect only after the creditor has about given up trying and is willing to salvage whatever is possible. Therefore, a creditor assigning an account for collection will pay anywhere from 25 to 50 percent of the amount due to the collector.

In what might be considered the "traditional" collection service, the collector must be quite persistent and firm; remember that these are accounts in which all efforts by the creditor have failed to produce the payment. It's not a job for the faint-hearted.

Most collection agencies first send a series of collection letters and notices, the first politely inquiring, the series becoming firmer and harsher, to the point where they promise (or threaten) legal action. Those efforts failing, the collection agency then usually resorts to the telephone to make personal contact.

Since you are working on, probably, one-third to one-half the amount due, as your own fee, you may be able to negotiate a settlement for something less than the full amount. For example, if you can settle a $100 debt for $80 and you are working on one-half, you still earn $30 for yourself, while the creditor is happy to get even $50 and the debtor is glad to get out from under at a saving of $20.

Collection-letter service

One man earned a great deal of money with a variation of the collection service, while at the same time risking nothing—not even his time pursuing hopeless collection problems. Instead, he sells a collection-letter service, and is paid "up front" for his service, without risking anything or being responsible for collecting anything.

His service is providing that series of collection letters and notices, and he sells the service primarily to doctors, lawyers, dentists, and other professionals (as well as many small-business owners) who simply do not have the time or desire to develop their own collection systems and who do not want to turn their accounts over to collection agencies.

Initially, he developed a series of several letters and notices, which are now standard. He packages the series in a quantity sufficient to cover collection efforts on a number of accounts—usually 50 (that is, the package contains 50 of each letter or notice)—along with instructions and a record-keeping system. He sells this package for $150, to be sent out by the customer. He reports that the package is easy to sell (he uses commission salespeople) and highly profitable. And he lives in a home and in a style that bears out his claim!

Although he does not offer additional services, a variation of this idea would be to offer such a package *and* the option of handling all the mailing too, for an additional fee.

Guide books

When the Washington, D.C., "Metro"—high-speed subway and above-ground electric cars—opened, a young couple got a bright idea. There were already several guides to Washington-area restaurants, theaters, and other recreational facilities being published, but how about such a guidebook geared to the convenience of the new Metro stations, for those who wanted to use the Metro to go out for the evening? It was a high-risk enterprise, but the couple managed to put out the first edition for an initial $10,000 investment. It proved to be a successful idea, and the enterprise is now reported to be in a desirably liquid condition.

Two booming businesses today are consulting services and seminars. The consulting business alone, it is estimated, currently accounts for about $3 billion of the gross national product and there are several multimillion-dollar seminar-giving organizations. Each of these fields appears to merit its own chapter.

16

THE SEMINAR BUSINESS

Seminars are today a burgeoning business. Originally an academic device to conduct special training or orientation sessions, seminars are increasingly sponsored and operated by for-profit organizations and individuals. If handled properly, they are characterized by low risk and high profits.

For some reason, people are more likely to pay out $100 or more for a seminar than $25 for a book, although the book may contain several times more information than will be presented at the seminar! Perhaps this reflects a growing reluctance of people to read, or a common lack of confidence in being able to learn from reading alone. Perhaps still another reason, in some cases, is that the employee whose firm sends him or her to a seminar looks forward to the experience—traveling, meeting other people, and so on.

Whatever the reason, experience indicates that seminars do attract participants in large numbers, and are usually profitable.

You can create a seminar on a great many subjects, and you can develop seminars to attract individuals as individuals or as employees of organizations. Both methods obviously work. However, some seminar topics are by their very nature suited to seminars for individuals, acting as individuals; some are well-suited to companies that will send employees to attend; and some may be adapted to either application.

Seminars to teach people how to start a small business, lose weight, buy real estate (residential, that is), and write a resume to get a better job are obviously aimed at individuals in their private capacity—it is not likely that a company will send its employees to a seminar to help them lose weight or learn how to seek a better job! (Although there are exceptions.) On the other hand, companies often send employees to seminars on how to write proposals for contracts, conduct labor negotiations, learn to cope with federal regulations, and dozens of other topics that will help them become more effective in their jobs.

There are seminars which are attended both by individuals who have paid for their own attendance and by people who have been sent to attend by their companies. Speed reading is one topic that fits into this category, but there are others. An individual might want to learn how to type more rapidly, but a company will often send its employees to such classes, as it will to seminars and/or workshops on effective writing, advertising techniques, and other business skills which benefit the company as well as the individual.

In selecting topics on which to conduct seminars, then, you will want to consider whose needs are best served by your offering.

HOW TO RECRUIT PARTICIPANTS FOR SEMINARS

This is another chicken-egg problem. There are two different ways of soliciting seminar attendance, with one best suited to soliciting the individual paying for his own attendance, and the other more effective in persuading organizations to send employees. Ergo, if you decide to design a seminar for individuals, you are pretty much married to an advertising plan which works for individuals. But if you are already married to some specific advertising/solicitation method, you are more or less compelled to devise a seminar program in accordance with the dictates of that approach.

There are two basic approaches to advertising and soliciting attendance: using mass media, such as newspapers, radio, and TV; and approaching selected targets via direct mail. To solicit organizations, direct mail works well and is the favored way by far. It has the advantage of enabling you to target your appeal to the best prospects—say, nonprofit associations, aerospace companies, insurance brokers, or whatever. You can rent mailing lists for almost any category of business, and it is not especially difficult, even, to compile lists of your own.

Mailing lists of the best-prospect individuals are much more difficult to get: lists of individuals tend to be more general in nature, and it would be difficult to compile or rent such a list, except in some specialized cases. Therefore, for soliciting individuals to attend seminars, mass media work much better.

It is not uncommon for organizations soliciting seminar attendance to mail out as many as 50,000 advertising brochures at a time to bring out from 40 to 150 participants. The most common practice, when direct mail is used, is to print an expensive, multicolored brochure and mail it under bulk-mail rates to rented lists. The cost for such a mailing is likely to run quite high. There are three costs: printing, postage, and list rental (not to mention labor). Such mailings will probably run to $250 to $300 per 1,000, running up a total bill of $12,000 to $15,000. Quite a front-end investment.

That is what accounts for the high cost of many seminars—averaging something like $400, or even more, for a two-day seminar. In most cases, it would be almost impossible to charge less without losing money. Yet, there are successful seminars conducted at rates of $95 to $125 for a one-day session. How is this possible?

SOME VITAL STATISTICS ABOUT SEMINAR COSTS AND REVENUES

It has been the experience of many seminar entrepreneurs and mail order dealers that bulk mail is not a bargain. Although the per-piece rate for bulk mail is less than one-half that of first-class postage, many bulk-mailers have found that the response is so much less as to make bulk mail a dubious bargain, in these days of high printing costs and high cost for list rentals.

The fact is that some seminar operators have been able to draw as many as 30 to 60 attendees from a mailing of less than 3,000 by using first-class mail and stuffing the brochure and other sales literature into an envelope instead of by mailing it flat and *announcing* that it is advertising matter. Let's look at the costs for doing it this way:

3,000 pieces, first class @ 15¢:	$450
Printing, black ink only (approx.):	200
List rental:	150
	$800

With this kind of cost, it takes only about 8 to 10 attendees, at $100 to $125 each, to recover all costs. Anything above that is profit.

It is possible, too, to compile several thousand names, which you then *own* and can use over and over, saving the list rental cost.

A hotel room to accommodate about 50 people will cost you from about $40 to $100, depending on day and location. Coffee service runs about $10 per gallon, and you will need 2 to 3 gallons, for most sessions.

It is possible—and it is being done by many seminar operators—to get total costs down to about $300 per seminar, which means that you can recover all your costs with the first 3 to 4 attendees! Here are some cost-saving methods.

Schedule and announce several sessions of your seminar in each mailing so that you distribute printing and mailing costs over perhaps a half-dozen sessions.

Order coffee by the gallon rather than by the estimated number of attendees.

Check in advance on best days with several hotels in your area. Some charge less on weekdays than on Saturdays. (However, if you are appealing to individuals as individuals, you will find Saturday a much more popular day than a weekday, because most of these people have jobs.)

In your mailings, ask recipients to pass on literature, if they can't use it, to someone else who may be interested. Also, ask recipients to let you know if they want to be notified of future sessions, if they can't attend this one, and use names obtained this way for special mailing lists.

Don't go overboard in your printing costs. It's not necessary to go for expensive multicolored brochures—as long as your brochure looks professional, it can be in black ink on a decent-quality white or pastel stock.

Organize your brochures so that nothing changes in the next printing except the dates and places of the sessions. In fact, an even better plan is to put the dates and places on a separate card, and don't change the brochure at all, once you have developed one which produces good results. Then you can print it in very large quantity at much better prices.

Most seminar operators establish an at-the-door admission price and offer some discount for advance registration. If you are using direct mail, include a registration form in your mailing. You'll get most of your money "up front" that way, and you'll have a better idea of how many attendees you can expect.

HOW ORIGINAL SHOULD YOUR SEMINAR IDEA BE?

Ideas for seminars are no different from those for any other business. If the seminar is about a really new and different subject, you have the old problem of resistance to new ideas. What probably works best is an accepted, well-established idea with a new twist to give it special appeal.

Government Marketing News's seminars on proposal writing were done that way, with great success. Seminars on proposal writing are not uncommon, and many are offered every year by large organizations. Most of them are oriented to proposals by high-technology companies pursuing technical business with such government organizations as the Defense Department and its military organizations, the Department of Transportation, the Department of Energy, NASA, and other high-technology federal agencies. But *Government Marketing News* took a different approach to proposal-writing seminars:

1. The seminar was announced as being on "proposalmanship," with emphasis on the *strategies* of winning rather than on proposal writing per se.
2. The seminar was generalized so as to be appropriate to *any* kind of organization, bidding for *any* kind of work. (Most others focus on defense contracts.)
3. The brochure was kept relatively brief and to the point, instead of being loaded down with so many technical details as to frighten prospects off.
4. A sales letter accompanied the brochure, with a "routing slip" printed at the head of the letter so as to suggest routing the literature around to different departments of the company.

In a first test, only 800 pieces were mailed, for a one-day session at $75. The mailing produced 54 participants! The biggest mailing used was 3,000, and the smallest turnout was 20 participants. (By this time, the price had been raised to $95.)

The main idea was to offer to teach *proposalmanship*—the art of winning through strategy. It was new enough and different enough to draw attention, yet familiar enough to enable the prospect to recognize his own need.

HOW TO CONDUCT A SEMINAR

A seminar is a study group, usually on a specialized subject or advanced aspect of a subject—a learning session. Presumably, the seminar leader—or leaders, if there are several—is (are) expert in the subject. Typically, the seminar is largely lecture, with participation by attendees in the form of questions and discussions. Participant exercises may be included, and are often a great help in sustaining interest.

Some seminars are all-day lecture sessions, which is acceptable if the leader is an interesting lecturer and has the instinct for sensing the attendees' needs and interacting accordingly. Otherwise, although the leader may indeed be expert in the subject, the lectures should be brief and relieved frequently with question-and-answer sessions, exercises, and other activities.

Participants should be encouraged to ask questions, and the session should include discussions.

Handouts or a manual of some sort should be provided. Reference to material handed out may be made, but the leader should not use the exact material in the handout, nor read from the handout material. The handout material is for reference, both during and after the seminar.

Visuals should be used—posters, transparencies, slides, or some other such attention-centering aids.

SPEAKERS' FEES

The matter of speakers' fees is pretty much an individual problem. Obviously, if you are going to pay high fees to speakers and use a number of speakers, your costs will go up sharply and you will be forced to establish a seminar registration fee high enough to cover these costs. That, in turn, means that you will have to make a larger (and costlier) promotion effort to bring out participants at the higher fees.

Our own choice has been to keep costs down to enable us to operate seminars at relatively modest prices. It is possible, we have observed, to get speakers at small cost, often at no cost. Government officials are often available at no cost except the cost of lunch and transportation reimbursement. If your topic lends itself to the interests of either federal or local government, the government will usually make a speaker available. You can, of course, offer the speaker a small "honorarium," if you choose to, but in many cases the official will decline even that, since he is already on the public payroll and is likely to consider it unethical to accept any kind of fee. Many companies will make speakers available, in the same manner, if they believe the "exposure" of their company is good advertising for them.

For example, one local organization always has a few

speakers from government bureaus, and usually induces a few consultants to speak for a token honorarium. The consultants are encouraged to distribute their own cards and brochures, which is their principal motivation for devoting their time.

A typical honorarium would be something on the order of $25 to $50.

ANATOMY OF A SUCCESSFUL ADVERTISING CAMPAIGN

Frank Tennant, to whom we have referred earlier, runs frequent seminars on how to launch and operate a successful consulting practice. Frank is a highly methodical and thorough person who operates in a highly professional manner. Hence, when I asked his cooperation in revealing some of the background behind his seminar promotion, he was kind enough to offer me his complete layout and the history of his campaign. Here, in his own words, is his explanation, complete with copies of the space advertisements he runs in newspapers:

> I have always had my ads done by a professional graphic design artist, and furnished to me in multiple repro proofs—the same glossy paper, good camera-ready quality that I am sending you. Then all the newspapers do is put in the insert regarding date, time, hotel, etc. This ensures consistency of typography, lessens likelihood for error (the only thing the paper can get wrong is the insert they typeset), and is generally easier when one is sending ads to papers in various cities.
>
> [Figure 15a] was my original ad for my consulting seminar. [Figure 15b] is the same ad, with a typical insert shown.
>
> [The ad shown in Figure 16] was my first revision. I had several things I wanted to do here. First, I directed the use of smaller type, with the overall idea (obviously) of a smaller ad, to save expense. I also removed the seminar fee from the ad. Having it already on the ad makes it difficult to change prices. Now, my seminar fee, which has gone up several times, is always put in as part of the insert. I also had what I consider to be the excellent idea of adding the sentence, "Clip and save this ad." I

Figure 15a. Frank Tennant's first advertisement.

Figure 15b. The same advertisement with insert.

250 / *Profit from Your Money-Making Ideas*

Figure 16. Reducing the size to save advertising dollars.

SEMINAR:

HOW TO BECOME A SUCCESSFUL

FREE-LANCE
CONSULTANT

You too can earn up to $500 a day as a part-time or full-time consultant to business and government. This exciting seminar will teach you how to turn evenings, weekends and other free time into more income, with no capital investment. The seminar is conducted by Frank Tennant, successful executive consultant, speaker, editor and writer.

Who should attend? Anyone with a marketable skill gained through education or experience—managers, administrators, executives, college professors, graduate students, engineers, military officers, scientists, teachers, authors, designers, investors, editors, photographers, businessmen, and others.

You will learn: consulting requirements; structuring your business; finding consulting opportunities; selling your services; the consulting job interview; overcoming client resistance; keeping clients happy; grantsmanship; determining overhead; setting your prices; collecting fees; getting repeat business; becoming well known; avoiding bad business, avoiding giving away your services; working with other consultants; and a lot more.

Clip and save this ad. You owe it to yourself not to miss this outstanding seminar.

Registration begins 45 minutes prior to each seminar. Visa credit cards and checks accepted.

THE FRANK TENNANT CONSULTANCY
1301 Forestwood Drive, McLean, Virginia 22101
(703) 893-8757

know that many people do it, too. I think this helps when one is not advertising every day. If the interested prospect clips the ad and saves it, he has a reminder—even if he doesn't attend the particular seminar advertised. If he comes upon the cut-out ad weeks later, he is likely to call or write about the data and time of the next presentation.

[The ad in Figure 17] was designed to be even smaller, to save space rates, by leaving out some of the words (the "Who should attend" portion) of the ad. I have come to the conclusion that the slight size reduction isn't worth it. Pointing out to people the various types of people who would be interested in the seminar is important.

[The ad in Figure 18 was] again designed to save space, and appeared in the same paper as one of the larger ads. My research and questioning of people who attended the seminar showed this

Figure 17. Reducing the size even further.

SEMINAR:

HOW TO BECOME A SUCCESSFUL
FREE-LANCE
CONSULTANT

If you have a marketable skill gained through education or experience, you can earn up to $500 a day as a consultant to business and government. This exciting seminar, conducted by Frank Tennant, successful executive consultant, will teach you how.
You will learn: consulting requirements, structuring your business; finding consulting opportunities; selling your services; the consulting job interview; overcoming client resistance; keeping clients happy; grantsmanship; determining overhead; setting your prices; collecting fees; getting repeat business; becoming well known; avoiding bad business, avoiding giving away your services; working with other consultants; and a lot more.
Clip and save this ad. You owe it to yourself not to miss this outstanding seminar.

Registration begins 45 minutes prior to each seminar. Visa credit cards and checks accepted.

THE FRANK TENNANT CONSULTANCY
1301 Forestwood Drive, McLean, Virginia 22101
(703) 893-8757

Figure 18. A small teaser ad.

SEMINAR:

HOW TO BECOME A SUCCESSFUL
FREE-LANCE
CONSULTANT

For details, see our ad in today's Finance section.

THE FRANK TENNANT
CONSULTANCY
1301 Forestwood Drive
McLean, Virginia 22101
(703) 893-8757

---

small ad not to be very effective (even though there are proponents of small ads around), and I rarely use it now.

[Figure 19 shows] another major revision. First, I added to

Figure 19. Final version of Frank Tennant's advertisement.

my list of types of people who should come, and put them in alphabetical order. Next, I put the subheads (*Who should attend?*) in boldface italics to make them stand out. Next, I took advantage of some excellent publicity I had in the *Washington Post*, by quoting from the article. Finally, I added a mention of the written handouts and the free question-by-mail privilege. This is the ad I still use today—a smaller version on Sunday when rates are higher, a bigger version on weekdays.

If you compare Tennant's first advertisement (Figure 15) with his current one (Figure 19) you can see how it has evolved, through constant testing—interviewing people, making changes, and measuring results of the changes. The basic text hasn't changed materially, but has been refined by adding subheads, set in boldface to gain special attention, and by adding several noteworthy items.

One thing you will note Tennant added was the notation that he is a former West Point professor. That adds to his credentials—a critically important point in this case, since he is asking readers to believe that he can teach them something they ought to learn.

A second point, which Frank notes in his remarks reproduced here, is the addition of more types of technical/professional specialists identified as those who should be interested—those whose skills may be put to work in a consulting capacity, that is. It's important, of course, that the largest number of readers possible be able to "identify" with an advertisement—that is, perceive that the advertisement is addressed to them, that it appeals to their own self-interests. (In the advertising profession, this is known as "positioning" the product.)

The subhead "You will learn:" is an especially important one. This gets down to *specifics,* and it is specifics, not generalities, which do the selling. "You too can earn up to $500 a day" is the *benefit* promised, which attracts attention and arouses interest, but to make the offer *credible,* to persuade the reader that you can and will *deliver* the benefit, you need the detail, the specifics.

Of course, the last paragraph is also important, especially since it quotes a newspaper story about Frank Tennant, "consultant to consultants." That adds greatly to Frank Tennant's credentials and credibility.

Finally, it was wise of Frank Tennant to specify the handout materials. No one likes to leave a seminar empty-handed. Part of the motivation in going is to get handout materials *not otherwise available*. That is one point Frank has not covered which would add value—*exclusivity* of the handout materials.

HOW BIG IS THE SEMINAR BUSINESS?

No figures are readily available on the dollar volume of seminars generally, but one Washington firm which started as a newsletter-publishing business today grosses about $4 million annually, running a variety of seminars virtually every business day of the year. While this firm has not abandoned the newsletter business, seminars are obviously its mainstay today. And it is worth noting that this firm prepares a special manual for each seminar, usually a rather thick manual, and makes no bones about the seminar manual being available to seminar attendees only: it will not sell the manuals separately for any price.

This firm also issues a certificate of completion to each attendee, a practice followed by many seminar promoters to add a bit more value to the session, especially when the seminar is designed to appeal to companies that send employees.

WHEN TO HOLD YOUR SEMINAR

The day of the week on which you schedule your seminar has much to do with its success—its appeal, that is. One large firm holding its first seminar found this out quickly. The company prepared a seminar on how to start and operate a small business, with obvious appeal to individuals rather than to large companies. It scheduled the same seminar—a one-day session—to run on two successive days, Friday and Saturday, in two Washington-area locations. And it promoted its seminar with mailings to leads generated through newspaper advertisements and radio spot announcements.

The Friday session did not do much better than break even, but the Saturday session was a financial success, producing a sound profit. Obviously, individuals, who are either already in a struggling, small business or still working at jobs, have some difficulty in being present on Fridays, a normal working day, but would far prefer to come to a session on Saturdays, when they are normally free.

On the other hand, attendees sent by companies are not eager to spend their day off at a seminar session, nor would companies want to pay overtime (which they would probably be legally bound to) for Saturday duty.

Even on weekdays—normal business days—Mondays and Fridays are usually bad days for seminars, particularly for those coming from out of town to attend. A Monday seminar means the attendee from out of town will have to travel on Sunday, and a Friday seminar means the attendee will be a bit late getting home to start the weekend, in addition to the inconvenience of traveling Friday evening, when airports are crowded and taxis are hard to get.

In practice, Tuesdays and Wednesdays generally prove to be the best days for one- or two-day seminars appealing to companies that will send employees, and Saturdays for seminars appealing to individuals who will pay their own way.

17

THE CONSULTING BUSINESS

If you missed the figure mentioned earlier, consulting is a $3 billion business today, according to the financial press. As in the case of seminars, the growth of the consulting business is probably the result of the increasing specialization of our age. In any case, the number of consultants and the work available for consultants increase steadily. But perhaps part of the reason is that the term itself has been broadened considerably in meaning, and virtually any specialist in virtually any field may be fairly termed a consultant today.

In its original use, a consultant was a specialist who was called in for advice only—consultants rendered counsel. Your family physician might call in a consultant to help him diagnose your illness. In the early days of transistors, when only a few specialists knew much about the new technology, one specialist made a regular appearance at the plants of various electronics firms to offer advice on the firms' problems concerning transistors and their use. In these days of energy problems, the government calls upon specialists from various firms to render advice on federal measures to conserve energy.

Today, many consultants do more than merely consult and render advice. Many *apply* their skills and do the work required. An artist might be called in to "consult" on creating a trademark or "logo" for a firm, but his contract will probably include the actual work to design the device. As a government contracting specialist, I am often called upon to give advice regarding efforts to sell to and contract with the government, but more often than not I will help prepare the bid or proposal. Hubert Bermont, who is a consultant in the field of publishing, reports his assignments as often including something more than merely rendering advice.

Consultants have got a bad name in some quarters, because many specialists—and even some generalists—have called themselves "consultant" when between jobs, hoping to pick up an assignment or two while seeking a new permanent position. Some wags insist that a consultant is anyone who is momentarily out of work. And some maintain that a consultant, whether of the permanent or temporary sort, is someone who borrows your watch to tell you what time it is.

THE HAZARDS OF CONSULTING

Consulting ordinarily requires no investment whatsoever, except perhaps for business cards announcing your proud profession and some advertising literature. Other than that, you are a consultant because you say you are. All that remains is to get some clients!

Many who venture into consulting do not long survive as consultants. Usually, if they have almost stumbled into the profession because they found a sudden demand for their help or suddenly found themselves divorced from their jobs, they soon discover the inherent feast-or-famine nature of the consulting profession. When they have a great many requests for help—their busy season—they are often forced to turn work away; they have no means for storing up reserves for what inevitably arrives: a slow season. Consulting, by its nature, is a necessity of the moment, and clients usually cannot wait for an appointment weeks hence. That's an inherent difficulty of the service, although there are exceptions.

By far the vast majority of those who decide to set up shop as independent consultants eventually find themselves seeking a position again. The feast-or-famine characteristic makes it impossible for them to survive in the profession. At least, they cannot survive as individual consultants.

One way out of the dilemma is to build up a consulting firm which can handle overloads of work. The problem with this solution usually is a financial one: the individual cannot support a payroll until there is work for everyone, but often he cannot even support himself until he can build a backlog of work. Few individuals start consulting firms successfully.

Some alternatives that work

One way consulting firms have begun successfully is through the teaming together of several consultants, as "associates." Each is independently established—or at least has a number of contacts (business sources). They form a loose association, in which they share a suite of offices, each handling his own work and paying his share of all expenses for the suite, and all of them working together when the combination is successful in winning large assignments that provide work for everyone.

Such arrangements can work out when each individual can find enough work for his own needs, initially. Ultimately, they can begin to work as a firm, although they are usually not truly a single firm in the beginning.

Another way many consulting firms have begun is by diversification. Some of the leading consulting firms were originally accounting firms or employment agencies. As they found markets for more sophisticated services, they broadened their bases of operation to include a variety of specialized services.

For the individual, consulting alone is usually not enough

Most individual consultants who succeed and survive do so by having more than one iron in the fire. Some are university professors with schedules providing adequate free time for consulting—a not unusual arrangement for professors. Others have long-term or semipermanent consulting contracts, which provide enough assured income to permit them to build a following. Still others run seminars, lecture, publish newsletters, and do several other things which fill in the lows of consulting.

Probably the most natural combination of talents, skills, and abilities for the typical consultant is lecturing and writing, in addition to whatever his technical/professional specialties are. With good abilities to speak and write, the typical consultant can usually broaden his base of activities to include several sources of income, all of which he may lump together as "consulting."

A FEW CONSULTING SPECIALTIES

Almost any skill or specialized experience and knowledge can serve as the base for consulting. Hubert Bermont, mentioned already, counsels clients in book publishing. Many of his clients are associations that wish to publish a book. (He also conducts successful seminars on the subject and publishes books of his own.) Frank Tennant is a specialist in speaking and in preparing presentations generally, and counsels others in the arts. Frank conducts seminars on how to be a successful consultant. I and a few other fellows are consultants in how to write proposals and win government contracts. But there are dozens of business consultants in accounting, inventory control, marketing, safety, energy, and a variety of other fields.

The fields in which consultant services are most appropriate (hence, most likely to be in demand) are those requiring highly specialized skills and experience, especially those which represent modern problems. For example, an industrial plant must cope with problems of federal regulations concerning many things, such as energy, safety, and environmental pollution. Unless the company is large enough to hire permanent, on-staff specialists, it is most likely to want the services of a good consultant to help management find a way through these labyrinths of regulations and requirements.

The principle is very much the same as the principle of sales and advertising: everyone has problems, and if you can relate what you offer to direct and effective help in solving one or more of those problems, you can't help but arouse a fair degree of interest. If you can help with the most severe problems, you will meet with the lowest degree of sales resistance—inevitably, these two factors have an inverse relationship.

To be a successful consultant, then, consider first whether your service involves specialized problems that require specialized skills or experience. Are they serious problems which the prospective clients cannot ignore but must find solutions for? Are they problems for which the prospective clients almost surely need some outside assistance—that is, do they indeed require special abilities? And can you really help solve those problems?

These are some main considerations, but there are others. For one, are the skills you can offer truly rare and unusual, or are they readily available? Or can you focus your offering on some rare aspect of your field? For example, the woods are full of computer-system specialists today, and it is not at all difficult to find people who represent themselves as programmers, analysts, and the like. But what are the lesser known specialties within the specialized field, where the know-how you have is not too commonly available, yet is in some demand? Word processing? Microprocessing? Micrographics?

In my own area of consulting, for example, there are many people, some of them consultants, who know how to write and assemble a proposal for a contract. I deliberately avoided competing with those fellows, but selected an aspect of the field in which I have yet to discover any serious competition—the *strategies* of the successful proposals.

It's an age of specialization, and there are specialists within specialties today. Not long ago, one could be an electronics specialist, but today electronics is so diversified that the field is full of specialists in terms of equipment—radar, computers, videorecorders, and so on—and even within those equipment categories there is specialization. Within the special field of computers, for example, there are numerous specialties. Some are specialists in memory devices, others in microminiaturization, and still others in new devices, such as "bubble" memories.

Your field need not necessarily be a technological one, either. Today, the social sciences are so varied and specialized, with some consultants especially knowledgeable in drug or alcohol abuse, while others may have concentrated their efforts in urban blight or the problems of the aged.

A large part of success in consulting, then, is in the selection of the field of effort or identification of the types of problems you can solve.

SELLING YOUR SERVICES, OR GETTING CLIENTS

Consulting is a profession, and the most effective way of selling consulting services in our society is through the methods used by professionals. But, as in the case of seminars, you must first identify your targets, which in most cases are going to be government and business organizations of various kinds, although you should not rule out the possibility that your service may appeal to some individuals as well.

In my own field, I have never made a concentrated effort to seek consulting clients. Instead, they have appeared unbidden, as a result of other activities, during which I make no secret of the fact that I am a consultant and available as a consultant. Probably the most fruitful source of consulting contracts has been the seminar session: almost every seminar I have conducted has produced inquiries into my availability for consulting work. However, consulting assignments have also resulted from my newsletter and special reports which my firm publishes. And, once my consulting practice was under way, word-of-mouth recommendations have resulted in a number of assignments.

Hubert Bermont, in his book *How to Become a Successful Consultant in Your Own Field* (Bermont Books, Washington, DC 20005, 1978), reports his own problems in getting his first assignments. He tried advertising in trade journals related to his field and found that it simply didn't work. And, as he studied his "calling cards" (business cards), the thought occurred to him that they couldn't help him unless he did some "calling"!

His first effort was probably typical of most newly announced consultants: he got on the telephone and began to call his professional acquaintances. He learned soon enough that *that* wasn't going to produce a rush of orders.

He finally resorted to the dodge Mark Twain reported he had used once. Twain offered to work on a newspaper at no salary, and was accepted, on those favorable terms. After a few weeks, during which he demonstrated his abilities, he offered his resignation, pointing out that he could not afford to work longer for the "salary" he was getting, whereupon he was offered a salary to stay! Bermont did something along these lines, won his first assignment for pay, and was able to go on from there, although he had plenty of struggles still ahead of him.

Of course, one of your first moves must be to let it be known that you are a consultant, and, of course, you must also let some specifics be known about exactly what you offer to do—what kinds of problems you can solve, what specific services you offer to render, and so on.

As in any advertising, it is essential that you are as specific as you can be in suggesting the benefits you can bring to your clients. List the kinds of problems you solve and the kinds of results you can deliver. Use something more than the mere word "consultant" on your business card. My own card, in addition to showing my address and telephone number and stating "Government Marketing Consultant" under my name, says in the upper left corner "Proposals & Presentations" and, below that, "Custom Seminars." As you can see, it offers some specific services in the field of marketing to the government—or, more specifically, aiding clients in both marketing to the government and *learning how* to market to the government (as a natural adjunct of advising clients in the field of selling to the government, my work also entails training their own staffs to aid them in becoming more self-sufficient in the work).

Now there were those who counseled me against being so

specific. They thought that I should "protect" my position by making my work as mysterious as possible, with a view to compelling the client to call me back each time he wished to pursue a government contract. I reject that concept. It is my opinion that such a devious approach is self-defeating. The client pays me the rate I demand, and in my opinion is entitled to know exactly what I am doing for him so he can learn from me. In any case, I have had no reason to regret making that decision. I deplore the psychology of fear and insecurity that motivates some people to rely on secrecy, rather than ability, to safeguard their position.

Your cards and a small, discreet brochure should go out to everyone you know who might either use your services or be able to pass the word along to others. Telephone calls just to advise old acquaintances of your venture are in order too. *Don't* put your old friends and acquaintances on the spot by pressing them for business, however; that can only embarrass them and possible estrange them. Call simply to *announce* your venture.

Develop a mailing list of suitable prospects and mail your cards, with a letter and your brochure. But try to keep a dignified, professional image. Blatant advertising is as out of place here as it would be for a doctor or lawyer. What is appropriate is a dignified announcement that you are a consultant (perhaps the type of announcement that a doctor or lawyer uses when setting up a practice), along with some clear identification of what you can do, and a clear description of your qualifications—some impressive past positions and achievements, modestly presented as examples of what you have to offer. And if you have already handled a few consulting assignments (perhaps on a moonlight basis), you should list past clients. However, it is a good idea to call those past clients and get their approval of being so listed; some clients will resent being listed without their prior approval. Prospects are likely to call them, so you want to be sure that your clients will not be angered by learning of the listing in that manner for the first time.

The real key to getting business as a consultant lies in

being well known to the right people—"contacts," as many put it. The successful consultant is usually one who "gets around," belongs to various organizations, and meets people. Get involved in any associations or societies, attend all relevant conventions and trade shows, and pursue every means possible to meet the right people. Keep a list of people you meet. Get birthday and anniversary dates and send out cards on such occasions. Send out dignified advertising specialties, such as wallet-size calendars.

Some of these things will of themselves produce an occasional consulting assignment, but that is not the prime purpose—that is, it's not advertising in the usual sense, but a means of knowing many people and making people remember you.

Write articles for magazines—even letters to the editor have been known to help. (In one case I know of, a letter to the editor appearing in *Nation's Business* brought the author of that letter an invitation to write a book for a prominent publisher.) Volunteer articles for the newsletters or magazines of relevant associations. Offer to speak, without charge, at meetings. Have yourself identified as a consultant as often as possible, through such means.

All these activities do three things for you:

- They widen your own circle of business and professional acquaintances—people who know you personally.
- They widen the number of people who know your name—know of your existence and services as a consultant, even if they do not know you personally.
- They add to your prestige and credentials as a consultant—make you far more credible than you would otherwise be.

WHAT SHOULD YOU CHARGE?

A prospect walked into my office one day (he had called for an appointment) to discuss his needs for a consultant. He had come to Washington for the express purpose of selecting a consultant. After some discussion, he asked me point-blank, "What do you charge?"

I told him with equal frankness that my usual arrangement was by the day and my daily rate was $500.

"That must be the standard rate in Washington?" he responded. It was a question.

I admitted that I had no idea of what the "standard rate in Washington" was, if indeed there was such a thing as a standard rate. He had obviously asked the question of several others and been given the same quotation. I still doubt seriously that there is a standard rate for consulting, in Washington or anywhere else. I think the rate varies widely, depending on quite a number of factors:

The economics of your locality—cost of living and so on.

Your own overhead costs.

How rare your own specialty is and how much in demand it is.

Your own idea of your worth.

How badly you need the work.

The first time I ever took on a consulting assignment, I was actually assigned to the task by my employer, who accepted a consulting assignment from a client. He charged the client $200 a day, plus expenses (of course) for my time. I was flattered. It seemed like a huge value placed on my abilities, for those times. But it gave me the notion that it was the right price for my time, even years later, after inflation had worked some of its evils. I then reluctantly raised my daily rate to $300, expecting a great deal of resistance.

Little by little, I came to the realization that $500, which I later established as a fair rate, was far from excessive for what I did, for several reasons. First, there was the fact that there seemed to be no one else doing just what I did; at best, my competitors were offering a quite different service, although it was similarly named and identified. Additionally, it was never my practice to watch the clock, and many $500 "days" proved to be 12 or more hours long, and some of them were Saturdays and Sundays (I never asked for overtime or premiums for weekends and holidays). Finally, I did two other things, which made my fee more than reasonable: I did my level best to work things out with the client so that he did those things he could do and was willing to do (that is, he was not unknowingly paying me for doing things which did not really require my special skills), and my rate of "production" was exceptional—I produced more in a day than most people can produce in two or three days.

In actuality, perhaps the rate I asked was low, considering these factors. But there is one overwhelming factor controlling your rate, one I failed to mention in the listing I provided a few paragraphs ago. It's this: *what the customer is willing to pay.*

There are customers who will think that $100 a day is an exorbitant rate, and there are customers who will pay $1,000 a day. These are extremes, and you can't work to the extremes—you won't find a great many customers willing to pay you $1,000 a day, in most cases, and you can't afford to worry about the occasional customer who is unwilling to pay you a fair rate. You must settle on a rate you can live with (literally!), somewhere between the extremes.

Handling the question and negotiating

At some point, every prospective client is going to ask you "How much?" and some even lead off with that question. However, it is not good practice to begin the discussion with a quotation, nor is it good practice to ever *volunteer* a quotation. You should first discuss the client's need or problem and what you can do to help. If the client has led off with the request for quotation, you can usually postpone an immediate answer by saying something such as "Let's take a quick look at your problem (or need) first. Then I'll be able to give you a more intelligent answer."

The point is that if your client is strictly price shopping, quoting your rate is unlikely to arouse more of a response than a grunt and an "I'll let you know." You'll probably get no opportunity to sell your services at all—perhaps not even a chance to find out what the client's problem is.

When it is time, finally, to quote, be sure to *explain* your rate. Explain exactly what it means, what it covers, what it does not cover. In my own case, it has always been my practice to explain that "a day" does not mean an eight-hour period, that there is no overtime or premium pay involved, and that the "day" may not necessarily be continuous, but may be four two-hour sessions or two half-days, according to the client's needs.

This may seem like either generosity or foolishness on my part, but it has proved to be an effective selling technique for me, without causing me any problems I wouldn't have had in any case. It sweeps on from the flat statement of $500 per day, which would otherwise hang like an iron curtain between us. The customer would see nothing but that $500 times some number of days.

Once I have had a chance to look the job over carefully, it has also been my practice to furnish my clients an estimate of the time I'll require, and to guarantee that as a maximum. And in those cases where something I could not have anticipated arose to invalidate my estimate, I have had no difficulties in negotiating a change with my client—rarely, if ever, will a client object to your being thoroughly businesslike.

Of course, there are many other ways to price your services. You can price each assignment as a fixed-price job, you can charge by the hour, with or without overtime and holiday premiums, and so forth. How you charge depends entirely on what you want and what your clients will accept. But you should have some definite standards—*your* standards—and stick with them consistently. Charging different clients different rates leads to trouble, besides being tinged with a suggestion of dishonesty.

CONTRACTS

I have used contracts in some cases, but not in all. There have been some prestigious, large-company clients with whom I have done business several times, and with whom a verbal agreement was adequate. However, it is far better, for the typical case, to have some sort of written agreement. But a word of caution here: don't go overboard in this with an elaborate, multipage document, with seals and witnessed signatures. Such excesses often kill the deal entirely. A client who is led to think that he must have his lawyer present (who would sign such a document without his lawyer's approval?) or that you feel you must bind him thoroughly on paper for a relatively small sum of money is likely to fall back to think some more about doing business with you.

For most consulting assignments, a simple letter is entirely adequate, and you can use a form letter. It can be a single page, on your regular letterhead, addressed to your client, and stating the terms of your employment in simple language: what you are going to do, what you guarantee, what the client agrees to do, the rate or price agreed upon. At the bottom is "Accepted," and the two parties sign it and date the day of signing. In a few cases, the customer prefers to have the agreement on *his* letterhead. If so, let him use your form for guidance and have his own secretary type it up. It's that simple.

The point of the agreement is not to serve as a bulwark against default or as a platform from which to launch a lawsuit; it's to (1) document the terms of your agreement so you don't have to trust to memory (which often leads to later dispute) and (2) demonstrate the seriousness of intent. The existence of the agreement, informal though it is, is normally enough to ensure payment.

18

THE WONDERFUL WORLD OF MAIL ORDER

WHAT'S SO WONDERFUL ABOUT MAIL ORDER?

It is estimated that some two million eager hopefuls enter what is referred to as "mail order" every year. No one appears to have a good estimate of how many of those two million are still in mail order at the end of that year, but it is surely a tiny fraction; otherwise nearly everyone would soon be in mail order.

The fascination of the mail order business is the array of advantages of doing business by mail offers, along with the indescribable fun of opening a bundle of mail every morning and finding money in many of the envelopes. Those who have been in the mail order business for many years all seem to agree that the fun of doing that never wears off. The apparent (if not real) advantages of doing business by mail are these:

- The investment, at least for many mail order plans, is so small as to be virtually zero. Almost anyone can afford to try his hand at the game.
- There are no required business hours. The mail order aficionado can work whatever hours are convenient.
- There is no need for a business address or extra rent. You can operate a modest mail order enterprise in your own home—even in a small apartment.
- You can be as small or as large as you wish—do it full-time or in your spare time, as a living or for extra money.

- You can get rich without leaving your home (occasionally it has happened).
- You can sell some things by mail order which would be difficult to sell any other way.

All this suggests that there is something different or special about mail order—that it is a specific kind of business all its own. But there are some who do not agree with that. Let's have a look.

JUST WHAT IS "MAIL ORDER"?

Sears (formerly Sears, Roebuck & Co.) sells a great deal of merchandise by mail and was, in fact, based on that concept. Likewise, Montgomery Ward. Fingerhut is a large mail order dealer, as are several other firms whose business is conducted solely by mail.

Most publishers of periodicals, including magazines, newspapers, and newsletters, sell and distribute at least a portion of their output by mail. (Newsletters are usually sold and distributed entirely by mail.)

Thousands of small dealers operate small mail order enterprises from their own homes, selling little publications—newsletters, reports, manuals, and the like—and merchandise ranging from gift items to rubber stamps and printing.

All these enterprises are using mail as a primary means for reaching customers and selling to customers—even delivering to customers. Are all in the "mail order" business?

The answer to that is, of course, "Just what is meant by mail order?" There are those who maintain that mail order is no different from any other business, except that dealer–customer relations are entirely via the mails. Some maintain that anything that can be sold at all can be sold by mail, although that seems to stretch things a bit. And there are those to whom mail order is something special and different, and who feel that the mere fact that business is conducted through the agency of the world's postal services does not automatically qualify an enterprise as "mail order."

For our purposes, the precise definition does not matter. Some of the businesses described and discussed—for example, retail stores—could be mail order businesses, or they could be conducted by face-to-face sales encounters; others are almost necessarily conducted by mail, or they could not succeed. (It would be most difficult to market newsletters any other way and still turn a profit. On the other hand, what are the probabilities of selling automobiles by mail?) Let's deal with mail order as a *means* of making contact with customers and closing sales, recognizing that it is the only practical means for some purposes and totally impractical for others. In any case, it offers unique advantages, by its nature, while it also presents certain specific disadvantages, also by its nature. Let's consider those.

ADVANTAGES AND DISADVANTAGES OF MAIL ORDER

Many of the general advantages of doing business by mail have been covered already, especially the advantage of being able to start and operate a mail order business with little or no capital and little or no real overhead expense. But it also offers a few other business advantages:

- Anyone—even the smallest entrepreneur—can do business on a worldwide basis by mail.
- Some items that would be impractical to market any other way can be marketed successfully and profitably by mail.
- It is not absolutely necessary to have merchandise in stock. It can be a catalog business, with the entrepreneur accepting orders and having them filled by someone else, who does have the merchandise in stock.
- Payment is ordinarily "up front"—in advance of shipping the order or providing the service.

- There is no minimum size to a mail order operation; it can be as small as you wish.
- It is quite simple to diversify or even switch over to a completely different kind of offer if a given proposition is not working out well.

This is not to say that there are no disadvantages. There are, inevitably, a few drawbacks to this apparently idyllic entrepreneurial environment:

- It's more difficult to sell something by mail—essentially, sight unseen—than in personal, direct confrontation with a customer.
- In many cases, the cost of making each sale—the cost of getting a customer—is quite high, relative to the sale price.
- There is never an end to advertising and active solicitation of customers, as there may be in a retail-store operation; a slowdown or stoppage in sales effort and advertising inevitably results in an abrupt slowdown in sales.
- There are numerous small problems, such as that of bad checks. It is most difficult to take action on a bad check with a customer who is thousands of miles away.
- The U.S. mails are not a perfect medium of delivery. A percentage of your shipments inevitably go astray and are never heard from again, compelling you to make duplicate shipments.
- You hear much about unscrupulous and dishonest dealers, but there are also many dishonest customers who will swindle innocent dealers and are much more difficult to take action against. There are those who will order on a credit card and then demand that the bank cancel the charge, claiming either to have not received the merchandise or to have returned it. There are also those who make a practice of ordering books and reports, reading them swiftly, and then returning them for refund.
- Risks can be great, as when a large promotion doesn't

work out. Losing a large sum of money on advertising and direct mail is not like making a bad buy of goods. In a bad buy of goods, you at least have the merchandise, such as it is, and can retrieve *something*. When an ad or mail campaign goes astray, *all* is lost; there is nothing to salvage.

The fact that the list of disadvantages is longer than the list of advantages has no significance—it does not suggest that mail order is not a worthwhile enterprise, but only that it is not all peaches and cream, despite its many attractions. Quite the contrary, mail order has great fascination for small entrepreneurs, and has proved highly rewarding as a business. Moreover, it offers great opportunities for added sales to established businesses of many types.

Take the neighborhood retail store as an example. The business done by such an establishment is usually limited to the walk-in trade. That may be stimulated somewhat by advertising specials and sales of various kinds, and even by other special promotions, but the trade is still one of waiting for the customers to walk through the door, and is still severely limited by such factors as size and location. Expansion is generally through physical expansion of the store (that is, taking additional property next door and breaking through), moving to a larger and/or busier location, and/or opening branch outlets.

However, for many retail businesses, mail order is a possible way of expanding sales with little or no physical expansion of facilities or increase in basic overhead. If the merchandise offered is amenable to shipping via mail or other means, without excessive shipping costs, the proprietor of such an establishment can open an entirely new set of markets, covering the entire world, no matter his physical location.

There are, in fact, other benefits also accruing from expanding into mail order sales: by increasing sales volume without increase in rent and other such fixed costs, the operator of a small retail business reduces his overhead rate (proportion of overhead dollars to gross sales) and increases his buying power, getting added discounts. Ergo, profitability in general should increase.

In my opinion, the single greatest advantage in mail order is that by using direct-mail solicitations, you are not waiting passively for customers to come to you, but going out aggressively after the customer, seeking him out with individual, virtually personal appeals. In my own view, that gives you much more control over your business. In conventional retail sales, you advertise and open your doors every day, waiting for customers. That's a passive way of doing business, giving you only limited control of your business.

WHAT CAN BE SOLD BY MAIL?

It is perhaps true that almost anything that can be sold can be sold by mail. There have been and are successful mail order campaigns selling live lobsters and fresh frozen steaks by mail, for example. Many custom services—for example, resume writing and making rubber stamps—are sold by mail. Even real estate has been sold that way. Yet there are limits. To judge what you can sell successfully by mail, you must take into account your minimum costs for even the smallest mail order effort, the margin of profit you have to work with, the degree of price competition you can afford, the transportability of what you offer (can you ship an ice cream cone?), and other practical matters. Bear in mind, too, that you might find it practical to sell by mail to customers in your own general locality, but not in distant localities. That is, the shipping problems might militate against shipping across the country or to foreign destinations, yet shipping might not be prohibitively expensive or difficult for local orders. Of course, that's easily adjusted by mailing only to local prospects.

In general, those who represent themselves as mail order experts tend to stipulate that a good mail order item is one not readily available elsewhere. (Ballpoint pens would presumably not be a good mail order item because they are available everywhere in retail outlets.)

In fact, a great many ballpoint pens and other commonplace items *are* sold by mail every day. Exclusivity or availability of the item is only one of several considerations. There are others. Probably the principal one is price.

Ribbons for my typewriter, purchased either through the manufacturer or through my local office-supply outlets, cost me about $3 each. I purchase them from the Quill Corporation, in the Chicago area, at 40 to 50 percent below that price. Likewise many other items: I can save a great deal of money by buying most of my office supplies through mail order.

Quill Corporation started in 1956 as a one-man business in the basement of its founder's home. Today the corporation employs 275 people, occupies a large warehouse with its own computer system, and serves over 200,000 customers throughout the United States. Yet, Quill obviously does not operate on that almost traditional and supposedly obligatory 1:3 minimum markup. The answer to this is obvious: volume. Quill does enough volume to operate profitably on much smaller markups than 1:3.

There are at least two reasons Quill is able to do this successfully. First, it sells items which need neither hard-sell nor introduction to the buyer. The buyer knows what the items are, the prices are attractive, and the buyer already has a felt need for them. Second, most Quill customers will order again and again. With repeat business—that is, steady customers—even if the cost of getting the customer initially was high and the first order a net loss, repeat sales will more than compensate, over the long term.

The Quill Corporation obviously bases success on service. No matter how low its prices, customers will not be back to reorder if they are dissatisfied with the products or the service. As in the case of IBM, the company realizes that service is always number one in satisfying and keeping a customer. And to prove to customers beyond reasonable doubt that customer service is more than a promise, Quill does two things which are unusual, if not unique:

1. Every shipment you receive from Quill includes a

Figure 20. Quill Corporation Product Return Information Form and Replacement Order Form.

PRODUCT RETURN INFORMATION FORM

So we may handle your return promptly and accurately, please complete this form and enclose in return package along with your invoice and/or packing slip, any correspondence and debit memos.

FIRM NAME _____

ADDRESS _____

CITY, STATE _____

FOR QUILL USE ONLY:	( ) C/S Rep.
( ) Product Code	( ) Comment Code
( ) Action Date	
( ) Credit Code	( ) C/M to Cust?

ZIP CODE _____ BUYER _____

QUILL ACCT. # _____ QUILL ORDER # _____

QUILL INVOICE # _____ INVOICE DATE _____

LIST HERE ITEMS RETURNED:

FREIGHT:

FOR QUILL USE ONLY:
TAX OVERRIDE CHECK

QUANTITY	U/M	CATALOG NUMBER	COLOR	DESCRIPTION	U/M	PRICE $	¢

REASON FOR RETURN: _____

☐ REPLACE (see below)   ☐ CREDIT MY ACCOUNT   ☐ REFUND

NOTE: ATTACH PACKING SLIP OR INVOICE

REPLACEMENT ORDER FORM

FIRM _____

DATE _____

CUST. ACCT. # _____

STREET _____

P.O. BOX _____

BUYER _____ TITLE _____
CUSTOMER
P.O. # _____

CITY _____ ST. _____ Z I P

PHONE ( ) _____

QUANTITY	U/M	CATALOG NUMBER	COLOR	DESCRIPTION	U/M	PRICE $	¢

SPECIAL SHIPPING INSTRUCTIONS: _____

Product Return Information Form and a Replacement Order Form (see Figure 20). If you receive anything not to your satisfaction, you return the first form with the merchandise, indicating whether you wish a replacement, a credit to your account, or a refund. If a replacement, you fill out the bottom half of the card, which is the Replacement Order Form.

2. Quill also uses a speed-letter form called the "Quill Service-Gram," which is used to advise customers promptly if something is out of stock or to respond to a customer complaint or inquiry. Quill personnel are required to write these by hand, and the form has a second page for the customer's use, should the customer wish to respond.

When I asked Jack Miller, President of Quill Corporation, for permission to cite Quill as an example of how to put good business ideas to work, he responded promptly and courteously, and straightened me out on whether Quill had been built on any radically new ideas. In fact, here is what he said:

> You are quite perceptive in picking out that concept—service—as one of the cornerstones of our success. However, in choosing that, you might have to change your concept of the examples you are using. It's neither a better idea nor a new idea. It is simply a much ignored old, tested, and proven idea that works.

In referring to the Product Return Information Form, Jack Miller said, "This form is included in every shipment to make it easy for a customer to return or exchange merchandise they don't want. In fact, we encourage them to do so." (Note that the only justification required is that the customer doesn't want it.) He concluded:

> Yes, Mr. Holtz, we think service is important. While so many people are frantically searching for that "new" idea that will make them a million, some of the old, proven ideas—such as service, quality, reliability, friendliness—are lying around unused.

Perhaps Quill's basic idea is not new. But it is implemented quite well with prompt and courteous service, good products, and prompt adjustment of complaints. Certainly, in my own experience, I can't think of anyone who makes it so easy for me to return something I decide I don't want or am disappointed with. And the company's method also provides great convenience—a powerful motivator—because it ships via United Parcel Service, which means prompt delivery to my door.

Note that Quill's success depends on *repeat* business—making *customers,* not sales. Unless the majority of new customers become steady customers, the high cost of making sales would be prohibitively expensive.

For some mail order dealers, only items which produce repeat sales—steady customers—are worthwhile; others sell one-time items. These are factors which must be considered. The principle is simply that getting a new customer by mail is, ordinarily, expensive. *Keeping* that customer for whom you have paid so much is the true payoff, for some kinds of mail order.

Therefore, the question is not so much what can be sold by mail, but what can be sold by mail *at a profit.* If it's a "hard sell," you will probably need that 1:3 (or greater) markup, especially if there is little prospect of repeat business from each customer. But if what you sell is something which the customer will need more of, or if you are handling a line of related items, the rules are different: you must think in terms of what a customer is worth to you over the long term, and be prepared to solicit added business.

Even with standard items, such as typewriter ribbons at a sale price, the new customer does not know what kind of quality he can expect; hence, the first order is likely to be a trial order, and probably a small one. If the customer is completely satisfied, his orders are likely to grow larger and larger, reflecting his confidence in you.

Consider, then, whether what you offer is something the prospect is already familiar with and is likely to have felt a need for or whether it is a new and different item and must be sold, sold, sold to get the order. For in the end, it all comes down to two questions: What does it cost me to win the customer? and What is the customer worth to me? Or perhaps it is even more meaningful to ask yourself this: Am I trying to win an order or a customer? If an order—that is, a one-time sale—that order must stand on its own feet and produce an immediate profit on the transaction. But if a customer, profit may be deferred.

THE MAIL ORDER "CIRCLE"

There are literally thousands of work-at-home entrepreneurs in what has come to be called "the circle" of small mail order operations. They are so called because they sell to each other, essentially, in an almost incestuous business relationship. Typically, they break down into three fairly well-defined subgroups:

1. Those who offer various plans and reports to "opportunity seekers" (those who are in, or are contemplating going into, the field and are looking for good business propositions).
2. Those who offer supplies and services to small mail order dealers. (Rubber stamps, mailing lists, mailing services, and printing are examples of the items offered in this category.)
3. Those who published "advertiser" type periodicals in which others advertise their offerings.

In many cases, these mail order dealers are engaged in all three activities. Some of them are at their little businesses full-time, some spare-time. And some of them manage to build up substantial enterprises.

There are some who are using mail order as an additional source of business, too. For example, while some of the printers working in the circle have small presses in their homes and work in the circle only, others have fully equipped print shops and get much of their business through conventional means, which they supplement with mail order work. Many of these operators advertise in more ambitious publications, also, such as *Income Opportunities* and *Popular Mechanics,* taking both classified and display advertising.

Some of these people never graduate out of the circle—they go on indefinitely, offering items running only a few dollars, mailing and advertising on a small scale, never growing appreciably. Many, however, do graduate into a more important class of mail order—important in effort and sales volume, that is. These operators tend to specialize in publications of several kinds, frequently self-published works. The most common of these are self-help books, self-help reports, and newsletters, mostly addressed to opportunity seekers and small-business people. Such publications offer many advantages—an ample markup to offset the cost of winning customers, repeat business for many items which are unique, complete control over supply, and ease of mailing—almost the ideal mail order business, in these respects.

Those who offer self-help reports and newsletters are creating customers. Usually, the publisher of reports (which are usually several typed pages bound with a corner staple, or small booklets) issues a series of related reports, so that the buyer of one is always a good prospect for the others. And newsletter publishers (who often also sell reports) sell subscriptions, of course, and so are trying to create steady customers. But quite often the publisher of a self-help book is trying only to win sales, with little hope of getting repeat business.

For example, there are several self-help books, self-published, on the subject of how to buy and sell real estate at heavy profits. Obviously, no customer has need for more than one copy of the book. And in most cases of such items, the seller offers only that single item. Therefore, although the book costs him from $1 to $3 at most, the selling price is rarely less than $10 and often as high as $20. Such a heavy markup is usually necessary to offset the heavy selling costs—full-page advertisements and thousands upon thousands of direct-mail pieces.

Some of the successful titles sold in this manner have included *The Lazy Man's Way to Riches* by Joe Karbo, *Writer's Utopia Formula Report* by Jerry Buchanan (who also publishes a newsletter), and *How to Form Your Own Corporation Without a Lawyer for Under $50* and *How to Self-Publish Your Own Book and Make It a Best Seller,* both by Ted Nicholas. Note that in most cases, the title of the book is its own headline. This is almost mandated by the fact that to make such promotions profitable, every effort must be made to sell. A full-page advertisement may easily run to $3,000, even in a periodical of relatively small circulation. That means that 200 or 300 books must be sold just to return the costs—before any profit can be realized. Or if the publication is offered by direct-mail pieces, a 2 percent to 3 percent response is needed to return costs, before a profit can be taken.

SELLING INFORMATION BY MAIL

In general, the business of self-publishing and selling the product through the mails is known as "selling information by mail." (Remember, this is what Hubert K. Simon finally concluded *he* was doing.) A great many small, work-at-home mail order entrepreneurs are doing just this, and almost as many are earning a living teaching it to others. This is what *Writer's Utopia Formula Report* and several other self-published books deal with. In this book, Jerry Buchanan relates how he was plagued with gophers and found that all the supposed remedies for that problem did not work for him. He therefore undertook a campaign of research, which was finally successful. Realizing that he had uncovered information not known to most people, and reasoning that there must be many others plagued with gophers and at a loss to cope successfully with the problem, he wrote a brief report on the subject and offered it for $2, using a small classified advertisement. From his successful experience in selling that small report, he developed his book and, later, his newsletter on the subject, *Towers Club*

USA, which he publishes from his home in Vancouver, Washington. He believes himself to be the originator of the field—that is, the author of the first book on the subject and still the only publisher of a regular newsletter on that subject. Whether he is or not, he is well known as a pioneer and leader in that field, although he has ample competition today.

Many of the "mail order plans" offered by others in this field are of most doubtful value and appear to rely for their success primarily on the gullibility of newcomers to the field. Some of the more worthless schemes are "envelope stuffing" offers, in which the readers of the advertisements are led to believe that the advertiser will pay them a flat fee per envelope stuffed. The reader is asked to send in some small sum of money to "register" and receive a "starter kit." This usually turns out to be a bunch of sales literature, asking for more money and explaining that the reader is to have the sales literature reprinted or to purchase a supply, and then to either take out advertisements or rent mailing lists, and start a mail order enterprise. The advertiser will fill the orders at some discount, and the reader will keep a commission. Such schemes are on the narrow edge of outright fraud, but usually manage to comply technically with the law. They are therefore difficult to stop under present laws.

Many of the other plans offered are legitimate enough, but old and worn out, offering scant chance for success. In many cases, when a self-publisher has pretty well exhausted his market—that is, when his advertisements and direct-mail pieces are no longer producing well enough to justify their continuance—he may offer "dealerships" in his book. Unfortunately for those buying dealerships, the market has been milked virtually dry, and the dealership is not profitable.

Even in those cases where the market has not yet been worked to death for the item, such dealerships have dubious value for this reason: working on a discount, which is usually 50 percent of the list price, does not offer the dealer that 1:3 minimum markup necessary. In actuality, the dealer is working 1:2, because the dealer is paying the publisher one-half the selling price. This makes it rather difficult to turn a decent profit on the proposition.

None of this is to suggest that those selling "information by mail" and other mail order plans are not honest business people. Most small mail order dealers are, in fact, honest and hard-working. But ready-made mail order plans ought to be studied closely before venturing into them.

WHAT TO CONSIDER BEFORE ENTERING MAIL ORDER

Most of the basic mail order principles have already been discussed in the preceding few pages. However, let's recapitulate them here:

1. Markup: Unless the item or service is one in which you expect to find little sales resistance, less than 1:3 is risky, and even 1:3 is far from being a comfortable edge today.
2. Supply: Are you sure your source of supply is dependable? Do you have a backup source in case of failure of your first source?
3. Does the item have wide appeal, or are you going to have a problem reaching the prospects you need to reach?
4. Is there some reason the prospect should buy from you? Is the item obtainable from you only? Or can you offer an attractive price or some other inducement?
5. Is the item easy to ship or mail?
6. Is it a consumable item, which must be renewed? Is it one item in a line of related items, all of probable interest to the same customers? (Are you going to make a *sale* or a *customer* with this item?)
7. Is it a fresh, new idea, or it it an old and worn-out one?

8. Is your line expandable, as you go? Or is it confined to a single item?
9. Is there some large front-end risk—that is, must you make a large investment in getting started, with little hope of recovery if it doesn't "fly"?
10. Has the item been tested, or can you test on a small scale before plunging?

CAN YOU SELL PERSONAL SKILLS BY MAIL?

In many cases, dealers sell their own personal skills by mail. Some mail order dealers are advertising copywriters, for example, who prepare advertisements and direct-mail pieces for clients. Personal writing skills are salable by mail in several ways, including the preparation of resumes and other such items.

One skill sold widely by mail for many years has been that of musical composition. A number of advertisers offer to write music to go with the customer's verse or lyric. Handwriting experts—"grapho-analysts"—do business by mail. For a small fee, they will analyze the customer's handwriting. Illustrating and typesetting are offered by mail, to help the customer prepare advertising copy or typeset and illustrate publications.

Of course, if you publish self-help books or reports, that is often selling your skills by mail too, for these offer instruction in something you are skilled at—how to dance, play the piano, write a resume, convert old English measures to metric, publish a book, or whatever.

One man in Washington publishes a newsletter of original laugh lines for those who want to use them in speeches or in their own newsletters. And a number of people publish newsletters on investment and business practices based on their own study of current conditions and their knowledge of investment—they are, in effect, investment counselors.

SOME FACTS OF NEWSLETTER PUBLISHING

Once you undertake to publish a newsletter, you have made a long-term commitment: you are pledged to produce that publication regularly, month after month, and the deadline each month rolls around more rapidly than you would have believed possible. It soon seems as though you have barely finished putting an edition to bed before the next one is staring you malevolently in the eye. The newsletter soon becomes a tyrant, oppressing you every month (or every week, if you have been foolhardy enough to undertake a weekly). Think carefully about this and be prepared for it before making that fateful decision to become a newsletter publisher.

Several books have been published on the subject of how to become a newsletter publisher. The authors of those books appear to agree that the nouveau newsletter publisher should expect to invest as much as $50,000 to make a success of the enterprise. Personally, I am extremely doubtful that any beginning entrepreneur ever began a newsletter—especially as his or her first business effort—with anything approaching that sum of money, a considerable bundle even today. Nor do I think it at all necessary to run that great a risk. It is possible to launch a newsletter on a much more modest scale, and many successful newsletters have been initiated for far smaller sums of capital.

The chief problem with a newsletter is that subscriptions are notoriously difficult to win, which means, of course, that they are expensive to win. In fact, the conventional wisdom of newsletter publishing is that the best a newsletter publisher can hope for on a new subscription is a breakeven the first year, and that he should expect to get profits only on renewals of subscriptions, which presumably cost very little to get. I must say that my own experience does not bear that out, although I must qualify that too: my *recent* experience does not bear that out, but my recent experience has been much better than my early experience, because I have learned a few things about selling my own newsletter. However, in a recent sales campaign for new subscribers, my cost per new subscriber has been only slightly over $9 per new subscription. This, together with the cost of fulfilling the subscription, leaves an adequate profit on even the first year's subscription. This may or may not be accepted as typical or average, but it does prove that it is possible to earn a reasonable profit on first-year subscriptions.

At the same time, I hasten to admit that getting subscriptions is not easy. You are asking customers to *invest* for a full year in an unknown product, in the hope that the investment will prove worthwhile. It takes a good bit of effective selling to do this, and customers do not exactly break down your doors to press their damp dollars into your hand.

But even that $9 is a best guess, for this reason: the sales campaign, conducted by direct mail, offered books, as well as newsletter subscriptions, at a special, reduced price. Orders of three types come out of the campaign: for books alone, for subscriptions alone, and for an entire package, consisting of a subscription and books. It is rather difficult to segregate costs and sales for this kind of offer, and to assign costs on some kind of pro rata basis. However, were I to make a "worst case" analysis and count only subscriptions against total costs (totally ignoring other orders), my per-subscription cost would still be "only" $25. Even this relatively high cost would leave me some net profit on each subscription.

As far as costs for getting started are concerned, they can be quite modest indeed. Here's how.

Let us suppose, first, that this is to be a part-time effort (a newsletter need not consume your entire time) and that you will not attempt to draw money from the enterprise until it is on its feet. This desirable beginning situation enables you to start for very little money and with relatively little effort.

Supposing your project is an eight-page newsletter, and supposing you are not going to try for an award for publishing graphics and cosmetics, you can produce 100 copies of your first edition for about $35 to $50, depending on whether you choose to collate and bind them yourself or have the printer do this small chore for you.

Mailings—and almost everyone agrees that direct mail is the way to go in promoting newsletter sales—will cost you approximately $250 per 1,000 pieces plus the cost of the list rental, if you use a rented mailing list. Or, if you choose to run small classified inquiry advertisements to collect names of interested people, you'll pay from about 50¢ to $5 per word in each advertisement, depending on where you run them. However, if your advertisement works well for you, you'll be mailing to better prospects—people who have already expressed interest by sending inquiries—and you should have a far better rate of closing than you would with a rented mailing list.

There is another way, however: depending on the kind of prospects you are seeking, you may be able to compile your own lists and save those costs. Here is what I did when I started a newsletter and had virtually no capital to invest.

My newsletter was designed to appeal to small-business people and opportunity seekers, to whom it offered useful business information. I made up a direct-mail package along the lines of that appeal, offering one-year, six-month, and "special trial" subscriptions of three months, at $18, $10, and $6, respectively. I then drew names from classified advertisements where the nature of the message suggested that the advertiser should be a good prospect. I got these names out of a variety of "opportunity" magazines, the Sunday edition of *The New York Times,* and other such sources.

My first subscriber was a six-month customer, a small firm in New Jersey. Others followed. I soon had approximately 100 subscribers, many for three months, a smaller number for six months, and a few for one year.

I next began to mail a special offer—for six-month and one-year subscriptions, I would add three and six months free, respectively, at the same price. This offer pulled quite well, and soon my subscriber list had more than doubled.

Ultimately, I raised the price to try to match the pace of our inflation, and refrained from giving anything away, from that point on, for I was well enough established by then to sell the newsletter entirely on its own merits at the price listed.

TYPICAL NEWSLETTER PROMOTIONS

Many different means are used by newsletter publishers to promote both initial subscriptions and renewals. Here are some of the typical ones:

- Related books, either free or at a reduced price, offered as an inducement along with a subscription or renewal.
- Sale price, for limited time, if the subscription is a new one.
- Free trial period of three months or more. Subscription will continue, unless the customer specifically cancels (à la book clubs—if customer fails to cancel, he has accepted the subscription).
- Special price for two-year or three-year subscription or renewal, usually at almost nominal increase over one-year price.
- One issue free, on request.
- A number of back issues with new subscription.
- Special publication free, containing reprints of most significant of last year's published items.

From all the evidence I've been able to gather, price breaks appear to work best at motivating customers to subscribe or renew. One publisher, badly in need of operating capital, offered his about-to-expire subscribers a second year at *one cent* over the one-year subscription. His renewal rate zoomed upward immediately, as most of his subscribers hastened to get two years for only one cent over the price of one. (Those with many months to run paid to get a two-year extension to their current subscription.) He reported the campaign highly successful in raising capital, but lamented that now it would be a long time before he saw any more subscription money from his old subscribers!

NEWSLETTER TOPICS AND MARKETS

In one sense, there are two newsletter markets: individuals and organizations. Organizations will subscribe to newsletters geared to their business interests, as individuals will subscribe to those related to their individual interests. There are many geared to each kind of audience. Newsletters are to be found in many fields—health, investment, business opportunities, hobbies, and myriads of other topics. In some cases, the coverage is quite broad, across the whole field, whereas in some cases the coverage is extremely narrow, focused on some specific aspect of the field.

There is hardly a topic which is not worth considering for a newsletter, but there are certain factors which must be kept in mind:

- Can you get enough subscribers to make the enterprise worthwhile—that is, how many people are likely to be interested in the topic?
- Can you get enough useful information, not readily available elsewhere, to fill your pages every month (or week, or whatever)?
- Is the information you can get worth the cost of subscribing to a special newsletter—is it useful enough?
- How much competition do you have?

People subscribe to newsletters to get either of two things, or perhaps both: information not readily available elsewhere (perhaps the story behind the story) and a condensation or digest of the important facts of the month, which they could not have kept up with unaided.

From the publisher's viewpoint, he therefore must either have some especially good sources for exclusive information or do an enormous amount of reading each month and abstract all the important items for his own publication. And often he must follow up an item he has picked up and see if he can get a few inside facts or backup information that will be truly exclusive. That, plus his interpretation of events (if that is the nature of the newsletter), is what makes the subscription a value.

The fact is that not all newsletters actually deal in "news." Many do, but many are interpretive, analyzing events and trends and offering advice, as in the case of investment newsletters.

Some newsletters depend on the reading and compilation of events, such as one newsletter which reports on contests every month, advising readers on the where, what, when, and how of contests throughout the United States.

PRICING YOUR NEWSLETTER

In general, the price of your newsletter depends on its size, its frequency, and its market. A daily newsletter (there are many of these) addressed to executives or wealthy investors may sell for several hundred dollars a year and be well worth it to the subscribers. A quarterly or even monthly newsletter, addressed to individuals who are average consumers or small entrepreneurs, may not be able to command more than $15 or $20 a year. And some newsletters used for promotional purposes (as mentioned earlier) may sell for nominal prices such as $5 or $10 a year.

Probably the best way to price your newsletter is to consider these facts and survey what other newsletters that are similar in nature or go to a similar class of reader are charging.

EVALUATING CHANCES FOR SUCCESS

Advice already published by those experienced in the newsletter business is along these lines: if there are only one or two, or even no competitive newsletters (that is, newsletters dealing with the topic you have in mind), beware! It may well mean that there is not enough of a market for *any* newsletter of that type. And if there are perhaps eight or ten competitive newsletters, beware! It may be very difficult to break into what appears to be a crowded market. According to the advice of such experts, the magic number is approximately five—the existence of four to six competitive newsletters suggests to these gentlemen that the market is ample and the competition not intolerably great.

Like most conventional wisdom, this is generalizing over such a widely varying sample as to be almost meaningless. Eight newsletters in a highly popular field may mean not nearly enough newsletters to provide adequate coverage, and the lack of even one may mean that the field is badly neglected. (There are still none directly competitive with *Government Marketing News,* and the potential is far greater than that newsletter will ever realize by itself.) The numbers have meaning only in relation to the *potential number of subscribers* in the chosen field, for one thing. For another, if you find some important aspect of a field that is not being covered well, and if you are right in your estimate of reader interest in that aspect of the field, you have an excellent reason for entering what may appear to be a crowded field.

In any case, if you approach the project along the lines suggested here, you can test quite easily, cheaply, and rapidly—and withdraw promptly if you are wrong, not greatly impoverished by the effort.

CATALOG SALES

A busy and productive area of mail order is a type of enterprise known as catalog sales. The Quill Corporation example cited earlier is an illustration of a general catalog, presenting all the items normally carried in stock, along with standard prices. Quill periodically—every month, in fact—sends out a special, abbreviated catalog, which carries a

Figure 21. Quill Corporation catalog cover.

number of items on special sale that month, with coupons. Figure 21 is a typical catalog front cover. Note that all the main sales arguments—the reasons for buying from the dealer—are listed clearly. That is, the catalog cover is in itself a sales presentation.

You may have been the recipient of catalogs of household items—"gift catalogs"—from such mail order houses as Sunset House and Giftime or Drake, especially as the Christmas season approaches. (This is their peak season, of course.)

Many catalog houses offer dealerships to beginners entering mail order. The dealer buys the standard catalogs, with his or her own name imprinted, and mails them out. The orders come to the dealer, with payment. The dealer immediately deducts the sales commission or discount and sends the order along to the catalog house, with the wholesale price, whereupon the catalog house ships, *under the dealer's label*. This protects the dealer, because the customer does not know where the order is filled and therefore reorders from the dealer.

This is the exception to the rule about the 1:3 markup, because most customers will order things from time to time— that is, the dealer is seeking to make customers, rather than single sales.

A VARIATION ON INQUIRY ADVERTISING

One profitable way in which many mail order dealers run their inquiry advertising is by offering some inexpensive bargain item. The objective is primarily to compile a mailing list of interested prospects, but on a basis that makes the advertising pay for itself—therefore the bargain price, which is an inducement to order yet yields a small profit so as to return the cost of the advertising. There is a bonus in this, moreover: experience shows that when the mailing list is of people who have actually bought something, the response is far greater. (There are many idle curiosity seekers who will make inquiries but never order anything, costing the advertisers time and money.)

One catalog firm that does this quite successfully is Drake, which offers name and address labels at a small price, as its "leader" in its inquiry advertising, and then sends the new customer a catalog of its main line of merchandise.

Beware of one peculiarity, however: the danger of pricing too low, as well as of pricing too high. Here is an illustration of what that means.

A Florida newsletter publisher ran some small classifieds, offering a special report at $2 a copy, an obvious bargain. He found the response quite satisfactory, so he reasoned that since he was after the names rather than the $2, he would greatly increase inquiries by cutting the price to $1. To his dismay, the response fell off sharply at $1. Reason? The readers simply didn't believe the offer at $1; they didn't find it credible that they could get anything worthwhile at $1.

That's one objective in testing, too: test to find out what price the customer finds most credible and most attractive. Suppose you want to test for this. You might mail out 3,000 direct-mail packages to three 1,000-name lists which are as much like each other in types of prospect as you can make them. (Or mix up a list of 3,000 names at random, and mail to all.) The packages are identical, except for price: one package is priced at $10, another at $12, and another at $15—1,000 of each. Here is one set of results you might get:

$10 orders:	40	($400)
$12 orders:	42	($504)
$15 orders:	26	($390)

Which is the best price to use? Probably the $12 price, since it brought the best results, overall. However, you might get this kind of result:

$10 orders:	60	($600)
$12 orders:	41	($492)
$15 orders:	45	($675)

In this case, the $15 price appears best—fewer orders, but greater volume. But suppose the results were these:

$10 orders:	55	($550)
$12 orders:	35	($420)
$15 orders:	33	($495)

In this case, which would you select? No, probably not the $10 price, despite the fact that it produced the greatest number of orders and the greatest number of dollars. Why? Because you probably make at least as much profit on the $15 price, with far less labor. You'll fill 40 percent fewer orders and get 90 percent as much money.

THE "DRAG"

There is one peculiarity—at least, everyone in mail order seems to regard it as a peculiarity—about mail order, and that is what some refer to as the "drag" in mail order sales. Orders will dribble in for many months after an advertisement has run for the last time or a direct-mail package has been mailed out for the last time. Obviously, a great many people save literature and advertisements they have clipped, and act on them a long time later. Here are a few examples from my own experience.

In a current direct-mail campaign, each mailing receives a different "key" to enable me to know how that particular batch did. My keys are "A," "B," "C," and so forth, printed inconspicuously on the order blank. As orders arrive, I record them and keep a tally for each mailing and an overall tally for the campaign. At present, batch "E" is being mailed, but occasional orders are still dribbling in from batch "A," which was mailed several months ago.

An advertisement that ran until April–May of this year is still producing orders six months later, although they are gradually abating now.

Occasionally an order will come in which we can identify as being from a direct mail of at least a year ago.

Over one and one-half years ago a syndicated columnist mentioned that we would send literature to anyone interested in what we offered. As of today, an occasional inquiry from that notice still arrives.

For that reason, it is most difficult to measure the response to any advertising or direct mail—you are never entirely sure that you have gotten all the response. However, in most cases the response is essentially complete within three to six weeks, and for practical purposes, that may be used as the measure. But that effect explains why catalog sales and direct mail in general increase in rate of response with repeat mailings to the same lists. A number of people who did not order are still holding your literature, and a follow-up mailing often prompts some of them to order then.

Because of that drag effect, every mailing creates some unknown number of "banked" orders—potential orders that will come through one day in the future. One mail order dealer therefore advocates steady mailing, which he refers to as "putting money in the mail order bank."

ABOUT GUARANTEES

Because you are asking customers to buy sight-unseen for most mail order offers, you have a bit of extra sales resistance to overcome, as already noted. This is especially the case if you are not a well-known firm such as Sears or Wards, of course. Customers want some reassurance that you are honest and reputable and will stand behind what you sell. Therefore, most mail order firms offer a money-back guarantee, and most writers on the subject of mail order insist that such a guarantee, prominently displayed in your advertising, is a must.

Here again, my experience indicates otherwise. I followed the apparently sound advice for a long time. During that time I discovered that not all customers were completely honest or ethical, but there were some who would take advantage of the mail order dealer even more unscrupulously than mail order dealers are sometimes accused of dealing with customers. For example, there are some individuals who make a practice of ordering everything that bears such a guarantee, and then returning the item for refund. And in the case of some items—information—they have virtually swindled the dealer: they have gotten the information, absorbed it, perhaps even made a copy of it, and are asking for refund! Why, I reasoned, *invite* them to return items?

I therefore decided to see what would happen if I did not trumpet such a guarantee, and eliminated the *statement* of guarantee (although I do accept returns for full refund). As far as I was able to tell from the results, it made not the slightest difference in sales.

Whether my case is special or not, I can't say. But I cannot verify that a *statement* of guarantee and a blatant exhortation to return the item for refund is even necessary, let alone advisable. (I do, however, recommend a money-back policy; just don't exhort the customer to return merchandise.)

CHARGES

One modern convenience that appears to help sales considerably is offering your customers the convenience of charge cards. VISA/Americard and Master Charge are especially easy to arrange, although small mail order firms also accept charges on other cards. Visa and Master Charge are "bank" cards, arranged through your local bank. You'll pay some percentage of interest for the convenience, but you'll find as much as 25 percent of your sales being charged, many of which you would not have got if your customer had not been able to charge it.

Getting a charge order is almost the same as cash. Once you have checked the card number and obtained approval, you write up a sales slip and deposit it as you would cash, and your account is immediately credited the full amount, less the interest. There is no need to wait for clearance, as with a check.

CHECKS

As in any business, you will occasionally receive a bad check from a customer. Because of this possibility, many mail order houses will not ship an order until the check clears, and this can take as long as 30 days, which may strain your relations with your customers. Many mail order houses see the problem as one of acceptable risk versus impatient customers, and ship immediately, taking their chances on the checks. By and large, judging from my own experience and that of others I know in mail order, the losses are small. First of all, only a few checks bounce. And usually the customers will make those good. However, where the checks are large and the merchandise is valuable, the dealer is reluctant to take that chance, understandably, and may therefore wait for the check to clear before making shipment.

MAIL ORDER COPY

The typical direct-mail sales package includes three standard items: the sales letter, the brochure/circular, and the order form. Many mail order operators also enclose a return envelope, often prepaid. The principles of sales and advertising applicable elsewhere apply here. However, there are certain "rules" and principles, some widely believed by mail order entrepreneurs, others simply the result of my own experiences and observations. But there is one overriding "rule" which I have learned to observe and which I find echoed by only an occasional other mail order entrepreneur. It is this: the only valid rules are the ones you discover for yourself. All others, no matter their source, are to be regarded with healthy skepticism and put to the test before you allow them to control what you do. Here are a couple of examples.

I write my own sales copy, and I "typeset" on a good electric typewriter (an IBM Selectric, in fact) that permits me to use several different fonts. I use transfer type for headlines, or have a local shop set them for me on a machine called a "headliner," at small cost. For illustrations, I use ready-made art work, which you can buy. (It's referred to as "clip art.") And I have most of my literature printed on relatively inexpensive offset paper, usually white (the least expensive), although sometimes I order colored stock, which raises the price about 20 percent.

I have been assured by those who are supposedly quite expert in mail order that this is a mistake: I should use more expensive papers, have my copy set by typesetting shops, and use prepaid return envelopes.

I experimented with all these things, at great expense. I was unable to detect any difference in results, except that my printing bills and other related expenses increased greatly.

Among the many pieces of advice I have received was the admonition to use two-color printing. I have tried this, too, with similar results. Again, the chief result was a near doubling of my printing costs.

I have been counseled on the virtues of bulk mail, to reduce postage costs. I tried bulk mail too. The problem, I found, was that customers can easily spot the fact that the envelope contains advertising matter, by virtue of the fact that it is readily apparent that bulk mail has been used. I have found that the response is so much smaller that the advantages of lower postage costs were not an advantage at all.

There are three main costs in mail order: printing, postage, and advertising. Advertising and printing are somewhat inverse costs—if you use advertising as your main method for getting orders or names of good prospects, your printing costs will be proportionately less, and vice versa. Printing costs are controllable to some extent, as explained, and there is no question that profits are almost as dependent on costs as they are on sales and markup; certainly, you should do everything possible to keep costs to a minimum. However, beware of false economies: they may cost you more than they save. The idea is not to save money per se, but to save money where it does not help your business, and spend it where it does help your business. Here is an illustration of what I mean.

Early in my mail order experience, I ran a small classified advertisement for a report. I received a goodly number of orders for the report, for which I was asking $2, but I soon found that I wasn't doing much better than breaking even at that price. I therefore expanded it considerably and priced it at $6.

At $6, I could no longer get orders directly from a small classified advertisement, so I switched to inquiry advertising, offering to send details. I received an ample response and sent out a sales letter and brochure, the last page of which included an order form, to be clipped off with scissors. (Avoids the added expense of a separate order card.)

The returns from that were fairly satisfactory, but I thought I could do better. At 15¢ for one ounce, I could get as many as five sheets of advertising matter in the envelope, but I was using only two. I decided to add a third, which increased my printing costs, although my postage was the same. I designed a third piece, another brochure, and included that.

The returns—orders coming back from the inquiries I responded to—shot up to an amazing 40 percent! The one-third increase in my printing costs proved to be a sound investment.

In general, just as you need a much larger advertisement to pull $10 orders than you would for $2 orders, you need a great deal more "selling" in your direct-mail package for a $10 order than you do for a $2 order.

One more example: There are two schools of thought among mail order people as to whether you should offer many items—"catalog" type appeals—or a single item. As time went on, I continued to build the number of items I had available, and finally I was sending out literature describing and listing about 30 different items, with my envelopes now stuffed with the five pieces I could squeeze in for 15¢ first-class postage. The most expensive single item was $89.95, and there were items for as little as $2. But many people ordered a variety of items, and soon it was not unusual to receive orders ranging to over $200, despite the fact that my literature was set mainly by typewriter and printed on inexpensive paper.

The rules in direct mail are only those someone believes in, on the basis of his or her own experience. Before following them slavishly, put them to the test. Try them out on your own offerings, on a small scale, and do what works for you. In the words heard widely at Fort Benning Officer Candidates School during World War II, "Anything that works is right."

19

SELLING TO THE U.S. GOVERNMENT

SELLING COAL IN NEWCASTLE

When the U.S. government's Consumer Products Safety Commission was in its early formative stages, a journalist named David Swit haunted the offices and corridors of the commission's building, getting acquainted with people and learning what was happening there. Soon enough, he began publication of his own newsletter, the *Product Safety Letter.*

His best customer for that letter about the doings of the commission was—the Consumer Product Safety Commission. Every executive wanted his own copy. It was far more informative about what was happening in the commission than anything else he could read! But it's also to be found in the libraries of many other government agencies, even those having nothing to do with consumer product safety.

Every government agency of any size publishes its own telephone directory in Washington, but almost all subscribe to the privately published *Federal Telephone Directory* because it's much more up to date and accurate than any of the official directories.

In any of the many agency libraries you will find dozens of privately published newsletters about federal agencies and their activities, some of them selling for as much as $250 a year.

The Office of Personnel Management (formerly the Civil Service Commission) runs a number of training classes for the employees of the various agencies. Many of the programs are written and presented by people from the private sector, even for such subjects as federal procurement. (It has been my own

302

privilege many times to lecture federal employees on federal procurement.)

Specialists are called in from the private sector for many kinds of assistance—to operate government computers, organize government offices, develop government training programs and publications, furnish expertise in technical matters, and even answer the government's mail and telephones.

When the National Park Service decided it would be a good idea to dress people in Colonial costumes and have them enact household scenes at the historic Nelson House in Yorktown, Virginia, a contract was issued to private groups. And when the Department of Housing and Urban Development (HUD) was organized and had to make notations in thousands upon thousands of federally guaranteed FHA mortgages, a contract was written to have the employees of a private firm do the work.

In spite of the immensity of the sprawling Government Printing Office (GPO), which processes over $500 million in printing every year for the federal agencies, the GPO contracts out some 70 percent—$350 million—of this every year to small and large private printers. Many of these do little else but print for GPO.

No one, either insider or outsider, knows exactly how much the government spends with private business each year for such services and supplies, but even the most modest official estimates now put the figure at $100 billion, and that is almost surely a large underestimate.

WHAT AND HOW DOES THE GOVERNMENT BUY?

There are, at this writing, 13 departments in the government, plus some 60 "independent agencies," some of which are even larger than some of the departments. (For example, NASA and EPA are independent agencies.)

However, the various departments and agencies are often sprawling "conglomerates" of bureaus and "administrations," headquartered in Washington for the most part, but having a mélange of offices scattered throughout the United States— throughout the entire world, for that matter. The Occupational Safety and Health Administration (OSHA) is one bureau within the Labor Department, for example, while the Department of Health, Education and Welfare (HEW) includes the Public Health Service, the National Institute of Occupational Safety and Health, the National Institutes of Health, and a great many other bureaus.

All in all, so vast is this tentacled monster that it includes over 15,000 "buying activities," which employ 130,000 of the 2.8 million federal employees simply to spend the money (in other words, there are 130,000 procurement specialists).

Much of federal purchasing is of supplies and money just to keep the establishment operating—office supplies, janitorial services, printing, security guards, vehicles, furniture, and the like. But there is much purchasing also to implement the many programs—specialists to program computers and operate them, field work for social programs, services to operate Job Corps centers, bumper stickers to exhort Americans to conserve energy, public-service commercials to have a medical checkup and refrain from using charcoal starter fluid on a lit fire.

Small wonder then that there are almost no kinds of goods and services which are not viable in the thousands of government markets, from renting mules and booking go-go dancers to making sandwiches and answering telephones. There is almost certainly an array of government customers for whatever you have to offer.

If the diversity of government needs is almost bewildering in its scope, the variety of government buying arrangements is almost equally dizzying. However, despite a wide number of different purchasing arrangements, all buying by the government is based on some form of competition, and there are only two basic methods: what the government refers to as "advertised" procurement and "negotiated" procurement.

Both are simple concepts. The complexity arises in the many variants of implementing these two basic methods.

Advertised procurement

At one time, virtually everything the government bought was bought through the method known as advertised or formally advertised procurement. That was, and is, simply asking for sealed bids. The sealed bids are due by some specified date and time, at which time they are opened publicly and read aloud. Barring some special circumstance, such as the low bid having been submitted by an unqualified bidder, the low bidder is awarded the contract.

To this day, the procurement regulations envision this as the primary method for government purchasing. However, in modern times the government has had many special needs, arising originally out of defense needs. Most of our military weapons—and "weapons" does not mean only guns and bombs, but also refers to missiles, radar, airplanes, ships, computers, and other modern systems—are developed and designed especially for the military. Obviously, they can't be bought in the open market from suppliers competing with each other for low bid, but must be procured through research and development contracts with firms that have the resources and staffs to do such work. The abilities of the bidders to do a good job—to develop the best equipment—is even more important than price. Therefore, such contracts are exceptions to the rule and are negotiated. Today, this situation is not peculiar to procurement by the military, but is also characteristic of procurement by many nonmilitary agencies. In fact, 85 percent of procurement today is "negotiated."

Negotiated procurement

The basis for negotiated procurement is primarily technical competition: the agency describes its needs in a solicitation package called "Request for Proposals" (RFP), and anyone who wishes to enter the competition for the contract must write and submit a proposal, describing what he offers, his qualifications for doing the job, and the price he asks. The agency reads the proposals and decides which ones it likes best and, consequently, which firms it wishes to negotiate with.

Low price counts for something, but is not necessarily decisive. In most cases, the technical proposal is decisive, unless the price accompanying the technical proposal selected is "out of the ball park." In that case, other acceptable technical proposals will be considered.

It is through procurements of this type that systems are designed for fighting wars, landing on the moon, establishing health-care systems, distributing food stamps, and carrying out thousands of other government programs and functions.

Exceptions

There are many exceptions to the practice of soliciting bids and proposals. The procurement regulations provide for exceptions that authorize federal agencies to make "noncompetitive" awards—that is, to begin negotiations with any firm of their choice. Sometimes the justification is time—it takes time to go through the competitive-proposal process, and in some cases the need is too urgent to allow time for that. In other cases, some given firm may have a unique ability or proprietary equipment the government wants to buy, which makes competition impractical. However, by far the majority of contracts are awarded through some competitive process.

WHO BUYS FOR THE GOVERNMENT?

Although there are 130,000 federal employees whose full-time function is to attend to the details of making actual purchases, they act on requests submitted by other federal employees—employees whose function is not purchasing per se, but who have the authority to buy whatever they need to conduct the government's business. Not every federal office has "procurement authority," but by far the majority are authorized to do at least some purchasing for their own needs.

At the same time, there are several centralized procurement and supply services among the agencies. These services buy in quantity, if the item is a standard commodity—for example, office supplies—and stock the items, then disburse them to the various agencies as needed. Chief among these is the Federal Supply Service, which is part of the General Services Administration. The military services also have a centralized supply service, the Defense Logistics Agency, and the Postal Service also maintains its own supply service. All of these have warehouses and supply centers in various U.S. locations.

As a result, all federal agencies, military and civilian, may purchase many of their supplies through the Federal Supply Service. The Postal Service units also buy from their Topeka, Kansas, supply center, and military agencies buy much from and through the various centers of the Defense Logistics Agency. At the same time, many of these agencies may buy their supplies elsewhere, at their own option.

The result is that there is only a surface uniformity in the system; overall, it presents a great many opportunities for business, to those who take the time to learn the system and make the marketing effort required. In fact, a large number of businesses, large and small, subsist entirely on government contracts, and were even organized solely for government business.

The General Services Administration

The General Services Administration was organized to support the rest of the federal establishment with a variety of supply and administrative services, from finding office space to providing vehicles and pens. GSA spends about $5 billion per year. It includes the National Archives and Records Service, the Public Buildings Service, the Automated Data and Telecommunications Service, and the Federal Supply Service, as well as the Federal Preparedness Agency and administrative offices. Chief targets for business in GSA are the Federal

Supply Service and the Automated Data and Telecommunications Service, with the former by far the more important.

The Federal Supply Service (FSS) spends well over $3 billion annually, and operates 10 warehouses and 75 stores to service the rest of the federal establishment with a variety of office supplies, furniture, and other staples of operation. To support this, FSS keeps about 6 million items in stock.

Much of the FSS buying is done through Federal Supply Schedules, which are annual agreements entered into with suppliers, against which FSS orders on an as-needed basis throughout the year.

It is relatively easy—almost an automatic routine—for a supplier to sign an annual agreement under the supply-schedule system. While this does not guarantee the supplier orders, it paves the way by authorizing federal agencies to buy from the listed suppliers through the simplified procedures of purchase orders, as distinct from formal contracting. There are about 300 such schedules, covering thousands of industrial and commercial items the agencies use regularly, as well as a few services, such as dry cleaning, shoe repair, food services, trucking, and many others.

The Automated Data and Telecommunications Service buys computer-type equipment and communications equipment, and some of the schedules for such supplies have been turned over to ADTS.

The Public Buildings Service is responsible for some of the government's construction work (although not all) and awards contracts for architectural and civil engineering services, as well as for construction work.

Each of GSA's ten regional offices (actually 13 offices, since three of the ten regions have two major offices each) operates a GSA Business Service Center, whose main function is to assist newcomers to government business in getting started. At these centers you can get detailed information and personal counseling on the system and how to work in the system.

Defense Logistics Agency

The Defense Logistics Agency (DLA) operates six supply centers in CONUS (Continental United States) and buys a wide variety of supplies and services needed by the military and not normally supplied through other government supply functions. However, DLA also operates six Defense Service Centers and four Defense Depots, all of which account for some military purchasing. Moreover, there are nine Defense Contract Administrative Service Regions, and these provide a service to small businesses to assist them in winning subcontracts from the large prime contractors.

Other government business prospects

With only a few exceptions, federal agencies are not required to do any of their buying through these centralized purchasing and procurement services. In any event, much that the federal establishment wants is not available through these supply agencies, either because the need is for a product or service developed on a custom basis or because it is a need encountered only occasionally. Therefore, the billions of dollars represented by such centralized purchasing, significant business though it is, is only a fraction of the overall total of federal procurement. The rest is on a contract-by-contract basis, agency by agency, as needs appear.

Some agencies do a great deal of outside buying, some buy occasionally, and a few buy only rarely from outside sources. Among the most active agencies—that is, those representing probably the most promising market targets—are these:

Department of Commerce (DOC).
Government Printing Office (GPO).
Department of Agriculture (USDA).
Department of Defense (DOD).
Department of Energy (DOE).
Department of Health and Human Services
Department of Education

Department of Labor (DOL).
Department of Transportation (DOT).
Environmental Protection Agency (EPA).
General Services Administration (GSA).
National Aeronautics and Space Administration (NASA).
National Science Foundation (NSF).
Postal Service (USPS).

FORMS OF CONTRACTS

The actual agreements or contracts between the seller and the agency fall into a variety of types, although, again, there are only two basic types: firm fixed-price contracts and cost-reimbursement contracts. The difference is simple. In a firm fixed-price contract, the agency can specify exactly what and how much of it it wants, which makes it possible to quote an exact figure to be paid. In the cost-reimbursement type of contract, for one reason or another, neither the government nor the seller can quantify the product or service exactly; hence, a contract is entered into which guarantees the seller that he will be paid all his costs plus some agreed-upon profit or fee. However, each of these two classes of contract has its own variations. Moreover, a "contract" is, technically, an agreement signed by the two parties to the agreement represented by the contract. However, some government purchasing is done by government purchase order, which is a contract for all practical purposes, although only the government signs the document. (The agreement is, technically, a verbal contract, backed up by a government purchase order.)

There are two situations in which purchase orders are used. One, the Small Purchases Act identifies a small purchase as any purchase under $10,000—that is, up to $9,999.99—and authorizes such purchases to be made through purchase orders rather than formal contracts. Two, orders issued under a Federal Supply Schedule or any other general purchasing agreement may be made by purchase order for amounts specified in the agreement (which may greatly exceed $10,000). The agreement is a formal contract itself and is the legal basis for orders.

For orders placed under the Small Purchases Act, the procedure is simple. No competitive bids are required for purchases under $2,500. From $2,500 to $5,000, the agency is supposed to get three bids, which may be made verbally, and select the lowest. And for purchases over $5,000, up to $10,000, the agency is supposed to get three written bids, although these may be quite informal. However, in actual practice, a government employee who has the buying authority can issue a purchase order under $10,000 to anyone he or she pleases.

In practice, therefore, it is entirely feasible to sell to federal agencies "across the counter," as one would to private businesses, for purchases under $10,000. Typically, this is the way it is done:

Having reached verbal agreement with the government executive, the seller is usually requested to furnish some kind of "letter proposal," which is simply a brief description of what is to be supplied and a price quotation. Using this as documentation, the federal executive then writes a purchase request, providing the information written up by the seller, and has the government contracting officer issue a purchase order to the seller. Upon delivery or completion of the service, one of the copies of the purchase order serves as an invoice. The buyer signs, certifying delivery or completion, and the purchase order cum invoice goes to the contracting office for listing on a payment schedule, then to the Treasury Department, which then issues a check to the seller.

It is entirely feasible, because of this, to make sales calls on government agencies exactly as you would make sales calls on private-sector business prospects. (We have made many sales to government agencies in this manner, some of them at the agency's own initiative, as a result of our advertising.)

There are a number of types of cost-reimbursement contracts. Most people have heard of the famous cost-plus contracts, used extensively by the military agencies originally, but used today by other agencies dealing in technology—NASA and EPA, for example. This is frequently the only practical kind of contractual arrangement when the seller must provide research and development to produce something entirely new and different, such as a high-speed fighter plane, a missile system, or a space vehicle. It is all but impossible to do more than guess at how much effort and cost will be involved in overcoming the technical problems of such projects; hence the contract provides for repayment of the contractor's costs plus some fixed fee or profit.

The actual procedures for this are along the following lines.

1. The government describes the need or the problem in a Request for Proposals (RFP).

2. The firms that wish to respond develop proposals, which can be quite large (running to thousands of pages, in some cases), describing how they propose to organize the project and accomplish the results called for, plus presenting their own credentials for the effort, and their estimates of costs, carefully detailed.

3. The government selects one or more of the most promising proposals and enters into negotiations. These negotiations result in a *ceiling* price, with a fixed fee based on that ceiling or on some lower estimated figure (the ceiling then being a safety margin). The contractor's books are subject to audit, as the contract proceeds or when the contract is over, to verify the contractor's costs and indirect rates.

Some of the other forms are either variants of this or hybrids between cost-reimbursement and fixed-price agreements. Here are two commonly used types:

Time and Material (T&M). In this, the government knows *what* it will buy, but not *how much*. Therefore, the contractor furnishes unit rates, and the government issues orders, as needed, to be billed at the agreed-upon rates.

Basic Ordering Agreement (BOA). This is a general arrangement, typified by the T&M, in which the agreement is to furnish goods and/or services, as needed, at rates agreed upon.

The contract is usually for one year and may cover goods or services. (T&M usually covers both, with main costs for services, such as in some construction projects or in publications support.)

Both types of contracts are also referred to as "task order" and "call" contracts or "work order" contracts, particularly when the contract is primarily for services, with materials or supplies only incidental.

Even so, the actual form and details of these may vary a great deal. In the case of the classic cost-plus contract, the fee may not be fixed but may be an incentive fee, which varies according to some indicator of quality and efficiency—for example, if the contractor brings the job in below the estimated cost, the government will increase the fee or award a share of the savings to the contractor. In another variation, NASA has engaged in contracts which include both a small fixed fee and an incentive fee.

SELLING NEW PRODUCTS TO THE GOVERNMENT

Any new product may be sold to federal agencies on a casual, individual-case basis. However, if you have something which you believe to be of such broad interest that it merits becoming a regularly stocked item, the Federal Supply Schedules include one for new or improved items. If, for example, you have some improved type of carbon paper or some new office machine, you may apply to have it placed on this new-item schedule for a year. If the item is well received (that is, if you sell enough of it to federal agencies during the year), it may be placed on a regular schedule, or a new schedule may be established for it.

If you are in the newsletter or other publishing business, there are several schedules for these, and new offerings are accepted readily, since each of the products on these schedules is necessarily unique and, in many cases, new. However, to give you some idea of the diversity of items you may offer on these schedules, here is a small sampling of the schedules:

Vehicles.
Automotive accessories.
Woodworking machinery.
Appliances.
Agricultural equipment.
Pipe.
Toiletries.
Hand and power tools.
Drugs and pharmaceuticals.
Cameras and photo supplies.
Furniture (office and household).
Recreational and sports equipment.
Chemicals.
Clothing.

In all, the approximately 300 schedules list over 5,000 individual items of supply and services, and most schedules list a large number of suppliers for the various items. (And all of this still represents at most 2 percent of federal procurement!)

The schedules do not issue from a single source within the Federal Supply Service but are assigned to various GSA regional offices. One function of the GSA service centers is to assist you in finding the right FSS office for the schedules that interest you.

Some items which are offered could logically be fitted into any of several schedules, so in some cases you have a choice of which schedule you wish to get on. (You may not list your item on more than one schedule, however.) Schedules are also subject to change—some are canceled, new ones are created, and some are transferred to other agencies (for example, some have been transferred to ADTS, another GSA bureau.)

If you have a new product that fits into an established category—say, a new type of check valve or pocket calculator—you may have it listed on one of the existing schedules, or you may apply to have it listed on the new-item schedule.

The FSS will determine whether it is "new" in the sense that it offers something not available before or is sufficiently improved to merit inclusion on the new-item schedule.

THE PROPOSAL GAME

Unless you supply some standard commodity—that is to say, if you offer any kind of custom-designed product or service—you are likely to need to know something about how to write proposals, to gain entree to government contracts. Proposal writing is an art in itself, and the companies that pursue government contracts regularly do a great deal of proposal writing. In fact, many of the large corporations that depend on government contracts, such as the major aircraft firms, maintain permanent proposal-writing departments and are engaged in writing proposals virtually every day of the year.

Briefly, the objective in writing a proposal is to sell your plan for doing the job the government wants done. In the proposal you must demonstrate that you are qualified in every sense—you understand the need thoroughly, you can offer all the skills, facilities, and resources needed, and your price is reasonable—not necessarily the lowest—for the job.

Very much the same principles which apply to advertising and sales apply here, for the proposal *is* a sales presentation, although extremely detailed. Unlike a proposal offered to a commercial prospect, however, a proposal to a government agency must present detailed proof of your qualifications to do the work. (Commercial enterprises accept that if you are in a business, you are qualified, but government agencies do not make that assumption—at least not officially, for proposal purposes.) You must offer not only those beneficial results you promise, but also some persuasive evidence that you *can* produce those results and that you *will* produce those results. ("Can" refers to your technical qualifications, skills, and plans; "will" refers to your "track record" of satisfactory performance in other projects.) So the credibility factor here comes down to establishing some confidence in your skills, abilities, and resources as well as your dependability as a contractor.

When the government issues the solicitation package or "bid set," it includes a "statement of work," which describes in some detail what is required. Included along with that are other information and a number of forms. You are also advised just what information is required in your proposal, how proposals will be judged and evaluated, what type of contract is contemplated, what price information is required, when and where proposals must be delivered or mailed, and any other details the agency thinks you need. In most cases, a form is provided for your cost estimates, and there are several other forms that require making check marks in boxes to indicate whether you are a small business, where you are incorporated (if at all), and other such background information.

Obviously, some writing skill is needed to present a clear and understandable proposal. But the contest is not one of writing skills, despite the importance of writing well; the contest is to select that bidder who offers the best plan and/or the best qualifications. Ordinarily, you must present at least the following information:

- Demonstrate a complete understanding of the government's need or problem.
- Analyze the need/problem technically to demonstrate the best method(s) to satisfy the need and/or solve the problem.
- Present a detailed plan or proposed program to carry out the work successfully.
- Present resumes of the principal staff members you propose to employ in the project, showing their individual competence and credentials.
- Present a "company resume" showing the qualifications and credentials of your organization to carry out the project proposed.
- Present a cost analysis to demonstrate the reasonableness of your costs and the validity of your estimates and rates.

The degree to which you accomplish all this—the "technical quality" of your proposal—is the chief factor on which you are judged, although your price must be in whatever is considered to be the acceptable range. (The customer has his own estimate of what the job ought to cost, and will negotiate with you only if he believes your estimate close enough to reach at least a reasonable compromise in negotiations.)

One important point: with only rare exception, there is only one winner in a proposal contest, and your competitors are usually experienced at writing proposals. Being as good as anyone else is not worth much. The objective is to offer a *better* plan and *better* credentials than anyone else. This is one place where superior writing abilities can make a substantive contribution in selling the plan.

INFORMATION ON GOVERNMENT NEEDS

Aside from the needs identified in the standard supply schedules, the federal agencies have hundreds of needs every day which require negotating individual contracts. These are announced every day in a Department of Commerce publication, printed by the Government Printing office, the *Commerce Business Daily*. (The GSA Business Service Center will usually furnish you a sample copy.)

The *Commerce Business Daily* (CBD) is published five days a week. It states on its front page: "A daily list of U.S. Government procurement invitations, contract awards, subcontracting leads, sales of surplus property, and foreign business opportunities." And it provides exactly that in from about 20 to 40 pages every business day. Services and supplies needed are listed under about 100 general headings, such as *Expert and Consultant Services, Maintenance and Repair of Equipment, Weapons, Lighting Fixtures and Lamps,* and *Clothing*.

Each such notice includes the address and sometimes the telephone number of the government office soliciting bids or proposals and the identifying number of the solicitation. To pursue the lead, you write or call that office for a copy of the solicitation ("bid set"), which will provide all the details you need to prepare your bid or proposal. In some cases, a special "pre-bid conference" is held to answer questions, but in most cases, the bid set is deemed to have furnished enough information to enable you to write your proposal.

BIDS INSTEAD OF PROPOSALS

However, not all solicitations so announced are RFPs calling for proposals. Many, especially those for materials and supplies, are of the formally advertised variety and call only for a bid. In these cases, the solicitation describes what is wanted—tools, machines, chemicals, foodstuffs, clothing, or whatever—and requires you to furnish your prices. (Forms are usually provided for pricing.) A bid-closing date and time is furnished, along with notice of where to deliver or mail your bid. That is ordinarily the same place where the public bid opening will be held, and if you choose to be present at the bid opening, you may deliver your bid at that time.

The bid opening is a simple affair. The contracting officer sits at a table, and anyone interested may be there at the table to listen to the bids being read aloud, with the bidders identified as the bids are opened. You are free to bring along a notepad and record the prices.

This is not the final act, however. After bids have been opened and read aloud, each will be checked to verify that all required information has been supplied, that the bid has been properly signed by someone authorized to bind the bidder, and that the arithmetic is correct. Then, with all bids so verified and all mathematics verified, the low bidder is officially identified and (usually) awarded the contract.

A mistake in arithmetic will not necessarily cost you the contract (although neglecting to sign your bid will). It depends on the kind of mistake. If it is such that you appeared to be the low bidder but are not, because of some mathematical error, you won't be disqualified, but you won't be the low bidder, either! On the other hand, you may be next to low, apparently, and actually low when arithmetic errors are corrected. (This was my experience once.)

Bidders lists

Each government contracting office maintains lists of bidders and sends solicitations to them automatically. To get on bidders lists, you need merely file a Standard Form 129, which you can obtain from any government contracting office, Department of Commerce office, GSA business service center, or Small Business Administration office. However, you must file a copy of this with each government contracting office from which you wish to receive solicitations.

Bid boards and bid rooms

Each government office that does a great deal of contracting on a regular basis maintains a "bid room" with a "bid board." All current solicitations are posted on this board, and you are free to visit such bid rooms regularly and inspect the bid boards. But even in those government contracting offices which do not do enough contracting to merit a special bid room and bid board, the equivalent exists in some form. Usually, it will be a loose-leaf binder with copies of all current solicitations. You are legally entitled to see this collection of bid sets whenever you please, during normal business hours.

BUYING FROM THE GOVERNMENT: SURPLUS PROPERTY

Property the U.S. government finds surplus and therefore available for sale to the public may be almost anything and in almost any condition, from new and unused to worn-out and suitable only for scrap. Perhaps the most sought-after item is the ubiquitous jeep, but few of these are sold in mint condition. The government sells many other vehicles, including passenger cars and trucks, but these, too, are generally sold only after long use. However, the government sells many items which are of interest to business people for business purposes—for example, timber, land, and buildings.

Most government surplus is sold via sealed bids, submitted after the prospective purchasers have had the opportunity to inspect the goods offered, although auctions are sometimes held.

There are some special cases, such as one in which the government sold a topless bar to the highest bidder. This unusual situation came about in this way: A government employee stole large sums of money through forgeries and falsifications, which amounted to something approximating $800,000 before he was caught. The government confiscated whatever it could, of course, from property he had bought with that money, including a topless bar in Washington, D.C. GSA then sold the bar to recover whatever it could of the $800,000.

In another case, a man bought several large crates of new electronics equipment for a few dollars at a government surplus sale. He discovered that the boxes contained new telephone switching equipment which had cost a great deal of money, but as far as is now known, he was never able to find an interested buyer!

On the other hand, a fair amount of government surplus is worth much more in scrap value than the selling price—in fact, this has caused the General Accounting Office to criticize federal agencies for unsound practices. For example, much electronic equipment contains precious metals—notably silver and gold, but often others. Much of the military electronics equipment sold as surplus contains large amounts of recoverable precious metals.

FOREIGN SALES LEADS

The Department of Commerce, among its many activities, tries to help American business do business in foreign countries, and has several programs to provide such assistance. For example, the Commerce Department will aid you in reaching foreign markets by exhibiting your products at trade fairs in other countries, frequently at no or little cost to you. At the same time, many foreign customers make their wants known to the Department of Commerce, and the department lists a great many of these in the *Commerce Business Daily* on an almost daily basis.

These appear under the general heading "Foreign Trade Opportunities, Department of Commerce." Under that general heading, some of them are "Department of State AID Financed" while others are "Direct Sales."

Listed then are a wide variety of needs—construction, heavy equipment, industrial development, consumer goods, and industrial equipment. In some cases the customer is a foreign government; in others it is a foreign company. Some cases call for writing and requesting a "tender" (equivalent to a solicitation), while in some cases a foreign buyer is in the United States and may be contacted directly. And in some other cases the contact is to be made through a Department of Commerce official who is identified in the notice.

THE SMALL BUSINESS ADMINISTRATION

Although SBA has been heavily criticized by Congress and others and has been a disappointment to many, some businesses have benefited from SBA and its programs. One of SBA's major responsibilities is to set "size standards" by which to determine what constitutes a small business for legal purposes.

In seeking to do this, SBA recognizes that the legal definition of a small business, as set forth in the Small Business Act, must be interpreted for each industry or industrial sector. The act provides that to qualify as a small business, a business must not be "dominant" in its industry, and SBA translates that provision into a measure of size, according to the nature of the industry. For example, for the petroleum refining industry, SBA established the size standard in terms of refining capacity and provided that only those refineries with a capacity not in excess of 40,000 barrels a day could qualify.

In other cases, size standards are set in terms of gross sales volume (say, not more than $3 million average sales over the previous three years) or number of employees (for example, not more than 500 employees).

To qualify as a small business, the organization must be counted in its entirety. It must be "independently owned," or if it has a parent organization or is owned by someone who also owns other such firms, the total holding will be counted. That prevents a large holding corporation from having its subsidiaries individually qualified as small businesses.

"Ownership" means controlling interest—at least 51 percent—and generally provides that the business must be "operated" by the owner(s). An absentee owner, especially one owning less than 51 percent, cannot normally qualify, especially if the business is part of a larger combine which in total size would not qualify.

Similar considerations apply to minority- and women-owned businesses: they must qualify as small businesses to get the benefits of the socioeconomic programs designed to help them. In reorganizing the SBA, in line with 1978 legislation amending the Small Business Act, SBA set up a minority small-business group to stress that qualification.

Small-business set-asides

One of the original facets of the small-business program, in addition to the loan and loan-guarantee programs, was the set-aside program, which is still in being, although less than 100 percent effective. (*Far* less!) In this program, the federal agencies' procurement offices are supposed to have established a small-business officer (sometimes an additional duty for the contracting officer rather than a separate position) to set aside contracts for small business only. That is, the requirements are to be studied, and whenever a requirement is such that the contracting office believes that small business can provide ample competition, the job is to be restricted to small business, larger business being barred from competing.

In making this judgment, contracting officers are faced with a problem: it may be quite difficult for them to determine whether there are enough small businesses qualified for and large enough to do the job to ensure an adequate amount of competition. Without this assurance, the contracting officer is inhibited from setting the procurement aside.

The result is that not nearly enough contracts are so set aside, although a number of them are every day. (The military, especially the Navy publications offices, have been probably the most effective at implementing this.) In some cases, such as that of Fort Belvoir, Virginia, a fixed policy has been established to further this program by deciding in advance that certain classes of procurement are automatically set aside for small business. For example, Fort Belvoir automatically sets aside "software" contracts—computer programming, technical writing, drafting, and so on.

Other SBA services

In addition to the services already described, the SBA provides a "certificate of competency" to firms whose technical qualifications have been questioned, and where such doubt was used as grounds for disqualifying the firm in a competitive bid. In such event, the firm may appeal to the SBA, which is then at liberty to order suspension of contract award while it performs an independent investigation of the firm's technical qualifications. Should SBA find that the firm appears qualified, it may issue a certificate of competency, which thereby invalidates the disqualification of the firm.

Similarly, if a firm is disqualified on the grounds of not demonstrating financial capability to carry out a project it bid on, SBA may again hold up award while it tries to provide financial aid to the firm.

SBA also publishes a large number of brochures and books on a variety of business subjects (for example, *Product Safety*

Checklist and *Store Location: "Little Things" Means a Lot*), which are furnished to small-business proprietors either free of charge or at nominal cost. These are written for SBA by executives and business people on a voluntary basis and cover a wide variety of business subjects. In net effect, they present the experience, wisdom, and advice of many successful business people.

20

IDEAS AND OPPORTUNITIES

THE WORLD OF TRADE

After more years in the business world than I will confess to here, I am still constantly amazed at the ingenuity of individuals in developing business ideas and putting them to work. We have had a look in these pages at a few business ideas that grew into truly big business. For each of those, there are thousands of small businesses which will never grow into major corporations or make their owners millionaires, but which will provide them with a comfortable living and something to leave to their children. It becomes quite obvious that you need not work for someone else if you prefer to work for yourself. And you need not wait for the muse—inspiration—to strike you either: there are many sources for getting ideas, new and used.

One way to have a look at a wide range of business ideas is to subscribe to a few of the many newsletters and other periodicals that offer help—"opportunity seeker" publications. Perhaps the premier newsletter of this type is the *Business Opportunities Digest,* originated in 1963 and published today by Jim Straw in Atlanta, Georgia. Each month, "BOD," as its many subscribers refer to it affectionately, lists literally hundreds of "wanted" and "available" offers of many kinds. Here are a few examples:

> SUBSCRIPTION AGENT wants magazines, newspapers, and newsletters to represent. (Name and address.)

> TV MARKETING FIRM seeks products to sell on TV for a percentage of profits.

FINDER will locate any type chemical needed for export.

ADVISER offers assistance to home owners who want to sell their homes themselves.

BOD usually has a number of "finder" offers in the monthly issue. A finder is someone who will find either a buyer or a seller and collect a commission from one party or the other, whichever one commissions the finder. In the current issue of BOD are listed a buyer who wants to find a sizable auto-leasing firm and will pay a fee to the finder and several other such offers. There are also notices from finders who list both buyers and sellers they are seeking. Any offer to buy or sell a sizable quantity of merchandise or parcel of real estate—any trade which involves a sizable amount of money—is a possibility for finders. Successful finders query everyone who runs a listing along these lines, offering a finder service in exchange for a commission. Many finders "earn a living"; there are others who earn well into six figures every year.

A gentleman from Chicago says, in the current BOD, that he is developing a microwave hot-water heater that will conserve energy and dollars for users. He wants to appoint regional representatives and accepts applications now. An engineering firm offers to send information on how to make your own alcohol to mix with gasoline. Recycled blue jeans and jogging shoes are offered in another notice, and a small publishing company announces that it is interested in seeing unpublished manuscripts on any subject and of any length, for possible publishing on a royalty basis. And if you have some use for eight or nine tons of Alaskan jade, a California subscriber has some to offer.

Business Opportunities Digest and other periodicals of the same nature (see the following chapter for specific listings) tend to specialize in trade offers—"wanted" and "available" merchandise, real estate, financing, partnerships, dealerships, franchises, and other business trades. But there are other publications which specialize in business *ideas,* both reports on what others are doing successfully and suggestions for new businesses.

THE WORLD OF BUSINESS IDEAS

Among the pioneers in publishing news of business ideas is George W. Haylings of Carlsbad, California. Haylings publishes the *Money Making Communiqué* every month, as well as a large number of self-contained business reports.

Another publisher active in publishing information of this sort is Thad Stevenson, now of Bellevue, Washington. He publishes the monthly periodical *Opportunity Knocks.*

Here is a sampling of ideas taken at random from such publications.

One man formed United Clergymen International, which registered bona fide clergymen and issued identifications, good for discounts at 30,000 retail establishments he arranged agreements with. His first mailing to clergymen brought in $15,000 in enrollments.

A New England man started a one-man delivery service for druggists and other retailers in his area who found his service more efficient than improvising their own deliveries. At the time of the report, his business had grown to several delivery vehicles and was grossing over $100,000 per year.

Some years ago, when computers were beginning to have a heavy impact on the business and scientific communities, a woman overheard two men discussing ideas for a new corporate name. She realized that there would be many new corporations formed around the new computer business, and that they would all be seeking good corporate names. She thought up about 70 corporate names using the word "computer" in them and incorporated each one as a corporate "shell." Over the next year she sold these names, for a total of well over $300,000.

A discharged Army veteran, proud of his service, had a local jeweler make him a ring showing the insignia of his former division. (All Army divisions have their own insignias.) He then hit on the idea that perhaps men still in service would like to have such rings. He had 100 sample rings made up, each with the insignia of an Army division, sent the samples to the various division commanding generals with an offer to supply such rings at $25 each. After a wait, he received his first order—$150,000 for 6,000 rings! And that was just from one division, the first of many orders that would ultimately arrive before he even expanded his business to rings for the other military services.

One woman whose name was Fox began wondering how many other people were named Fox. She soon discovered that Fox is a rather common name, and began to collect mailing lists of Foxes, to whom she began offering jewelry, stationery, and many other items which were either monogrammed "Fox" or bore some relation to the name. The common linkage proved an effective sales motivator.

One man sells pipes on approval, and he advertises that if the customer does not like the pipe, he may *break the pipe up and send back the pieces,* whereupon he owes nothing! He has been running this novel promotion for many years successfully.

The man who conceived the electronic language translator was not an engineer. He knew nothing of the technical problems involved in designing such a device. But he was familiar with all the pocket calculators, some of them, despite their small size, almost computers with amazingly sophisticated and complex abilities. He reasoned that it should be possible to build a pocket-size instrument capable of storing a small, working vocabulary of any language, with a counterpart in another language—a translator. He sought out engineering help and persevered until he succeeded in producing a practical device that holds up to 3,600 words and translates them from one language to another. The device is a commercial as well as a technical success. In addition to a 3,600-word capacity, it also stores 47 common phrases, all of which may be summoned up by pressing a key button, making it an almost indispensable travel companion for those going to foreign lands whose language they do not speak.

Chase Revel, operator of International Entrepreneurs Association and a man with a broad variety of business ventures in his personal history, claims a track record in predicting business trends. He predicts that with the petroleum shortages (and steadily increasing cost), a by-product of petroleum, plastics, will become increasingly expensive, giving rise to a boom in plastics recycling. He's also bullish on dainty feminine underwear (which he says is coming back), laundromats, and insulation. And he has a word to say about pioneering new things: in his opinion, such ventures are for fools and millionaires, because millionaires can afford the risk and fools simply do not know better.

The energy problem has also brought back into prominence an old profession: chimney sweeping. With many people turning to wood-burning fireplaces (many new homes are offering fireplaces as options), there is a need for chimney sweeps today, and many of the new chimney sweeps are educated men with master's degrees. But the lure of chimney sweeping is the profit to be made: one Harvard graduate claims to have grossed $240,000 in one year, and there are many who say that business is "fantastic." Going rates are on the order of $40 to $50 per chimney, with extra charges of $25 for each additional flue, and a chimney, it is reported, requires about one hour to sweep. There are an estimated 25 million chimneys in the United States, most of which are probably in need of cleaning right now. Working sweeps say that the work is dirty but not physically difficult. There is even a 110-pound, 5-foot, 2-inch mother doing the work successfully, completing five jobs a day.

If you prefer to have someone else start you in a business, there are many companies producing equipment and products designed to put you into your own enterprise. Here are some typical ones advertised in such publications as *Income Opportunities* and *Specialty Salesman*.

One company offers cassettes with special sound waves

designed to relax people, claiming that hospitals use them. It offers a "starter kit" and full instructions on how to sell these cassettes as a business.

At least two companies advertise furniture- and carpet-cleaning equipment, and promise to show you how to build a profitable business using their equipment.

You can also buy equipment and get instructions to do all of the following as a business:

Make rubber stamps.
Bronze baby shoes and other objects.
Sharpen saws.
Make badges for meetings' and conventions, souvenir shops, and so on.
Print bumper stickers.
Print signs and posters by silk-screen method.
Repair porcelain fixtures.
Repair cracked windshields.
Install fire and burglar alarms.
Repair small engines.
Convert TV sets to big-screen projection sets.
Become a locksmith.
Become a bookkeeper.
Make jewelry.
Repair tools.
Repair torn vinyl.
Be a printing broker.
Put decals on T-shirts.
Make Kentucky fried chicken.
Repair upholstery.
Customize cars and vans.
Make custom furniture.
Repair fiberglass boats, cars, and the like.
Become a professional photographer.
Make draperies, become an interior decorator.
Make picture frames.
Be a tax consultant.

Be a handwriting analyst.
Beat the odds at race tracks and casinos.
Stuff fish and animals.

For the most part, these offers are badly oversold in the advertisements, and caution is a good idea when investigating them. The equipment is generally rather high-priced, and the fields are crowded. The business of the advertisers is to sell their equipment and/or their books and training courses and, in many cases, the supplies you need with the equipment. However, as part of your general education and to help stimulate your thinking, browsing through these advertisements is good practice.

Many of these ideas—and the ideas you have read in these pages—have worked well for some people but may or may not work well for you, for a variety of reasons. Give some thought to what your idea requires of you to make it successful. For example, how are you at selling? Some of these ideas work only for the individual who is a good salesperson and who doesn't mind meeting people as a salesperson. On the other hand, if you are a good salesperson and like such work, you really do not need to invest in expensive equipment: there are myriads of opportunities for those who can sell on a personal basis.

But even if you find the idea of selling appealing to you, do you prefer to sell to consumers or to business people—say, dealers? The environment is quite different, and salespeople who are successful dealing with business people are not always happy selling directly to consumers.

Consider also whether your idea requires you to have some mechanical skills. There are those who simply do not get along with tools or anything mechanical. Also, do you prefer to be out and around constantly, on the move, or do you prefer a more sedentary situation? Consider hours, too: a retail establishment which caters to walk-in trade generally requires long hours.

Think about whether additional investment will be

needed, if you buy into one of the advertised plans. Carpet-cleaning equipment is rather bulky and will probably require a small truck or van. Saw-sharpening equipment is likely to require that you rent a workshop somewhere and advertise for business to come to you. Some plans require you to carry a substantial inventory.

But most of all, think about what other ideas these plans suggest to you—how you can modify or adapt a plan to create something better, whether it is a better way to do the job, a better product, a better service, or a better marketing method.

Take advantage, too, of all the "free" government assistance you can get. (I say "free" because it isn't really free; we all pay for it with our heavy tax load, and it makes good sense to use as much of the service as possible.)

I confess that I originally planned to include an appendix to this book, in which I planned to list other publications and miscellaneous useful information. But by the time I had nearly finished the manuscript, I came to the realization that it would be almost grotesque to call that kind of information "appended," in this case. Such information is very much a part of this book, a part of perhaps the most useful information. Therefore, I decided to devote the entire final chapter of this book to information I hope you will use frequently and with results as good as those I have got from much of it.

21

THE REFERENCE FILE

One thing we have learned about creativity is that those who expose themselves to ideas get the greatest number of ideas themselves. If you don't read, don't talk to many people, don't pay a great deal of attention to what goes on around you every day, but spend most of your time wondering what's on the tube tonight, you are obviously not spending much time thinking—and you are not going to generate any good ideas without thinking.

Of course, the opposite is also true: if you scoop up as much input information as possible, you can hardly help but do some reflecting on things and come up with a few ideas of your own. Therefore, I urge you to expose yourself to as many ideas, as much information, as you possibly can. Be aware of problems and what others are doing in trying to solve problems. Learn of new products and new business ideas, and think about how you might put some of these to work or adapt them to your own situation. Turn the tube off, once in a while, and read just a bit of the tremendous wealth of information available from hundreds of sources.

In this final chapter, I am going to try to help you in this endeavor as much as possible by listing for you a number of information sources and reference sources, many of which have been exceedingly helpful to me. Take advantage of them.

FEDERAL AGENCIES

One thing the U.S. government produces in abundance is "paper"—printed material. Much of it is most useful for starting the logs in your fireplace, but there are also many government brochures, pamphlets, books, and booklets which provide useful data.

The Small Business Administration produces a great many publications to aid small business. Many of them are free, while others are offered at almost nominal prices. Most of these are written by individuals in private industry, as a public service. They fall into several classes. Free literature may be found in the following general classes:

Management aids—for example, *Planning Your Working Capital Requirements* and *Getting Facts for Better Sales Decisions.*

Small-marketer's aids—for example, *Preventing Retail Thefts* and *Sales Contests for Wholesalers.*

Small-business bibliographies—for example, *Home Businesses* and *Financial Management.* (These are totally lists of recommended books and other publications, but most SBA publications include such recommendations.)

Preliminary SBA forms for loan applications—for example, *Personal Financial Statement* and *Monthly Cash Flow Projection.*

Counseling notes—for example, *Service Stations* and *The Nursery Business.*

Government procurement assistance—for example, *SBA Programs for Veterans of the Armed Forces* and *Minority Vendor Profile.*

Fact sheets—for example, *Seasonal Line of Credit Program* and *Physical Disaster Loan Program.*

Equity financing—*Starting a Small Business Investment Company.*

Title 13, CFR, SBA rules and regulations, and so on—for example, *Disclosure of Information and Privacy Act of 1974.*

SBA publications for which a charge is made must be purchased from the Government Printing Office. They are in three series:

Small Business Management Series—for example, *Handbook of Small Company Finance,* 83 pp., $1.50; and *Guides for Profit Planning,* 59 pp., $1.90.

Starting and Managing Series—for example, *Starting and Managing a Pet Shop,* 40 pp., 75¢; and *Starting and Managing an Employment Agency,* 118 pp., $1.30.

Nonseries Publications—for example, *Buying and Selling a Small Business,* 122 pp., $2.30; and *Managing for Profits,* 170 pp., $2.75.

Lists of these aids are available free of charge from any SBA office or may be requested from the following address:

Small Business Administration
P.O. Box 15434
Fort Worth, TX 76119
   or call toll-free 800-433-7212
   (Texas only call 800-792-8901)

In addition to these, all SBA offices can offer an abundance of small pamphlets and brochures, usually available on help-yourself display racks in SBA offices, that describe SBA services available.

The two lists to request are Forms SBA 115A (list of free publications) and SBA 115B (list of SBA publications for which a charge is made). Ask also, however, for Form 115 ML, which is an application form to have your name placed on a distribution list for new SBA free brochures, as they appear, and Form 348 SBA, which lists all SBA offices and their telephone numbers.

In the meanwhile, you can find your nearest SBA office listed in your own telephone directory under "U.S., Government of." (Or see *The $100 Billion Market* by Herman Holtz, published by AMACOM, 1980.) SBA offices are in these cities:

Boston, MA	Harrisburg, PA	Washington, DC
Holyoke, MA	Wilkes-Barre, PA	Atlanta, GA
Augusta, ME	Baltimore, MD	Biloxi, MS
Concord, NH	Wilmington, DE	Birmingham, AL
Newark, NJ	Clarksburg, WV	Charlotte, NC
Buffalo, NY	Charleston, WV	Greenville, NC
St. Thomas, VI	Pittsburgh, PA	Columbia, SC
Philadelphia, PA	Richmond, VA	Coral Gables, FL

Jackson, MS	Minneapolis, MN	Wichita, KS
Jacksonville, FL	Dallas, TX	Denver, CO
West Palm Beach,	Albuquerque, NM	Casper, WY
Tampa, FL	Houston, TX	Fargo, ND
Louisville, KY	Little Rock, AR	Helena, MT
Nashville, TN	Lubbock, TX	Salt Lake City, UT
Knoxville, TN	El Paso, TX	Rapid City, SD
Memphis, TN	Harlington, TX	Sioux Falls, SD
Hartford, CT	Corpus Christi, TX	San Francisco, CA
Montpelier, VT	Marshall, TX	Fresno, CA
Providence, RI	New Orleans, LA	Sacramento, CA
New York, NY	Shreveport, LA	Honolulu, HI
Camden, NJ	Oklahoma City, OK	Agana, Guam
Chicago, IL	San Antonio, TX	Los Angeles, CA
Springfield, IL	Kansas City, MO	Las Vegas, NV
Cleveland, OH	Des Moines, IA	Reno, NV
Columbus, OH	Albany, NY	Phoenix, AZ
Cincinnati, OH	Elmira, NY	San Diego, CA
Detroit, MI	Hato Rey, PR	Seattle, WA
Marquette, MI	Melville, NY	Anchorage, AK
Indianapolis, IN	Rochester, NY	Fairbanks, AK
Madison, WI	Syracuse, NY	Boise, ID
Milwaukee, WI	Omaha, NE	Portland, OR
Eau Claire, WI	St. Louis, MO	Spokane, WA

The U.S. Department of Commerce also offers many publications, as well as a number of services, to businesses. One valuable publication is its *Guide to Federal Assistance Programs for Minority Business Enterprises,* which may be requested from the department, Washington, DC 20230. However, the Commerce Department, like SBA, has a large number of offices scattered around the United States, and a personal visit to one will bring you an armload of informational brochures describing the many Commerce Department services which can be of substantial aid to you in your enterprises.

Over the past year, the Commerce Department has established revolving loan funds for small-business assistance in a large number of areas. One thing you might ask for is a list of these (new ones are constantly being established) to see if there is one so located as to be of aid to you.

In general, the Economic Development Administration of

the Commerce Department operates a large program of financial assistance to state and local governments, to community organizations, and to private businesses, with grants usually awarded to the local governments and community organizations, and loan guarantees to private firms. The basic justification for a grant or loan must be to create or save jobs, but loan guarantees may be sought by businesses to aid them in almost any set of circumstances, if they can demonstrate that jobs will be created or saved by such assistance.

If you belong to that class of Americans generally acknowledged to be "socially and economically disadvantaged minorities," you can probably get some assistance from one of the 300-odd organizations supported by the Commerce Department. Ask for its publication "OMBE Funded Organizations Directory," which is issued every year.

Government periodicals

It is not generally known to the public, but the U.S. Government publishes hundreds of periodicals through its many agencies, far too many to list here. Here is just a small sampling:

Business America (bi-weekly)
Business Conditions Digest (monthly)
FDA Consumer (monthly)
Food and Nutrition (bi-monthly)
Statistical Bulletin (monthly)

To get the complete listing, along with instructions for subscribing to any periodicals that interest you, ask for a free copy (practically the only thing that *is* free today from the Government Printing Office) of the publication *Government Periodicals and Subscription Services, Price List 36*. Order this from

Superintendent of Documents
U.S. Government Printing Office
Washington, DC 20420

If you wish to keep in touch with federal requirements, you may subscribe to the *Commerce Business Daily,* published five days a week by the U.S. Department of Commerce and printed by the Government Printing Office. Cost is $80 per year mailed second-class, $105 per year mailed first-class. However, you can now get a six-month subscription for $45 mailed second-class, $60 mailed first-class. To order, send payment to the Superintendent of Documents in Washington.

Some other government manuals

If you are interested in doing business directly with the government—that is, in pursuing government contracts (in which case I refer you again to the AMACOM book, *The $100 Billion Market*)—you can get a number of publications to assist you in learning of the various agencies' needs and procedures. Here is a sampling, which is by no means all-inclusive:

Small Business Guide to Federal R&D, National Science Foundation, Office of Small-Business R&D, 1800 G Street, NW, Washington, DC 20550.

Proposal Preparation Manual, U.S. Department of Transportation, Research and Special Programs Administration, Office of University Research, Washington, DC 20590.

Doing Business With the Department of the Interior, U.S. Department of the Interior, Division of Procurement and Grants Branch of Minority Procurement, Washington, DC 20240.

Government Business Opportunities, General Services Administration, Washington, DC 20405.

List of Commodities and Services, GSA Form 1382, General Services Administration, Washington, DC 20405.

GPO publications

The Government Printing Office (GPO) claims the printing of "tens of thousands" of publications each year, ranging from pamphlets to bound volumes and multivolume sets of books. GPO's booklet *Consumer's Guide to Federal Publications* (available free from GPO, as listed here earlier) claims that "some of them are free," while others are offered for sale. The fact is that GPO offers nothing free today, except sales brochures and announcements of its publications, although many of its publications *are* free at other federal agencies. Approximately 25,000 GPO publications are offered for sale, including the periodicals referred to here. These are divided into approximately 300 general categories, and the GPO offers to send you free copies of bibliographies or catalog sheets for those categories which interest you. Instructions and an order form are included in the *Consumer's Guide* referred to above. Upon your request, GPO will also place your name on a mailing list for announcements of new books, *Selected U.S. Government Publications*.

GPO also advises that many other government offices have descriptive literature available, which they will send you on request. Here is a list of such government information-publications sources.

For statistical and economic information on mineral resource development, including exploration, production, demand, stocks, prices, imports, and exports, write

> Branch of Publications
> Bureau of Mines
> 4800 Forbes Ave.
> Pittsburgh, PA 15212

For nautical charts and topographic maps:

> Defense Mapping Agency
> Topographic Center
> ATTN: 55500
> 6500 Brooks Lane
> Washington, DC 20315

For aeronautical charts, domestic and foreign, and nautical charts of U.S. waters, the Great Lakes, and possessions (over-the-counter sales at all offices listed; mail orders to Riverdale, Maryland office only), write:

National Ocean Survey
Distribution Division (C-44)
Riverdale, MD 20840
(301) 436-6990

National Ocean Survey
Chart Sales Office
6001 Executive Blvd.
Room 101
Rockville, MD 20852
(301) 443-8005

National Ocean Survey
Chart Sales Office
439 West York Street
Norfolk, VA 23510
(804) 441-6776

National Ocean Survey
Chart Sales Office
1801 Fairview Avenue East
Seattle, WA 98102
(206) 442-7656

National Ocean Survey
Chart Sales and Control Data
   Office
632 Anchorage Avenue
Room 405
Anchorage, AK 99501
(907) 265-4470

For publications, facsimiles, and reproductions of historical documents available to the public, request *Documents from America's Past,* a publication of the National Archives and Records Service:

General Services Administration
Publication Sales Branch (NEPS-G)
Washington, DC 20408
(202) 523-3164

A large number of government-sponsored technical reports on a variety of subjects are available from the following office:

National Technical Information Service
5285 Port Royal Road
Springfield, VA 22161
(703) 557-4660

The Smithsonian Institution also publishes many books and pamphlets on a wide variety of subjects, and has a catalog available. Write:

Smithsonian Institution Press
Publications Distribution Section
1111 North Capitol Street
Washington, DC 20002
(202) 381-5021

Many topographical maps and reports of mineral and water resources investigations on federal lands are available from the following offices:

(For areas east of the Mississippi River, including Minnesota, Puerto Rico, and the Virgin Islands)

Branch of Distribution
U.S. Geological Survey
1200 South Eads Street
Arlington, VA 22202
(703) 557-2751

(Maps only, for areas west of the Mississippi River, including Alaska, Hawaii, Louisiana, Guam, and American Samoa)

U.S. Geological Survey
Denver Branch of Distribution
Box 25046
Federal Center
Denver, CO 80225
(303) 234-3832

Residents of Alaska may also order Alaska maps from:

Alaskan Distribution Section
Branch of Distribution in Alaska
U.S. Geological Survey
Federal Building
P.O. Box 12
101 12th Avenue
Fairbanks, AK 99701
(907) 456-7535

GPO bookstores are located in the following cities:

Atlanta, GA	Jacksonville, FL	Washington, DC:
Birmingham, AL	Kansas City, MO	GPO
Boston, MA	Los Angeles, CA	Department of
Chicago, IL	Milwaukee, WI	Commerce
Cleveland, OH	New York, NY	Department of State
Columbus, OH	Philadelphia, PA	Pentagon
Dallas, TX	Pueblo, CO	USIA
Denver, CO	San Francisco, CA.	Department of
Detroit, MI	Seattle, WA	Health and
Houston, TX		Human Services

For help in information research in Washington

Washington contains the greatest store of information in the world. But finding it is most difficult for those not familiar with the Great Bureaucracy. One enterprising gentleman, Matthew Lesko, perceived this problem several years ago and proceeded to do something about it by organizing Washington Researchers. His firm publishes several manuals on the subject of how to research the information you want in Washington, conducts seminars on the subject, provides researching services, and even publishes a little newsletter about the subject. Two publications the firm sells are *Researcher's Guide to Washington* and *Washington Information Workbook*. For details, write and request literature from:

> Washington Researchers
> 918 16th Street, NW
> Washington, DC 20006
> (202) 828-4800

BOOKS RECOMMENDED

Some of the following books are world-famous and recommended by many people as among the best ever written in their fields; others are simply my own choices, most of them with a place on my own shelves. And where I choose to make comments, the comments reflect my personal opinion and I accept full responsibility for them.

Free Enterprise, the story of the Aronson Machine Company, written and published by Charles N. Aronson, and available directly from him at RR 1, Hundred Acres, Arcade, NY 14009. This is a mammoth book in many ways—approximately 1,700 pages (available in hard or soft covers), revealing the most intimate details of how the author battled his way up from the most discouraging and difficult beginnings to a sale of his company, after 23 years, for over $2 million *cash*. The book is loaded with Aronson's wry humor (even in rage at man's cupidity and treachery, he is often able to jeer at himself). It is especially rich in what I choose to call "Aronsonisms," his own always perceptive, often humorous observations about business life. Example: "You can't beat a man who refuses to quit. You can kill him, but you can't beat him." He also observes that companies are "little and mean" because the men who run them are little and mean. Altogether, this giant book contains a lifetime's worth of business wisdom for the thoughtful reader.

Up Your OWN Organization, by Don Dible, The Entrepreneur Press, Fairfield, CA 94533, 1971. Now available in your bookstore in paperback edition. This book would have impressed me even if I had never known Don Dible or heard him speak publicly. Having had that privilege, as the result of sharing the platform with him at a seminar for Control Data Corporation customers who were all small-business owners, I was far more able to appreciate the wealth of information contained in his book, and even borrowed some of his more pungent expressions.

The Complete Book of Money Making Opportunities, by J. F. Straw, published by Frederick Fell, New York, 1979. Jim Straw is also publisher of the newsletters *Business Opportunities Digest* and *Business Intelligence Network*. He is a business generalist who draws largely on his own experience for the content of his book, which makes many cogent observations for which I am indebted to him. His book, which is relatively recent at the time of this writing, has been well received, and many have praised it highly for its commonsense attitudes and approaches to business problems. Brutally frank, this book offers the harsh realities of the author's own experience.

How I Raised Myself from Failure to Success in Selling, by Frank Bettger, published originally in 1949 by Prentice-Hall, Englewood Cliffs, NJ, and still found in the bookstores after many successive printings. This book has been widely acclaimed, and the latest edition has a foreword relating the history of this amazing success. Must reading for anyone engaged in trade. (You'll almost certainly find yourself rereading it many times over the years, as I have.)

How I made $1,000,000 in Mail Order, by Joseph E. Cossman, published by Prentice-Hall, Englewood Cliffs, NJ, 1963. Cossman's is one of the great success stories about "mail order" (although his promotions were not always strictly mail order), and he reveals a great deal of valuable inside information in this account of his experiences and practical business education. Full of sound advice.

The Publish-It-Yourself Handbook, a collection of separately authored chapters, edited by Bill Henderson, published by The Pushcart Press, Yonkers, NY, 1973, itself an example of how to publish it yourself. This is a widely recommended book on the subject of how to be your own publisher, and offers a great many ideas and much detailed information.

How to Form Your Own Corporation, by Cotton Howell, Hamilton Press/Citizen's Law Library, 6 West Loudon St., Box 1745, Leesburg, VA. Cotton Howell is an eminent and highly experienced trial lawyer, with a background in general law practice. He has been busy for several years now writing an entire series of books on do-it-yourself legal practice, and he, among many others, agrees that forming a corporation is quite simple and easily done by the intelligent layman, given adequate instruction, which he hereby furnishes. Citizen's Law Library will send you literature on the entire law library, together with a sample copy of the quarterly newsletter *Citizen's Law Adviser* and announcements of new volumes being written by Howell.

The $100 Billion Market, by Herman Holtz, published by

AMACOM, New York, 1980. This is a detailed description of the vast U.S. government marketplace, with equally detailed instruction and advice for selling your goods and/or services to the federal agencies. Modesty prevents me from telling you how great this piece of work is. Just write AMACOM and ask for literature about it, or just order your own copy and judge for yourself.

You, Inc., by Peter Weaver, published by Doubleday, available now in your bookstore in soft covers. Weaver is an energetic free-lance writer who also does some TV commentary regularly on consumer-interest topics. He is a firm believer in free enterprise, particularly in the individual striking out on his own, and he offers both advice and encouragement in his book.

My First 65 Years in Advertising, a wry title by Maxwell Sackheim, Tab Books, Blue Ridge Summit, PA 1975; paperback. Sackheim was a specialist in mail order advertising (he's now semiretired in Florida). He developed many outstandingly successful advertisements and earned a leading reputation in his field. His book is loaded with examples, as well as observations and explanations. You are quite likely to find at least one example which is close to your own situation or need.

The Writer's Market, by the staff and others, published annually by Writer's Digest, Cincinnati, OH. Available in most bookstores. Useful to all writers, of course, but also most useful to photographers, illustrators, researchers, and advertisers for its peerless lists of periodicals and other types of publications.

The following books are offered with little or no comment. This is not damning with faint praise, but little or no comment appears necessary or helpful with these titles.

Where the Money Is and How to Get It, by Ted Nicholas, published by Enterprise Publishing Co., Wilmington, DE 1973.

Government Contracts, by Herman Holtz, published by Plenum Publishing Corporation, New York, 1979.

How and Where to Get Capital, by David Magee and staff, Counselor Reports, Kerrville, TX.

Membership Directory, National Association of Small Business Investment Companies, 537 Washington Building, Washington, DC 20005.

The Encyclopedia of Little-Known, Highly Profitable Business Opportunities, by Jack Payne, published by Frederick Fell, New York, 1971.

Complete Guide to Making Money with Your Ideas and Inventions, by Richard E. Paige, Prentice-Hall, Englewood Cliffs, NJ, 1973.

The Rogue of Publisher's Row, by Edward Uhlan, Exposition Press, Jericho, NY, 1970.

Up the Organization, famous title by Robert Townsend, Alfred A. Knopf, New York, 1970. This book was a sensation, inspired Don Dible's title, offers many unique viewpoints.

How to Start Your Own Business on a Shoestring and Make Up to $100,000 a Year, by Tyler Hicks, Parker Publishing Co., Nyack, NY, 1970. Hicks is prolific, has turned out many titles on getting financing and making money in business. This is one of his most successful efforts.

How to Turn Your Idea into a Million Dollars, by Don Kracke, with Roger Honkanen, published by Doubleday, New York, 1977. The title makes it sound easy, but this is no "get rich quick" fantasy; Kracke is frank about the problems and the agonies, not just about the joys of success.

Handbook of Home Business Ideas and Plans, by the staff of the periodical *The Mother Earth News,* published by Bantam Books, New York, 1976.

Marriott, by Robert O'Brien, Deseret Book Company, Salt Lake City, UT, 1977. Perhaps a typical vanity book commissioned by a corporate executive, under a subsidized publishing program. This one, however, provides many interesting and useful facts about the modest beginnings of what has become a giant corporation (over $1 billion annual sales today), starting with an almost literal hole-in-the-wall root beer stand.

How to Start and Manage Your Own Business, by Gardiner G. Greene, published by McGraw-Hill, New York, 1975.

100 Surefire Businesses You Can Start with Little or No Investment, by Jeffrey Feinman, published by Playboy Press, Chicago, 1976.

How Mail Order Fortunes Are Made, by Alfred Stern, Selective Books, Clearwater, FL, 1974.

Creative Selling Through Trade Shows, by Al Hanlon, published by Hawthorn Books, New York, 1977.

The Exhibit Medium, by David Maxwell, published by *Successful Meetings Magazine,* Philadelphia, 1978.

How to Participate Profitably in Trade Shows, by Robert B. Konikow, published by Dartnell Corporation, Chicago, 1977.

Advertising, by James S. Norris, Reston Publishing Company, Reston, VA, 1977.

Advertising Procedure, by Otto Kleppner and Norman Govini, 7th ed., published by Prentice-Hall, Englewood Cliffs, NJ, 1979.

How to Get Big Results from a Small Advertising Budget, by Cynthia S. Smith, Hawthorn Books, New York, 1973.

The Marketing Communications Process, by M. Wayne De Lozier, published by McGraw-Hill, New York, 1976.

There are, of course, many other excellent books, and the exclusion from this listing in no way suggests that they are not worthy of inclusion.

NEWSLETTERS YOU OUGHT TO KNOW ABOUT

No one knows exactly how many newsletters are published, but the number almost surely runs well into the thousands. Following are just a few I know about and which I believe are useful for you to know about. However, a more complete listing is contained in a directory published by Howard Penn Hudson, who also publishes *The Newsletter on Newsletters.* I find it most useful to have this directory on my desk, especially when I am preparing publicity releases:

The Newsletter Yearbook Directory (currently in 2nd ed.)
Newsletter Clearinghouse
44 West Market Street
Rhinebeck, NY 12572

Here are a few that I read and use:

Business Opportunities Digest and *Business Intelligence Network,* published by J. F. Straw, Straw Enterprises, 3110 Maple Drive NE, Suite 114, Atlanta, GA 30305. "BOD" is probably the oldest and most successful newsletter of its type, carrying literally hundreds of leads for business trades every month. "BIN" is not really a newsletter but an idea and information service for entrepreneurs. Monthly issues.

Fund Raiser's Exchange, Steve Savage, White River Designs, 237 Brookfield Gulf Road, Randolph, VT 05060. This is an excellent example of the newsletter art, highly professional, with many good ideas for fund raisers and suppliers of fund raisers. Published ten times a year.

Peephole on People, or "POP," as author-publisher Charles N. Aronson refers to it. All about many things that Aronson thinks worth commenting on or reporting on, including business topics. Inexpensive and fun reading, with many sparkling gems of both personal and business wisdom glittering among the recipes and sermons. Monthly issues. Charles N. Aronson, RR 1, Hundred Acres, Arcade, NY 14009.

Government Marketing News, primarily about proposal writing and related subjects. Government Marketing News, Box 6067, Wheaton, MD 20906. Published ten times a year.

Direct Marketing News Digest, 708 Silver Spur Road, Rolling Hills Estates, CA 90274. About direct marketing, including fund raising, mail order, advertising, newsletter publishing, and other aspects of direct marketing. Contains a gem or two every month. Published twice a month.

Boardroom Reports, 500 Fifth Ave, New York, NY 10036. Published 24 times a year. Twenty pages of business information, totally varied, a potpourri for executives and business people at all levels.

Brainstorms, H. K. Simon Co., Inc., 1280 Saw Mill River Road, Yonkers, NY 10710. Monthly assortment of ideas on business. May be on advertising or other promotion, but always on how to do more business.

Key, Voice Publications, Goreville, IL 62939. Ideas and information on sales promotion and advertising.

Small Business and Mail Order Views & News, DOL's House Press, 7801 Desen Drive, Lanham, MD 20801. Bi-monthly. A tabloid-style publication, full of "circle" advertising, but with many helpful articles and reports, some of them exclusive.

Towers Club, USA, 3601 E. 11th Street, Vancouver, WA 98661. Ten times a year, Jerry Buchanan, the Vancouver guru of the self-publishers, holds forth on the subject. Buchanan has a devoted following, also sells many books on subjects related to writing and publishing.

Profit Seminar, H. K. Simon Co., Inc., Dept. H, 1280 Saw Mill River Road, Yonkers, NY 10710. Published monthly. Information on business, ideas; answers questions, solves readers' problems. First-class information.

The Editorial Eye, Editorial Experts, Inc., 5905 Pratt Street, Alexandria, VA 22310. Published twenty times a year. Primarily on editorial/writing/publishing matters, useful tips, guidance, partially a house organ for the company, which provides editorial services, including temporary editorial specialists to work on the customer's premises.

Kellner's Moneygram, Kellner's Photo Services, 1768 Rockville Drive, Baldwin, NY 11510. A monthly letter service for free-lance photographers, offering a variety of tips, advice, leads for selling photos.

*Ca$h Newsletter,* Ca$hco, Box 1999, Brooksville, FL 33512. Published monthly. Written and published by G. Douglas Hafely, offering financial and investment advice, inflation-fighting tips. Useful for both personal and business applications.

The NAFCO Letter, Ivy Publishing Co., Box 1, Ischua, NY 14746. Published monthly. The publisher, Dick Brisky, furnishes a medium of exchange for those engaged in financial brokering and related fields. The newsletter carries both "wanted" and "available" notices, is outstanding in its field, highly successful and rapidly growing, due to conscientious and ethical effort by the publisher. *The* newsletter for free-lance financial people.

Direct Mail Briefs from Bringe, Paul J. Bringe, Inc., Box 139, Hartford, WI 53027. Published monthly. Bringe is a re-tired direct-mail executive, passing on the benefits of his many years' knowledge through his newsletter. He has a knack for stripping the mystery away and explaining logically why cer-tain approaches work while others do not.

The Writers/Publishers Digest, National Writers Syndicate, Box 1745, Leesburg, VA 22075. Newsletter for writers of all types.

Easy Chair Shopper, GMF Publications, Box 2506, Arling-ton, VA 22202. Published monthly. This has been one of the best of the tabloid papers devoted to mail order, carrying "cir-cle" advertising and helpful articles and reports. Now merging with another successful tabloid, *National Opportunities Clas-sified,* it promises to be bigger and better than ever.

The Photoletter, Ron Engh, Osceola, WI 54020. A bi-weekly. Engh offers a newsletter that is crammed full to the brim, every issue, with specific leads for free-lance photog-raphers, providing great detail on exactly what each source wants. Engh is a professional photographer who "retired" to the country but still is an active photographer when he isn't busy getting his newsletter together. Highly regarded.

"OPPORTUNITY" PUBLICATIONS

A number of publications are directed toward the "oppor-tunity seeker" market—those individuals just getting started in small enterprises or studying the field, trying to select the best ideas on which to base a business. In some of these publica-tions steady advertisers, particularly those who take full pages, are given free "editorial space." That is, all the "editorial" matter is actually free advertising, with the advertiser permitted to write his own copy as though it were an objective article rather than free advertising. A few of these publications have legitimate editorial content, with editorial staff completely independent of the advertising salesmen. Therefore, you may or may not get useful articles to read when you subscribe to these. (A couple, at least, give free trial subscriptions of several months' duration.) But many people read these publications primarily for the advertisements anyway, since their main purpose is to see what is being offered and/or what the competition is doing. All have extensive classified advertising sections, as well as display advertisements, and for many entrepreneurs, these publications are productive advertising media. Most of those listed are likely to send you at least a sample issue, if not a free trial subscription.

Income Opportunities, Davis Publications, 380 Lexington Avenue, New York, NY 10017.

Salesman's Opportunity Magazine, 6 N. Michigan Avenue, Chicago, IL 60602. (Offers free five-month trial.) Published monthly.

Specialty Salesman Magazine, Communication Channels, Inc., 307 N. Michigan Avenue, Chicago, IL 60601. Published monthly.

Money Making Opportunities, 13263 Ventura Boulevard, Studio City, CA 91604.

There are a number of other publications that carry large classified advertising columns, along with display space, for mail order dealers, and a number of them run "display-classified" advertisements today. This innovation permits the advertiser to use small display advertisements that will appear in the classified columns, interspersed with the classified advertisements. The advantage to the advertiser is that he brings his announcement to the attention of the many people who read the classified advertisements but not necessarily the display ads.

Among the most popular media for classified advertisements (in addition to the "opportunity" publications cited earlier) are these newspapers:

National Enquirer, weekly tabloid newspaper, Lantana, FL 33464.

Grit, weekly tabloid newspaper, 208 W. 3rd Street, Williamsport, PA 17701. An old-timer, *Grit* has been in publication since 1882. Appeals especially to rural folk.

The Star, weekly tabloid, 730 3rd Avenue, New York, NY 10017. Large circulation, among the leaders in this field of publishing.

Capper's Weekly, Stauffer Communications, 616 Jefferson Street, Topeka, KS 66607. Similar to *Grit* and slightly older (since 1879).

Midnight Globe, 200 Railroad Avenue, Greenwich, CT 06830. Same genre as *The Star* and *National Enquirer.*

A certain group of magazines also boast heavy classified ad sections, which are favored by mail order people because they produce good results. They include:

Mechanix Illustrated, 1515 Broadway, New York, NY 10036.

Popular Mechanics, 224 W. 57th Street, New York, NY 10019.

Popular Science, 380 Madison Avenue, New York, NY 10017.

Science & Mechanics, Davis Publications, 380 Lexington Avenue, New York, NY 10017.

If you want to reach military or civil-service people, you might try the "Times" magazines: *Army Times, Navy Times, Air Force Times,* and *Federal Times.* All are published by the Army Times Publishing Company, 475 School Street, SW, Washington, DC 20024. You can order advertising for any or all of these.

WAYS TO KEY ADS

There are many ways to "key" your advertisements so that you can measure just what responses you are getting from various media and from various offers. Here are some of the many ways:

Additions to your street address—Drawer M, Suite K, Room 22, and so forth.

Fictitious names: R. Jones, P. Smith, and the like.

Fictitious titles: Advertising Manager, Shipping Chief, and so on.

Add building name: Jones Building.

Alter company name: James P. Jones, Inc., James P. Jones Co., James Jones & Co., and so on.

Vary spelling of name: James Joanes & Co., James Jones & Co.

Add middle initial to company name: James X. Jones & Co.

Use alternate street-name spellings: Avery Rd, Averrie Rd.

Many advertisers use a mnemonic (memory-aiding) code by adding the initials of the publication, as in Dept NE (*National Enquirer*), Rm PM (*Popular Mechanics*), or Box 731MMO (*Money Making Opportunities*).

GETTING MORE ADVERTISING MILEAGE OUT OF YOUR ENVELOPES

Many advertisers use the outside of the envelope to add a sales message by using "envelope copy" or "teaser copy." This, hopefully, will offset the instinctive action of throwing away what appears to be advertising matter without even opening it. One instance, which I used myself successfully in soliciting attendees for a seminar, had these words in bold type in the lower left-hand area of the envelope:

Learn the art of
Proposalmanship!

During this one day workshop on
Winning Government Contracts!

Many dealers who run inquiry advertising use the envelope to advise the reader "YOU SENT FOR THIS," when sending out the literature the respondent has requested.

The pros of doing this are fairly obvious: theoretically, at least, such copy is additional advertising at no additional cost, and may reduce the number of direct-mail pieces thrown away without being opened. The drawback, at least for those cases where the envelope is not obviously carrying advertising matter inside, is that it telegraphs that the envelope contains advertising literature, which may then *increase* the number thrown away. The best way probably is to test and see whether envelope copy is beneficial.

A FEW LEADING CATALOG HOUSES

There are a number of companies that do all or most of their business by appointing agents to mail catalogs supplied by the company and imprinted with the agent's name. Others supply catalogs for use in taking orders by personal contact. In either case, the agent deducts the commission and sends the order on to the company to fill. Here are the names of a number of prominent catalog companies:

Giftime
4700 Wissahickon Avenue
Philadelphia, PA 19144
(Gift items)

Specialty Merchandise Corp.
6061 DeSoto Avenue
Woodland Hills, CA 91365
(General merchandise)

The Hanover Shoe, Inc.
Hanover, PA 17331
(Shoes)

Cameo Collection
171 Madison Avenue
New York, NY 10016
(Jewelry)

KC Business Forms Co.
Box 128
Tecumseh, KS 66542
(Business forms)

Jobbers Distributing Co.
Box 2128
Durham, NC
(Jewelry and general
  Merchandise)

Mail Order Associates
120 Chestnut Ridge Road
Montvale, NJ 07645
(General merchandise)

Show n' Sell Jewels, Inc.
Box 66291
Chicago, IL 60666
(Jewelry)

TRF Industries, Inc.
40 E. 49th Street
New York, NY 10017
(Rings)

National Press, Inc.
North Chicago, IL 60064
(Printing specialties)

Knapp Shoes
601 Knapp Center
Brockton, MA 02401
(Shoes)

Johnson Smith Company
35075 Automation Avenue
Mt. Clemens, MI 48043
(General merchandise)

SELLING TO MAIL ORDER FIRMS

There are literally thousands of mail order firms selling through catalogs and other means. Many are continually on the watch for new and better products to offer, and are good sales prospects for anyone with merchandise to offer. Here are the names of just a few of the leading such houses, with information following on how to get a directory listing nearly 6,000 such firms:

Sunset House Distributing
Corp.
3485 S. La Cienega
Boulevard
Los Angeles, CA 90016

Emerson Enterprises
Box 338
Fallbrook, CA 92028

Stanley Home Products Co.
4500 Campus Drive
New Port Beach, CA 92660

Warner Electric Co.
1512 W. Jarvis Avenue
Chicago, IL 60627

Midwestern Card Company
Box 530
St. Louis, MO 63166

Edmund Scientific Company
300 Edscorp Building
Barrington, NJ 08007

Lafayette Radio Electronics
Corp.
165-08 Liberty Avenue
Jamaica, NY 11433

Hoffritz for Cutlery
20 Cooper Square
New York, NY 10003

National Dynamics
Corporation
145 East 32nd Street
New York, NY 10016

The New Process Company
220 Hickory Street
Warren, PA 16365

Montgomery Ward & Co.
619 W. Chicago Avenue
Chicago, IL 60610

Frederick's of Hollywood
6608 Hollywood Boulevard
Hollywood, CA 90028

Walter Drake & Sons
4510 Edison Avenue
Colorado Springs,
  CO 80915

Fingerhut Corporation
11 McLeland Drive
St. Cloud, MN 56301

Spencer Gifts
Spencer Building
Atlantic City, NJ 08411

Edmar Creations
35 Mohegan Street
Clifton, NJ 07011

Jamestown Stamp Company
341 East 3rd Street
Jamestown, NY 14701

Lew Magram
830 Seventh Avenue
New York, NY 10019

Wall Street Camera
  Exchange
82 Wall Street
New York, NY 10005

The Drawing Board, Inc.
256 Regal Row, Box 505
Dallas, TX 75221

A Florida firm publishes an annual directory of nearly 6,000 firms, listed by states and cities, and identifying those which are the largest in their respective fields. The listings are also available on gummed labels. The volume and publisher are as follows:

Mail Order Business Directory
B. Klein Publications
P.O. Box 8503
Coral Springs, FL 33065

SOURCES FOR MAILING LISTS

There are many mailing-list brokers who can supply lists of all sizes and types, and at virtually all prices. Following are the names of a few who are generally recognized as being among the leaders in this field. The omission of others, however, does not signify that they are not also dependable and ethical, but merely that it is necessary to restrict the entries here, due to space limitations.

Dependable Lists, Inc.	257 Park Avenue So., New York, NY 10010
	1025 Vermont Avenue, NW, Washington, DC 20005
	333 N. Michigan Avenue, Chicago, IL 60601
	16661 Ventura Boulevard, Encino, CA 91436
Dun & Bradstreet, Inc.	7400 York Road, Baltimore, MD 21212
	1600 Wilson Boulevard, Arlington, VA 22209
Accredited Mailing Lists	15 E. 40th Street, New York, NY 10016
American Mailing Lists	7777 Leesburg Pike, Falls Church, VA 22043
Willa Maddern, Inc.	215 Park Avenue, New York, NY 10016
Florence Wolf, Inc.	919 N. Michigan Avenue, Chicago, IL 60601
Direct Marketing, Inc.	90 S. Ridge Street, Port Chester, NY 10573
	20 N. Wacker Drive, Chicago, IL 60606
	8720 Georgia Avenue, Silver Spring, MD 20910
Januz Direct Marketing	3553 W. Peterson Avenue, Chicago, IL 60659
Wm. Stroh, Inc.	568 W. 54th Street, West New York, NJ 07093
Uni-Mail	134 E. 73rd Street, New York, NY 10021
R. R. Bowker Co.	1180 Avenue of the Americas, New York, NY 10036
Ed Burnett Consultants, Inc.	176 Madison Avenue, New York, NY 10016
Cahners Publishing Co.	5 S. Wabash Avenue, Chicago, IL 60603

Chilton Direct Mail Co.	Chilton Way, Radnor, PA 19089
Herbert Dunhill Association, Ltd.	273 Columbus Avenue, Tuckahoe, NY 10707
Dunhill-Hugo Mailing Lists	444 Park Avenue, New York, NY 10016
R. L. Polk & Co.	6400 Monroe Boulevard, Taylor, MI 48180
Selmar Brooks Publishing Co.	126 Homecrest Station, Brooklyn, NY 11229
American Library Association	50 E. Huron Street, Chicago, IL 60651
American Student List Co.	98 Cutter Mill Road, Great Neck, NY 10021

SOME SPECIAL PUBLICATIONS

There are a number of publications that are little known outside "the trade" but are likely to be of great interest to you, depending on what business you are in or plan to enter. The following is only a partial listing:

Direct Marketing, 224 Seventh Street, Garden City, NY 11530. This is a periodical, published monthly, and considered by many to be the bible of mail order and other direct-selling businesses.

Insiders' Magazine, P.O. Box 879, New Hyde Park, NY 11040. This is a monthly periodical addressed to flea-market sellers, wagon jobbers, party-plan and mail order sellers, rack merchandisers, and other sellers of merchandise. The publisher promises to bring readers continuous tips on where, how, what to buy at lowest prices, and offers a trial issue for $2.

How to Copyright Literary Works, written and published by Judge Lee Ward, 165 S. 3rd Avenue, Piggott, AR 72454. Lee Ward is a retired jurist. This 47-page manual explaining the new copyright law which became effective January 1, 1978, is thorough and easy to understand.

Secrets of the Close-Out Business, written and published by

Art Newman, 9245 No. Regent Road, Milwaukee, WI 53217, recounting his own experiences which led to his success in handling closeouts and surplus merchandise, and incorporating his open offer to work with anyone on a profit-sharing basis or to pay for useful information on where/how to buy or sell closeout and surplus lots.

Incentive Marketing, Bill Communications, Inc., 633 3rd Ave., New York, NY 10017. Monthly magazine dealing with sales-promotional devices.

Marketing Communications, United Business Publications, Inc., 475 Park Avenue S., New York, NY 10016. Monthly magazine, deals with marketing and promotion.

Small Business Magazine, Small Business Service Bureau, Inc., 544 Main Street, Box 1441, Worcester, MA 01601. Bi-monthly, presents how-to articles on various phases of small-business operations and problems.

INDEX